A Life for the Spirit

Rudolf Steiner in the Crosscurrents of Our Time

Rudolf Steiner (center) with medical coworkers at the clinic in Stuttgart in 1924

A Life for the Spirit

Rudolf Steiner in the Crosscurrents of Our Time

Henry Barnes

Ⓔ Anthroposophic Press

© 1997 by Henry Barnes

Published by Anthroposophic Press
3390 Route 9, Hudson, NY 12534

Library of Congress Cataloging-in-publication Data

Barnes, Henry, 1912–
    A life for the spirit : Rudolf Steiner in the crosscurrents of our time
/ Henry Barnes.
        p.   cm. — (Vista series ; v. 1)
    Includes bibliographical references and index.
    ISBN 0-88010-395-7 (pbk.)
    1. Steiner, Rudolf, 1861–1925. 2. Anthroposophists—Biography.
3. Anthroposophy—History. I. Title. II. Series.
BP595.S895B37   1997
299'.935'092—dc21   97-22243
[B]   CIP

10 9 8 7 6 5 4 3 2 1

Printed in the United States of America

Contents

VISTA SERIES

VOLUME 1

The Vista Series

FOREWORD BY ROBERT MCDERMOTT

This book recounts the life and work of Rudolf Steiner, the early twentieth-century European philosopher, scientist, artist, and educator committed to imbuing all areas of social and cultural life with a revived consciousness of the reality of spirit in our lives. Because Steiner worked in so many areas and was so prolific, readers new to his influence and ideas will benefit from a combination of Steiner's own words and the advice of an experienced guide. This is precisely the purpose of the Vista Series. Each Vista volume will include selections of Steiner's writings and lectures on a significant contemporary theme, with substantial pages of introductory material by an editor who is expert on Steiner's work and on the theme of the book.

For an introduction to *Anthroposophy*—wisdom of the completely human being—one must sooner or later go to Steiner's own work. For a guide through Steiner's life and works it would be hard to surpass Henry Barnes, master Waldorf teacher and a leader of the Anthroposophical Society in America for more than fifty years. It is for good reason that the Vista Series, devoted to Steiner's actual and prospective contributions, has as its lead volume a tour through Steiner's life and times, guided by one who can recount and interpret both, each in light of the other.

Throughout the past century Steiner's work has had very practical consequences. C. G. Jung's remark in his autobiography that his life "is not on the surface for people to see" applies with equal or greater force to Steiner's life. Consequently, this volume includes not only material available to the usual range of intellectual effort and capability, but also material that is spiritual, esoteric, and made intelligible only by a special effort and capacity. The entire book points to

Steiner's spiritual life esoterically considered—that is, those dimensions of his life which are truly accessible only to supersensible perception.

While many of Steiner's writings and prescriptions are esoteric, some are entirely exoteric and some a combination. The discussions concerning eurythmy, the Goetheanum, the Christmas Foundation Meeting of 1923, as well as the deep spiritual source, content, and significance of his mission, his development, his influence, and his teachings, will require of the reader a willingness to consider deeply spiritual meanings woven throughout Steiner's life and times.

The entire Vista Series, and this book in particular, takes seriously the recognition that Rudolf Steiner was indeed an initiate in the modern Western tradition whose specific task was to help humanity liberate itself from the grip of alienation and materialism. Thanks to Henry Barnes's detailed recreation of both Steiner's ordinary life and the profound mystery of his esoteric-spiritual mission, we can glimpse the subtle weaving of the spiritual world in the destiny of this individual life and in his historical period. Following Steiner's lead, Henry Barnes strives to guide the reader past immediate surface meanings to inner realities. He presents and interprets events, influences, and ideas with which Steiner was familiar due to the spiritual-esoteric capacities which he developed methodically during his lifetime.

While Steiner's works and teachings might appear to focus exclusively on the ideal method and fruits of spiritual thinking, they are really best understood as a testimonial to the heart, to feeling, to love. Steiner learned and taught by sacrifice. His work as creator of the Goetheanum, the wooden building which was destroyed by fire on New Year's Eve, 1922, and the 1923 Christmas Foundation Meeting, are examples of the intimate relationship between his work and the needs of the time. Knowing that those who would be drawn to seek spiritual knowledge would need to find each other and to work together for their individual spiritual development as well as for the renewal of culture, Rudolf Steiner founded the Anthroposophical Society; knowing that such work would require ongoing spiritual-scientific research, he founded the School for Spiritual Science, the esoteric core of the Anthroposophical Society.

All of Steiner's 30 volumes of writings and 250 volumes of lectures display in some degree the method and results of spiritual science, or Anthroposophy. Throughout his writings and lectures, spread over twenty-five years, Steiner offered few if any requirements and no dogmas. Instead, he made suggestions or indications for others to test experientially. He answered many requests for help from spiritual seekers, artists, scientists, farmers, physicians, educators, Christian ministers, civic leaders, and others.

Steiner recognized that the paramount problem of modern Western culture lies in its cold reductionist thinking. As a way of helping each individual to know the deeper worlds of spiritual experience that can bring into cultural life desperately needed creative forces, Steiner developed and advocated a way of thinking which is reverent, filled with heart and will, and spiritually alive. It was because he was so remarkably capable of such thinking that he was able to penetrate the subtleties of science and the arts, philosophy, and child development.

In addition to giving indications for research by specialists, including scientists, social scientists, artists and educators, Steiner gave a method for anyone eager to see and to think spiritually, and to know the workings of the spiritual world. It was his great hope that more and more individuals would set foot on the path of inner spiritual development that leads eventually to direct insight into the realities that underlie the world of outer phenomena. It is out of such insight that we can hope to meet the needs of the complex and deeply challenging times in which we live.

~

The first ten volumes in the Vista Series of books have been generously supported by Laurance S. Rockefeller, a visionary with a deep and generous commitment to spiritual ideals. He is an exemplary and beloved philanthropist (*philo*, "love"; *anthropos*, "humanity") with his own highly developed version of human wisdom (*anthropos-sophy*).

Introduction

BY HENRY BARNES

A Personal Note

It is with gratitude that I have taken up the challenge of following the biographical path that led Rudolf Steiner (1861–1925), step by step, to the unfolding of anthroposophy. His life and work have profoundly influenced my own biography. I now believe there may be reason to share a few details of my own life history that led me both to anthroposophy and to this task.

I met the work of Rudolf Steiner in the summer of 1933, just before my twenty-first birthday. The occasion was the first conference to be held in North America to present anthroposophy and some of the practical initiatives arising from it.

Just a year and a half before, in January 1932, the suicide of my roommate and dearest friend had struck like lightning into the protected and unquestioning confidence of my young life. Peter and I had been schoolmates for many years at the Lincoln School of Teachers College in New York City, and we had gone on together to Harvard College. The Lincoln School pioneered what came to be known as "progressive education" in the United States. The school had been established in 1917, and we entered the first grade the following year. It was a privilege to attend this truly outstanding school, yet Peter's death raised deeply troubling questions. Had our education in some way failed us? I was roused to begin a search for an education that could go beyond the intellect and reach deeper than self-expression. Destiny intervened.

Peter's mother, in her effort to understand a death that had so little apparent outer cause, remembered a book she had read before

Peter was born. It was by Rudolf Steiner and was entitled *Knowledge of Higher Worlds and Its Attainment*.[1] After Peter's death, she returned to the book and discovered that Rudolf Steiner had written other books, and that there was even a small group of people in New York City who knew of his work. She also learned that a school based on this work had been started there a few years before. It was Peter's mother who invited me to the conference in Spring Valley, New York, in July 1933.

Two of the three guest speakers at that conference were teachers at the school in Stuttgart, Germany, which Rudolf Steiner had founded in 1919. What they said about the school, and about the view of the human being on which it was based, stirred me deeply. I determined to go to Stuttgart—one way or another—but I had already committed myself to a teaching job for the fall, a position I considered myself fortunate to have obtained during those Depression years. My even greater good fortune, however, was that when I told the school's headmaster that I wanted to leave at the end of the first year to study this new "Waldorf" education, he smiled wisely and said, "Why don't you go now and get it out of your system? Then come back to Choate."

As a result, I arrived in Stuttgart eight months after Hitler had been elected chancellor of Germany on January 30, 1933. As a student in the Waldorf Teacher Training Course, I came to realize that the Nazi government was gradually tightening a noose in the hope that the school would sooner or later close on its own. The Jewish teachers had to leave, and there was to be no new first grade. Every lesson had to begin with a "Heil Hitler" salute, and parents got into trouble if their children were not enrolled in a Hitler Youth Group. The school, however, did not give in. Finally, in March, 1938, the school was forced to close by government order. It was publicly stated that the function of education was to prepare the coming generation to be citizens of the state. There was no room in Germany for a school whose goal was to educate children to think

---

1. The current translation is entitled *How to Know Higher Worlds: A Modern Path of Initiation*, Anthroposophic Press, Hudson, NY, 1994.

for themselves as adults. It is significant also that the Anthropo-sophical Society and the Christian Community—an independent movement for religious renewal, inaugurated with Rudolf Steiner's help—had been banned earlier by the Nazi government in 1935. Hitler knew that a free spiritual life is by far the greatest danger to totalitarian state control.

By 1938 I was a class teacher in the first Waldorf, or "Rudolf Steiner," school in England, the New School, later called Michael Hall. That September I witnessed the British public's almost hyster-ical relief when Neville Chamberlain stepped out of the plane from Munich and announced "Peace in our time!" Staid, self-contained Londoners danced in the streets. Twelve months later, World War Two began.

These external world events and their consequences affected human beings worldwide and brought unimaginable suffering to millions. My own life continued to unfold in dramatic interplay with the larger circumstances of world affairs.

Two days after the war began, Christy MacKaye and I were mar-ried in Dornach, Switzerland, and we spent the first year of the war in that country. On June 1, 1940, Christy and I—with her father Percy MacKaye (her mother had died in St. Germain-en-Laye near Paris, June 1, 1939), her sister Arvia, brother Robin, and my younger brother Alfred—sailed from Genoa with the last American ship to leave the Mediterranean. We landed in New York on June 10, the day Italy declared war.

In Search of a New Thinking

Can we, from our vantage point at the end of the twentieth cen-tury and the beginning of the twenty-first, learn to read the reality underlying the complex chaos of events on life's surface? Can we dis-cover a *seeing thinking* that truly distinguishes outer events from their deeper causes? Can we learn to read individual events as symptoms of the historical currents struggling for expression beneath the sur-face? These events cry out to be understood, because they are born from the social and spiritual needs of our time.

One of the greatest pioneers to have blazed a path to the sources of such a thinking was Rudolf Steiner. This book is an attempt to trace how the path recognized and described by Steiner was also the one he himself followed in his individual biography. In doing this we will also touch on some of the practical results of his extraordinary insights.

We will encounter Rudolf Steiner first amid the turbulent cross-currents of this century, as the First World War entered its final phase. Steiner was one of the few who had seen from the beginning that this war was a symptom of the social and spiritual crisis of our time. When his help was requested, he responded from the understanding he had won through a lifetime of observation grounded in disciplined perception of the realms of soul and spirit as well as physical phenomena.

The path of knowledge through which Steiner came to such understanding, and to many resulting innovations, was the scientific method of inquiry, extended to include the investigation of realities that are not physically sense-perceptible. He came to speak of this path as *anthroposophy*, using a term already familiar to several thinkers of the nineteenth century. Derived from two Greek words, *anthroposophy* signifies the wisdom (*Sophia*) of the human being (*Anthropos*). Never one to cling to terms, Steiner said he would gladly have changed the name every week if it would not have confounded the authorities and everyone else. Nevertheless, the word *anthroposophy*, in the breadth and depth of its meaning, wonderfully describes the scope of his work. In his own words, Steiner characterized anthroposophy "as a path that would lead the spirit in the human being to the spirit in the universe."

Anthroposophy, however, is not a mystical path, but one of discovery and of objective reflection built upon the foundations of a *scientific* method of knowing. As a method, it invites the same scrutiny that any scientific discipline must undergo. What distinguishes the path of anthroposophy, or *spiritual science*, is that it refuses to accept the conclusion of modern thinking that the only knowledge acceptable as scientific research is knowledge gained through the physical senses (including every technical extension of the senses) and interpreted by logical, intellectual analysis. From the standpoint of spiritual science, it is not the *content* of knowledge that characterizes science but its *method* of inquiry. Anthroposophy's research method, which it extends into the fields of nonmaterial reality and experience, is the ground for its claim to recognition as a genuine scientific discipline.

Whether or not Steiner's insights are valid is for each of us to determine. His work is not easy, and he challenges our usual thinking every step of the way. The insights are radical, in the original meaning of that word: they go to the roots. We are forced more and more to realize that only through such thinking can actions arise that are truly healing and constructive.

We will meet Rudolf Steiner in the watershed year of the twentieth century, 1917. His entire work, however, stands within the tides of the century as a whole and leads us far into the next and beyond. He challenges us to think in ways that can engage the heart and will, as well as the mind.

Henry Barnes

1

The
Twentieth Century

Battleground for Human Individuality

Thank God our time is now when wrong
Comes up to face us everywhere,
Never to leave us till we take
The longest stride of soul men ever took.
Affairs are now soul size.
The enterprise
Is exploration into God.
Where are you going? It takes
So many thousand years to wake,
But will you wake for pity's sake![1]

Private Tim Meadows, in Christopher Fry's one-act play, utters this cry out of the heart of the twentieth century. And, out of the Underground, as the Cold War came to an end, another voice, tempered and tested during prison years: "The essence of the conflict is not a confrontation between two ideologies, but between an anonymous, soulless, immobile, and paralyzing power and life, humanity, being, and its mystery."[2] This same voice, once again, now speaking at Independence Hall in Philadelphia as President of the Czech Republic: "Only someone who submits to the authority of the universal order and of creation, who values the right to be a part of it and a participant in it, can genuinely value himself and his neighbors,

---

1. Christopher Fry, *A Sleep of Prisoners*, Oxford University Press, 1951.
2. "Power of the Powerless" in *Living in Truth*, Faber and Faber, London, 1986, p. 133.

and thus honor their rights as well" (Vaclav Havel, on receiving the "Liberty Medal," July 4, 1994).

. . . .

November 10, 1923. The day after the attempted Hitler-Ludendorff Putsch in Munich, Rudolf Steiner wrote in response to the vivid impressions of a friend who had inwardly experienced Berlin in flames:

> So may the lightning shatter into dust
> Our sense-built houses.
> We will erect instead soul houses
> Built on knowledge,
> Upon its iron-firm, light-woven web.
> And downfall of the outer
> Shall become uprise
> Of the soul's own innermost.
>
> We do not want this clear illumining
> To be in future brightnesses denied us
> Because we have not now,
> In pain, implanted it within our souls.[3]

Three voices from the twentieth century—the first directly out of an experience of World War Two, the second out of the century's closing years, and the third from the years immediately following World War One, with a clear view of what was yet to come.

Now, on the threshold of a new millennium, we look back, and we look ahead. What can we do? Out of this question, we turn to the individual whose life was placed in the service of exactly our current needs. We meet him in a moment of intense conflict. Europe is in flames. The First World War has entered its final phase. It is May, 1917.

---

3. From "To the Berlin Friends," in Rudolf Steiner, *Truth-Wrought-Words*, Anthroposophic Press, Hudson, NY, 1979, p. 49. See Note A, in Appendix, page 265.

Otto von Lerchenfeld, a German diplomat in Berlin, was searching for ideas that might offer a basis for genuine peace once the war finally ended. He decided to turn to the one person whom he believed might have insights that could penetrate to the sources of the social sickness that underlay the war. The person to whom he turned was Rudolf Steiner, whose work he knew. Von Lerchenfeld made an appointment and poured out the despair in his heart, speaking of his realization that Germany and Middle Europe had allowed themselves to be driven into a dead end. Steiner listened intently, asked a few questions, and invited him to return the next day. The result was that these two men worked together daily for more than three weeks to hammer out two memoranda in which Rudolf Steiner presented the ideas that he believed could serve as a foundation for peace.[4]

Von Lerchenfeld circulated the memoranda in the highest echelons of the German government. Somewhat later, through the interest of a mutual friend whose brother was then the cabinet chief of the old Austrian Emperor, the memoranda reached a few officials in the government of Austria-Hungary.

Although, as von Lerchenfeld writes, the ideas expressed in the memoranda awakened momentary interest and even recognition in a number of highly placed individuals, the dead weight of conventional, routine thinking, and the overwhelming pressures of daily events, rendered these people incapable of the radical initiatives necessary to change the course of events.

In both memoranda, Steiner sharply characterized the causes that had led to the outbreak of the war, as well as the justification for its continuation, presented by the Entente Powers. His essential message, however, was the need for a fundamental rethinking of the dynamics of social life. He hoped that, if Middle Europe could find within itself a commitment to move toward a social restructuring, the peoples of Middle Europe might then discover the inner strength to negotiate real peace. As expressed in the memoranda, Steiner's thinking was in essence as follows: The day of the centralized,

---

4. See Note B, in Appendix, page 266.

national, political state is past. The deeper currents flowing power-fully beneath the surface of external events are seeking to differenti-ate themselves in new ways. The single unitary state, in whose hands ultimate power over all branches of public life has come to be invested, must give way to social forms in which each branch—cul-tural, economic, and political—finds its own characteristic way of working within the whole social organism.

Cultural life, including everything that can arise only through the creative activity of individual human beings, in whatever sphere they are active, needs to be grounded in individual freedom. Only in this way can it bring forth the new ideas, the initiatives bearing the future, on which everything depends.

Economic life, which is concerned essentially with the production, distribution, and consumption of goods and services necessary to daily life—whether local, regional, or global—needs freedom to find practical ways of working in cooperative associations in a spirit of human brotherhood.

Political life, whose responsibility should be to guarantee every cit-izen equal access to justice, can be based only on the recognition of fundamental human rights. Individual cultural *freedom, equality* in basic human rights, and *fraternal association* in the economy, each administered and organized according to the necessities of its own sphere, are the basis for a threefold social order. In Steiner's view, this is the direction in which the underlying social forces are actually moving. The time has come, Steiner said, for the great ideals of the French Revolution—liberty, equality, and fraternity—to come into their own. When forced into the straitjacket of a single, centralized power structure, these ideals can lead only to conflict and confusion. Now they must be allowed to develop side by side, like the body's organs, each functioning according to the laws of its own life, yet working together harmoniously within the greater unity of the organism as a whole.

These thoughts, recapitulated briefly here, opened up radically new ways for understanding and solving the social problems that were enmeshing humanity ever more deeply. They led to significant action on the part of a remarkable vanguard of socially committed individuals, from many walks of life, during the years immediately following the war. These efforts came to be known as the "Threefold Movement for Social Renewal," which is described in a later chapter.

The fact that Rudolf Steiner could respond so directly to von Lerchenfeld's appeal with a radical rethinking of the relationships between the cultural, economic, and political life within the social organism was itself the result of thirty or more years of spiritual-scientific research into the nature of the human being. He had searched, through detailed observation, to understand how soul and spirit penetrate the body and manifest as the activity of thinking, feeling, and the will. It was only during the years of war that he had finally achieved full clarity in this regard. These years of research confirmed his perception of the threefold nature of the human organism. They enabled him to observe how soul and spirit engage, not only with the brain and nervous system in thought, but also directly with breathing and circulation in bringing about feeling, and with the metabolic processes in acts of will. These insights made it possible to see how these differentiated forces penetrate and interact within the social body.

In the spring of 1917, Rudolf Steiner spoke for the first time about the conclusions to which this research had led him. He gave them in written form later that same year.

~

On March 15—the fateful day of Czar Nicholas's abdication— Rudolf Steiner interrupted a series of public lectures in Berlin to present his conclusions. He began by describing the cognitive "no-man's land" that had arisen during the last centuries between those who were exploring the inner aspects of human experience and their scientific colleagues who were exploring human physiology and biochemistry. Western humanity was losing the ability to see the inner and outer aspects of human experience as two sides of a single whole. The modern worldview, based more and more exclusively on the material sciences, was being driven into an apparently irreconcilable dualism, so that the individual had to choose between a worldview that claimed to hold the keys to objective truth and one that could

call on only the hesitant authority of subjective experience. Faced
with these mutually exclusive alternatives, the human soul lost confidence in its innate powers of judgment.

Through insights gained over three decades of research, Rudolf
Steiner addressed this potentially fatal dualism. The lecture in which
he first undertook to rebuild the missing bridge that unites knowledge of the human soul and body began this way:

> On this subject, one can say that two recent spiritual directions
> of thought and investigation have led to the greatest possible
> misunderstanding. And if one becomes engaged in these misun-
> derstandings one finds, on one hand, that the thinkers and
> researchers who have sought recently to penetrate the field of
> psychological, or soul phenomena, do not know where to begin
> when they approach the admirable achievements of natural sci-
> ence—especially in relation to knowledge of the human physical
> organism. They cannot build a bridge rightly from what they
> understand as observation of soul phenomena, to the manifesta-
> tions of the body. On the other hand, it must also be said that
> those who represent natural-scientific research are, as a rule, so
> estranged from the realm of soul phenomena, or observation of
> psychic experience, that they also cannot build a bridge from the
> truly awe-inspiring results of modern science to the field of soul
> phenomena. One finds, therefore, that soul researchers, or psy-
> chologists, and natural scientists speak two different languages
> when they speak about the human soul and the human body;
> one finds that, basically, they do not understand each other.
> And because of this, those who seek insight into the great rid-
> dles of the soul realm, and the connection between the riddles
> of the soul and the universal world riddles, are misguided—
> indeed one could say that they find themselves completely con-
> fused.[5]

5. "The Human Soul and the Human Body" (March 15, 1917), included in
The Foundations of Human Experience, Anthroposophic Press, Hudson, NY,
1996, p. 247.

Contemporary science had concluded that the brain and nervous system trigger and control human thinking and, indirectly, feeling and volition as well. Contrary to this, Steiner realized that the brain and nervous system merely reflect the processes we call thinking and, consequently, make them conscious. He further observed that feeling arises in connection with the soul's engagement with breathing, and that an act of will is made possible when the human being penetrates and directly takes hold of specific metabolic processes.

Steiner now saw the human being as the living integration of three basically autonomous, yet interpenetrating and interacting, organic systems: the *nerve/sense system*, centered primarily in the head; the *rhythmic system* of breathing and blood circulation, centered mainly in the chest; and the *metabolic/limb system*, seated primarily in the lower organs and legs. This threefold organization emerged in Rudolf Steiner's perception as the living reality of the human physical constitution; it was first spoken of in this detail in the lectures referred to. Also in these lectures, Steiner first publicly challenged the current distinction between motor and sensory nerves in the human organism. In his view, all nerves are basically sensory. In the lecture of March 15, he introduced this conclusion as follows:

For spiritual science—I know how heretical this is—such motor, or motor-producing, nerves do not exist. Indeed, I have occupied myself for many years with this matter, and, concerning this very point, I know of course that one can refer to much that seems to be well-founded. Consider, for example, someone who is ill with locomotor ataxia, or whose spinal cord has been pinched, and, as a result, below a certain organ the lower organism is deadened. These things do not contradict what I am saying, rather, if one indeed sees through them in the proper way, they actually substantiate what I am saying. There are no motor nerves. What contemporary physiology sees as "motor nerves," or nerves that cause motion, will-impulse nerves, are actually sensory nerves. If the spinal column has been damaged in a particular section, then what happens in the leg or foot is simply not perceived, and thus the foot, because it is not perceived, cannot be moved; not because a motor nerve has been severed, but because a sensory nerve has been severed and cannot perceive what happens in the leg. (ibid., p. 268)

To a layperson this observation may seem remote from practical reality, yet it is fundamental to the understanding of the human being that underlies Steiner's educational, therapeutic, and medical work. If Steiner's finding is correct, and the soul—in which the impulse to action originates—works directly into the metabolic processes wherever the movement is to be enacted, then the function of the so-called "motor" nerve is to perceive, or register, the subtle changes in the corresponding metabolism. On such a view, the hypothesis that distinguishes two types of nerves with opposite functions cannot be valid.

Rudolf Steiner dealt with this question again during 1917 in a book published in November, *Riddles of the Soul* (*Von Seelenrätseln*), which includes three essays that deal, in very different ways, with the life and function of the soul.[6] Steiner appended a number of commentaries to these essays, and in the sixth note he once again presented in lapidary concentration his analysis of how the soul, in its thinking, feeling, and willing, penetrates the organism to effect what we experience as mental, emotional, and willed expression.

Those approaching Rudolf Steiner's work for the first time may find the aspect touched on here to be specialized and theoretical, but through persistence one enters into the whole scope of his spiritual science, or anthroposophy, and comes to realize that these seemingly theoretical conclusions actually go to the heart of what it means to be a modern human being. If there is a real possibility of bridging the widening gap that still threatens to estrange the realm of soul and spiritual experience from the world of sense-perceptible phenomena, then there is firm ground for the individual's struggle to become whole.

---

6. *Riddles of the Soul*, Mercury Press, Spring Valley, NY, 1996; originally available in part as *The Case for Anthroposophy: Selections from "Von Seelenrätseln,"* translated, edited, and introduced by Owen Barfield, Rudolf Steiner Press, London, 1970.

Barfield translated, edited, and published essential sections of Rudolf Steiner's very crucial work *Von Seelenrältseln* in the little book *The Case for Anthroposophy*. In choosing his title, Barfield recognized that Steiner indeed "rested his case" for anthroposophical spiritual science on the observations that he presented for the first time during the watershed year 1917. In the opening paragraph of the commentary note, which Barfield entitled "Principles of Psychosomatic Physiology," Rudolf Steiner states his intentions this way:

> My object here is to present in outline certain conclusions I have reached concerning the psychic and physical components of the human being. I may add that, in doing so, I place on record the results of a systematic spiritual investigation extending over a period of thirty years. It is only in the last few of those years that it has become possible to formulate these results in concepts capable of verbal expression, and thus to bring the investigation to at least a temporary close. I must emphasize that it is the results, and the results alone, that I shall be presenting, or rather indicating, in what follows. Their foundation in fact can certainly be established on the basis of contemporary science. But, to do this would require a substantial volume, and my present circumstances do not permit this. (*The Case for Anthroposophy*, p. 69)

And Steiner concluded his preface to the book by saying,

> It might well seem that the interests of human beings in the present time must necessarily go in a direction very different from that of the considerations that follow here. Yet, I believe that one will not only *not* be drawn away from the earnest duties of the immediate present through such considerations, but that the present times can be directly served by the impulses that lie within them. These impulses may be less immediately obvious, but therefore may have all the stronger relationship to the experience of the present time. (*Riddles of the Soul*, p. 5)

~

We have met Rudolf Steiner in his immediate concerns for the social future and as researcher into the nature of the interpenetration of the human body, soul, and spirit. Our encounter with Steiner in this decisive moment of our century would, however, be one-sided if we were not to see him also in his workman's smock and high leather boots, carving and painting in the building he designed, which was then nearing completion on a hillside in the northwest corner of Switzerland. We shall meet him first in the early days of construction, through the eyes of Natalie Turgeniev-Pozzo, one of the Russian artists who found their way to Dornach to help carve and paint the interior of the building.

Carving the capitals

On the first day of our job as sculptors, a row of wooden blocks stands before us. They are more than a meter in height and in breadth. Dr. Steiner had made small models of the capitals. (We were to hew their forms out of these prepared blocks.) We take hold of the chisels and mallets. Most of us timidly begin cutting away at the corners. The wooden mallets are very light; unpracticed hands could not hold heavier ones. It takes a big effort to split off just a couple of chips. We turn to each other for advice, tap again on the wood, and we are already tired. Even the few sculptors among us have never tried anything like this before. Our arms ache, and there is nothing to show for the work. The second day, Dr. Steiner comes, picks up a mallet and chisel, steps up, as we did, onto an overturned crate, and begins to work. It is the first time for him, too, but after just a few blows, he is completely oriented in the work and steadily cuts off one little chip after another. He hammers away like that for ten minutes, an hour, without pause. Without even moving off the crate, he continues for nearly two hours. We stand around him at a slight distance, pale with fatigue, our eyes staring wider and wider in speechless astonishment, unable to move. We had already experienced ourselves how difficult it was.[7]

The time must have been late 1913 or early 1914; the occasion: the very start of the sculptural work on what were to become the capitals of the great columns that would eventually support the larger of the two domes, already rising.

By 1917 Steiner had been engaged for nearly four years on the great project for which the wood-carvers had gathered. The work on the Dornach building absorbed him in his deepest being. When he was able to be in Dornach, he was involved as Natalie Turgeniev-Pozzo describes. When he had to be away, he carried the love for this work in his heart and mind. The English sculptor Edith Maryon became his closest collaborator in carving the sculpted group that was to become the focal point of his artistic efforts; she gives us yet another picture of Steiner amid this extraordinary undertaking:

Every morning Steiner, with Marie von Sivers and the leading coworkers, reviewed the building site. The groups that gathered around him were reminiscent of Raphael's *School of Athens*.

---

7. Natalie Turgeniev-Pozzo, *Zwölf Jahre der Arbeit am Goetheanum*, Dornach, Switzerland, 1942; quoted in *The Language of Color in the First Goetheanum*, Hilde Raske, ed., Walter Keller Verlag, Dornach, Switzerland, 1987, p. 26.

Some would unroll architectural sketches of window frames or doors for him to look at; others showed him pieces of wood primed for painting in various colors. Then again, others came to him with plaster models of the capitals to get help in solving some sculptural problem. Each one, aware of his or her own limitations, wanted only to learn, in order to serve the tremendous task. And Rudolf Steiner, who, with this task, had taken on the greatest exertions and concerns—with what gratitude he welcomed each small contribution of collaboration and help![8]

To complete the picture of Rudolf Steiner as we meet him in this new and very different aspect of his life during this crucial year, we must briefly fill in the background to the construction work. Chapter 6 describes the building in greater detail.

~

It became increasingly clear to those involved that the ideas of anthroposophy were alive, and—as life begets life—these ideas sought outer expression. As we shall see in later chapters, these living thoughts gave rise to a new art of movement and to four dramas, produced summer after summer in Munich, and these in turn evoked new initiatives in speech, painting, and sculpture. From this awakening of creative life came the longing that these activities might find a home in a building whose architectural forms would speak a language not unlike their own. There arose a plan to erect such a building in the interior of a residential city block in Munich. Rudolf Steiner created the design, but the city authorities rejected the plan. Swiss friends, however, offered land, and in 1913 the building began to be realized on the hill at Dornach.

It was to be a double-domed structure; two domes of unequal size intersected to form a single architectural whole. Constructed of wood, the domes rested on a concrete foundation at ground level,

---

8. Rex Raab, *Edith Maryon: Sculptress and Coworker with Rudolf Steiner*, Verlag am Goetheanum, Dornach, Switzerland, 1993, p. 131 (H.B. trans.).

and Steiner's design called for sculptural forms and flowing colors. Great windows of colored glass, into which designs were engraved using a technique adapted to the purpose by Rudolf Steiner, bathed the interior with color. The larger dome faced west and was supported by seven pairs of columns, which enclosed the auditorium for as many as nine hundred people. The smaller dome was carried by twelve columns that enclosed the stage. The entire structure, with the domes sheathed in Norwegian slate, reflected the lights and shadows from the sky.

Steiner returned again and again with heartfelt joy to work on this building, whose exterior was virtually complete by 1917. Men and women from seventeen nations—several of which were at war with each other—had gathered around this monumental project. Working as volunteers along with the Swiss workers, some, following Steiner's sketches, painted the arched ceilings of the two domes, while others carved the great wooden capitals and the architraves, whose living, moving forms united the individual statements of the capitals into a symphonic whole.

The imagination from which this great structure grew—as it lived in the inner vision of its designer—culminated in a central image that would speak both in color, from the interior of the smaller cupola above the stage, and in the sculpted form of a powerful and dramatic, free-standing figure carved in elmwood. Standing nearly ten meters high, this central figure strides forward in quiet freedom between two forms—one a mighty winged being above, the other a tortured, cramped, and pain-filled being, chained in a rocky cavern below. Steiner intended this sculptured group to stand within the central panel at the back of the stage, with its counterpart in color on the ceiling just above. He spoke of the central striding figure as the *Representative of Humanity*. In 1917, with much of the interior work accomplished, Steiner repeatedly turned his attention to carving this group whenever he was able to be in Dornach. Thus, within sound of the great French and German guns to the north along the Rhine, he strove to make visible in form and color the living experience and laws of the invisible, supersensible forces.

~

On June 28, 1914 the young Serb idealist Gavrilo Princip slipped across the Drina River into Bosnia and waited in Sarajevo for the arrival of Franz Ferdinand, Archduke of Austria. Princip was prepared to die for the dream of a "Greater Serbia." It was for this that he pulled the trigger on that fateful day, which eventually led to the outbreak of war. Over eighty years later, how many more have had to suffer and die for that same ideal in Bosnia?

In January, 1918, another idealist, Woodrow Wilson, proclaimed the fourteen points on which world peace should be established. We learn them in history books: freedom of the seas in times of peace and war; open treaties, openly arrived at; the right of each nation to choose its own government and determine its own destiny. And it may be remembered how their author was hailed by the desperate peoples of Europe as the savior of humankind.

In a more recent Bosnia, the right of a nation to self-determination has been translated as "ethnic cleansing." As with every assertion of exclusive power by a group willing to ignore the even more fundamental right of the individual to think and act freely, the experience of Bosnia has become a tragic symptom of the dead end into which every form of totalitarianism sooner or later leads.

Rudolf Steiner expressed his observations on the same difficult issues in a memorandum in 1917:

> Questions of common human concern and related questions concerning the freedom of folk groups and nations require, as their foundation, the freedom of the individual human being, both now and in the future. One cannot even begin to look at these questions realistically as long as it is believed that one can speak about freedom and the freeing of peoples and nations without basing this on the freedom of the individual human being.... Individuals must be able to acknowledge their relationship to their folk, to their religious community, and to every connection that arises from purely human aspirations, without interference from political or economic influences.[9]

9. Roman Boos, ed., *Rudolf Steiner Während des Weltkrieges*, Verlag der Sozialwissenschaftlichen Vereinigung am Goetheanum, Dornach, n.d. pp. 67–68.

The First World War—the first truly global war in human history—set the stage for the twentieth century and for our time. Modern technology was, for the first time, totally committed to war. The tank, the airplane, the submarine, the radio, as well as poison gases and the chemical industry were among its perfected gifts to humanity. Sixty-five million human beings under arms; twenty-two million wounded; nine million killed; five million missing in action; and, prophetically, around nine million noncombatants perished. It quickly became referred to as the "Great War," and the peace that concluded it has come to be called called the "peace to end all peace."

The year of 1917 may be considered the watershed year. Until then, peace might still have been negotiated, if it had been sincerely sought, but by April, 1917, it was clear that such a peace was not to be. Two events, within days of each other, indicated that a war would be fought to the bitter end. The German High Command hit on the brilliant strategy of shipping Lenin, in a sealed railway car, from Zurich, through Germany, Sweden, and Finland, into Russia. And in the West, Woodrow Wilson—reelected just five months before on the promise of keeping America out of war—went to Congress to ask that war be declared, and on April 6, Congress did as requested. On November 7, a handful of Bolsheviks led by Lenin overthrew the provisional government in Petersburg and declared the Revolution. The war into which Europe stumbled during the summer of 1914—its leaders literally "walking in their sleep"—finally engulfed the world.

Rudolf Steiner had no illusions about its outcome, but he knew that no effort could be spared that might help humanity to awaken from its troubled sleep. His entire life is a call to awaken. We have met him in the crossfire of the First World War. We now turn to follow the path that led him to this point and beyond, into the incredible initiatives that distinguish his final years.

Rudolf Steiner in the late 1880s

2

Child
of Middle Europe

Biographical Foundations

To be an Austrian in the mid-nineteenth century was to live at the heart of Europe; Vienna, Prague, and Budapest—all jewels in the Hapsburg crown—were truly European cities. The old Austrian Empire was a complex, cosmopolitan, political network of many peoples and cultures held together in a loose federation by the ruling house. When the emperor wished to address his people, his message had to be presented in thirteen different languages. Germans, Italians, Magyars, Slavs were all citizens of the empire, which in 1866–1867 became the dual monarchy of Austria-Hungary.

Rudolf Steiner was born into this Austria on February 27, 1861, but not into the beautiful forest land of Lower Austria, which had been home to the families of both his parents for generations. As the oldest of the family's three children, he first saw the light of day in an area far to the south, on the border between Hungary and Croatia. The family was then living in the village of Kraljevec, where Rudolf's father Johann Steiner had been recently appointed station master and telegraph operator on the Southern Austrian Railroad.

Rudolf Steiner himself found the circumstances of his birth significant for all that he later had to do in life. Deeply rooted as he was in the spiritual culture of Middle Europe—so well expressed in the language and literature of Goethe, Schiller, and Novalis—anything of a narrowly nationalistic or merely traditional form was foreign to him. He considered it no accident that he was born where Middle and Eastern Europe met, and where the Germanic and Slavic cultures mingled. He briefly mentions in his autobiography that he was born far from the geographical region of his ancestral roots. In April, 1912, in Helsinki, Finland he spoke at greater length of the importance of this fact: "The bearers of the bloodlines from which I am descended originally came from the German region of Austria. I could not have been born there. I was born in a Slavic region, in an area completely foreign to the whole milieu and character of the place from which my ancestors came."[1]

Franziska and Johann Steiner

We are able to follow Rudolf Steiner, step by step, along the inner as well as the outer paths of his biography, because, toward the end of his life, he perceived the necessity of "setting the record straight." He had emerged as a public figure in the crosscurrents of the time, especially in the years immediately after the First World War. He was often attacked on grounds that had little or no real foundation, and he reluctantly accepted that it was necessary to write about his life and work. Beginning in December, 1923, he wrote his autobiography,

---

1. Contained in *Spiritual Beings in the Heavenly Bodies and in the Kingdoms of Nature*, Anthroposophic Press, Hudson, NY, 1992, p. 224.

and each week a new chapter appeared in *Das Goetheanum*. The life story ends abruptly in 1907, which was the point Steiner had reached in his writing at the time of his death on March 30, 1925. These chapters were then published in a single volume under the title *Mein Lebensgang* (*The Course of My Life*).[2]

In this autobiography Steiner writes about himself with objective reticence, as though writing about someone else. We come to know his teachers, friends, colleagues, and contemporaries, and through them we gain insights into the one who writes about them with such transparent interest and affection. In a few brief pages we meet Rudolf Steiner as a child and youth, surrounded by the landscapes and people whom he came to know in the villages where his father was stationed for various periods of time. Of primary concern to us in this introductory sketch, however, are the circumstances that provided the biographical foundations for his later work.

That the boy lived in two worlds of experience is of decisive significance: an inner world of supersensible perception and an outer world of everyday experience. For Rudolf as a child the surrounding nature, which he loved, was alive with elemental beings. From an early age he was also able to follow the further journeys of those who had died. The world of nonphysical perception was more real to him than the one that spoke through his bodily senses, and he assumed that this was also true for others. He soon learned that this was not the case, however, for when he spoke matter-of-factly of these experiences, he was met with disbelief, embarrassment, and often ridicule. The boy thus learned to keep silent about his inner perceptions. This "keeping silent" was a characteristic of Rudolf Steiner's life well into his adult years, when—as we shall see—he finally met contemporaries who wanted to share this realm of his experience.

We can understand the joy that Rudolf, as a child, experienced when he discovered one sphere of knowledge that was fundamentally nonmaterial, yet generally accepted as real. He had formed a close connection with the village teacher, who allowed him—in his

---

2. *The Course of My Life*, Anthroposophic Press, Hudson, NY, 1986; also *Rudolf Steiner: An Autobiography*, Steinerbooks, Blauvelt, NY, 1977.

eighth year—to borrow a geometry textbook. Steiner wrote in his autobiography:

> Soon after my entrance into the Neudörfl school, I discovered a geometry book in [the teacher's] room. I was on such good terms with him that I was permitted take the book without further ado and to keep it for a while. I plunged into it with enthusiasm. For weeks at a time my soul was filled with the congruencies, or correspondences, among triangles, squares, and polygons; I racked my brain over the question: Where do parallel lines actually meet? The Pythagorean theorem fascinated me. (*The Course of My Life*, chap. 1)

This incident throws light on Steiner's whole relationship to the experience of knowledge. He wrote: "The fact that you could live inside yourself and shape forms that were purely within your own soul, without any impression on the outer senses—this gave me the greatest satisfaction" (ibid.). It was, he says, through this experience of geometry that an idea first awoke in his childlike mind that continued to evolve, finally taking on definite form around his twentieth year:

> I said to myself: The objects and events that the senses perceive are in space. But just as this space is outside of us, there is also a kind of soul space within, which is the arena for spiritual realities and events. In thoughts I could not see anything like the pictures we form of actual things, but in this soul arena I saw the manifestations of a spiritual world. To me, geometry seemed to be a knowledge that people have apparently produced but, nevertheless, its significance is quite independent of them. Naturally I did not, as a child, say all this to myself very clearly, but I felt that we must carry the knowledge of the spiritual world within ourselves just like geometry. (*The Course of My Life*, chap. 1)

Even earlier, before he was seven years old, Steiner had recognized the difference between things that are "seen" and those that are "not seen." The experience of this inner, outwardly invisible world in which he loved to live illuminated the phenomena of visible, sense-perceptible reality. He concludes this episode in his autobiography by saying, "I would have had to experience the physical world as a sort of spiritual darkness around me if it had not received light from this [inner, spiritual] side." (*The Course of My Life*, chap. 1)

~

It was customary in Europe at that time to select the boys who, at the age of eleven, showed intellectual promise. They were sent to a secondary school that offered either a classical humanistic curriculum, leading to the university, or a scientific course of study, leading in all probability to a technical institute. Thus it was that Johann Steiner decided to send his son to the scientific-technical school, or *Realschule*, in neighboring Wiener-Neustadt. He assumed that Rudolf would eventually find work as an engineer on the railroad. Thanks to his father's decision, Steiner spent the next seven years primarily studying mathematics, physics, and chemistry. Many of his courses were taught by truly outstanding teachers, and we meet them, engagingly portrayed, in the pages of his autobiography.

When he was fifteen, Rudolf's attention was caught one day by a book in the window of a local book shop. Without ever having heard of its author, the philosopher Immanuel Kant, the boy felt inwardly drawn to buy this book and to read it—which he did, once he had saved the necessary schillings, which were scarce and hard to come by in his young life. Of this experience Steiner wrote:

When Kant came into the sphere of my thinking, I did not yet know the slightest thing about his place in the history of human thought. Whatever anyone else had thought about him, in approval or disapproval, was entirely unknown to me. My boundless interest in the *Critique of Pure Reason* was entirely stimulated by my own quite personal inner life. In my boyish way I was striving to understand just what human reason could achieve as real insight into the nature of things. (*The Course of My Life*, chap. 2)

The study of Kant continued for many weeks despite the very limited time available to Rudolf. He was faced with several hours of travel and many hours of home assignments each day. But the determined student solved his problem ingeniously. Having observed that his history teacher "appeared to be lecturing but was actually reading from a book," which was later assigned to be read anyway, he decided not to waste his time during these history "lessons." He instead took the *Critique of Pure Reason* apart and interleaved it in his history book. Thus, while he appeared to follow the history lecture attentively in his text, he was actually thinking through Kant's thoughts. He wrote:

> Of course, from the point of view of school discipline, this was a serious offense; yet it did not disturb anyone, and it detracted so little from what was required of me that the grade I received for that history course was "excellent." (*The Course of My Life*, chap. 2)

We can appreciate Steiner's youthful subterfuge, but in the biography of this student (who was destined to refute Kant's hypothesis that there are inescapable limits to human knowledge) what is significant is his intense preoccupation with the nature of human thinking itself. He wrote:

> The reading of Kant went ahead briskly during vacations. I read many pages more than twenty times. I wanted to reach a decision about how thinking was related to the creative work of nature.
>
> At the same time, I was endlessly occupied with the scope of the human capacity for thought. I sensed that thinking could be trained and developed into a real power that could actually encompass the things and events of the world. A "substance" that remains outside of thinking, that we can merely think "about," was an unbearable idea for me. Whatever is in *things*, I said to myself again and again, must also be within human thoughts.

What I read in Kant, however, repeatedly opposed this sense. But I hardly noticed the conflict. For more than anything else, I wanted to gain a firm enough foothold through the *Critique of Pure Reason* to come to terms with my own thinking. Wherever and whenever I took my holiday walks, I always needed to sit down quietly somewhere and ask myself once again how we pass from simple, clearly-surveyable concepts to the mental pictures we make of natural phenomena. At that time my attitude toward Kant was quite uncritical, but through him I made no further progress. (ibid.)

~

In the summer of 1879, after Rudolf Steiner's graduation from the *Realschule* in Wiener Neustadt, the family moved close enough to Vienna for their son to attend its Technical Institute, an internationally known school of science. He enrolled in mathematics, natural history, and chemistry courses, but he was still primarily focused on his intense struggle to understand the role of thinking as the foundation and support for all knowledge. The spiritual world was open to him as a matter of direct perception, but nature, as he said, "would not enter into the spiritual world that I experienced" (*The Course of My Life*, chap. 3). Further, and in relation to these questions, he was increasingly concerned with the nature of human freedom, and with whether freedom is, in fact, attainable.

At this point, through his association with Karl Julius Schröer, Steiner met the work of Goethe in its full intensity and scope. Schröer was a professor of literature at the University of Vienna and also gave courses at the Technical Institute. Not only was he one of the foremost Goethe scholars of his day, but one might say that Goethe's poetic, artistic soul came to life within Schroer's own being. Soon the young student and the mature scholar were close friends. Schröer was the one who, two or three years later, recommended Steiner to Joseph Kuerschner, who was in charge of the Kuerschner editions of German literary classics. Thanks to Schröer's recommendation, Rudolf Steiner was asked to edit Goethe's scientific works.

Rudolf Steiner in 1879

However, in the summer of 1879, before Rudolf Steiner actually entered the Technical Institute, he met a person who deeply impressed him, and who would play a significant role in his life. This was the herb-master Felix Koguzki, whom we meet thirty years later as the character Felix Balde in Steiner's mystery dramas. Koguzki and Steiner both traveled to Vienna each week, the young man to visit bookstores and libraries, the older man to sell his medicinal herbs to the city's apothecaries. Riding on the same train every week, they became acquainted, and in Felix, Steiner met a man in whom an original nature wisdom and spirituality of a kind very rare in Western humanity still lived. Steiner wrote:

> It was possible to talk about the spiritual world with him as with someone who had his own experiences of it…. He revealed himself as though he, as a personality, were only the voice for a spiritual content that wished to speak out of hidden worlds.

Felix Koguzki
(taken in 1906)

When you were with him you could get deep glimpses into the secrets of nature.... According to the usual conception of "learning," you would have to say that you couldn't "learn" anything from this man. But if you yourself were able to perceive a spiritual world, you could obtain very deep glimpses into this world through someone who had a firm footing there. Moreover, anything fantastic or illusory was utterly foreign to this man. (*The Course of My Life*, chap. 3)

In this way, life brought the young man together with a representative of an ancient, unspoiled spirituality, and gave evidence that continuity is indeed a law of esoteric life.

Rudolf Steiner wrote about this period of his life (from the age of nineteen through his early twenties):

It was not easy for me then to realize that the philosophy I was learning from others could not, in thought, bring one to the perception of the spiritual world. Out of the difficulties I was experiencing, I found that a kind of "theory of knowledge" was taking shape within me. Living in thought gradually appeared to me to be the reflection, radiating into the physical human being, of what the soul experiences in the spiritual world. To me, thought experience meant to exist within a realm of reality where doubt could not arise, because this reality was inwardly experienced, through and through. To me, the world of the senses appeared less easy to penetrate with experience. The sense world is there, but we do not grasp it in the same way that we grasp thought. Some unknown realm of being could be hidden within it, or behind it. Yet, as human beings we are placed amid this world.

The question then arose: Is this world a reality, complete within itself? When we think our thoughts in relation to this world—thoughts that come from within us but nevertheless light up the sense world for us—do we introduce something that is actually alien to this world? This does not accord at all with the experience we have when the sense world lies before us, and we break into it with our thoughts. On the contrary, the thoughts show themselves to be just that through which the sense world expresses itself. Further pursuit of these reflections was an important part of my inner life at that time. (*The Course of My Life*, chap. 3)

Was there a bridge that an intellectually trained and scientifically disciplined thinker could cross in freedom, from the familiar land of sense-perceptible experience to the ordinarily unknown land of supersensible reality? Steiner knew from direct personal experience that human beings were actually at home in the latter, but he was constantly wrestling with the question of finding or building a bridge. He found help in Friedrich Schiller's discovery of a realm that offers human beings inner freedom. This realm lies between the compulsion of sense perception, on the one hand, and of rational, logical abstraction, on the other. In his *Letters on the Aesthetic Education of Mankind*, Schiller pointed to a middle realm, between the two spheres of necessity, in which the uncompelled human soul can freely act and create. Out of this middle sphere, beauty can arise. Steiner recognized that the path leading toward the potential of freedom lay in this direction. Looking back on this moment in his own development, he wrote:

> These directions in which Schiller was thinking were very interesting and attractive to me. They implied that we must first have our consciousness in a certain state, or mode, before we can achieve a relationship to the phenomena of the world that correspond to our own being. This direction gave me something that clarified the questions posed by my observations of nature and my spiritual experience. Schiller spoke of the state of consciousness that must be present to experience the *beauty* of the world. Could we not also think of a state of consciousness that would mediate the *truth* lying in the being of things? If this is a justified premise, then we must not, as Kant would do, observe everyday human consciousness and investigate whether it can enter into the true being of things. Rather, we must first explore and study the state of consciousness necessary to place ourselves into the kind of relationship with the world that allows things and phenomena to reveal their being to us.
>
> I believed I knew that such a state of consciousness is reached to a certain degree when we not only have thoughts that reproduce external things and events, but also *thoughts that we experience as thoughts themselves*. This living in thoughts revealed itself to me as quite another thing from the thinking carried out in our usual daily existence and in ordinary scientific research. When we penetrate farther and farther into the experience of thoughts, we find that spiritual reality comes to meet this experience. We then take the path of the soul toward the spirit. But on this inner soul path, we arrive at a spiritual reality that we also find again in the inner being of nature. We win through to a deeper understanding of nature when, after having beheld the reality of the spirit in living thoughts, we once again meet nature.
>
> Every day it became clearer to me how, through moving beyond our customary abstract thoughts to spiritual perceptions

of this kind (which, however, still retain the calmness and luminosity of thought), we grow into a reality that our normal, everyday consciousness prevents us from meeting. This everyday consciousness has the great liveliness of sense perception, on the one hand, and the abstract quality of pale thought on the other. Spiritual vision perceives the spirit just as the senses perceive nature, but with its thinking it does not stand apart from the spiritual perception—as everyday consciousness, with its thinking, stands apart from sense perceptions. Spiritual vision thinks *while* it experiences spiritual reality, and it experiences *while* it brings the awakened spirituality in us into thinking. [emphasis added]

A method of spiritual perception presented itself to me that did not rest on dim, mystical feeling. It proceeded much more through a spiritual activity that, in its transparent clarity, was fully comparable to mathematical thinking. I was approaching a level of inner experience within my soul that I could believe allowed my inner perception of the spiritual world to be justified before the forum of scientific thought.

At the time of these inner soul experiences, I was in my twenty-second year. (*The Course of My Life*, chap. 3)

~

It might seem that this young man was entirely absorbed in his own inner life, yet a glance into his autobiography tells a very different story. For Steiner this was a time of intense friendships, of youthful love affairs and active participation in the cultural and political issues of the day. Throughout these years he also had to support himself by tutoring students of varying ages and backgrounds in a wide range of subjects. This was by no means a new occupation—he had been tutoring classmates and younger students since he was fifteen, even while still a high school student in Wiener Neustadt. Nor were the subjects he tutored limited to mathematics and the physical sciences (which he himself was studying), but also included composition, German literature, history, and occasionally even Greek and Latin, which he had taught himself. Steiner wrote of his early Vienna days:

My work as a tutor, which at that time provided my sole means of livelihood, kept me from one-sidedness. I had to learn many things from the ground up in order to teach them. I even found my way into the "mysteries" of bookkeeping, when the opportunity arose to teach it. (*The Course of My Life*, chap. 5)

At this time, fate gave Steiner an unusual task. He was asked to take on the tutoring of four boys in a family by the name of Specht, one of whom required special care. In his autobiography, Steiner describes this boy's situation when he first went to live in the home. It was considered highly doubtful that the child, who had a pronounced hydrocephalic condition, could ever learn anything beyond the rudiments of reading, writing, and arithmetic. His young tutor, however, recognized that the boy's soul was only as though asleep and first had to be awakened—which could only happen if he found a loving relationship with the one who sought to help him. Steiner describes how he prepared the briefest of lessons to engage the boy, since his strength only allowed him to concentrate for very short periods of time. Through this careful, homeopathic approach, Rudolf Steiner succeeded in guiding his pupil so far that he was able to join a class in a secondary school. As the boy developed into young manhood, Steiner had the great satisfaction of seeing him enter the university and become a medical doctor; during World War I he lost his life while serving in this profession. Through the whole of this experience, Steiner came to realize that teaching and instructing must "become an art based on a genuine understanding of the human being."

When we look at the worldwide curative, or special, education movement that has developed in this century out of the therapeutic and pedagogical insights of Steiner, as well as at the Waldorf school movement, we realize how decisive and far-reaching his experience with the Specht boy really was.

Rudolf Steiner was in his twenties during the Vienna years. In his later spiritual-scientific and anthroposophical work, he characterizes this third decade of human life as the time when the newly awakened I begins to penetrate the soul in its life of feeling, of sentience, of emotion. This is the aspect of the soul he called the *sentient soul* (*Empfindungsseele*). We recognize the flowering of this side of Steiner's nature in the innumerable friendships he formed, which drew him out into circles where he met a wide range of personalities.

Some of these acquaintances were deeply involved with poetry and drama, some with painting, and some with religious and mystical thought. Among these personalities were quite a few who were strongly attracted to Eastern spiritual teachings and theosophical wisdom. Such studies were beginning to engage the hearts and minds of many who found themselves uncomfortable with the utilitarian and materialistic tendencies that increasingly dominated the thinking of the time. Within a number of these gifted souls there lived an underlying mood of melancholy and pessimism, a longing to retreat into a more spiritual age or to ascend to an otherworldly idealism that often found it hard to deal with life as it was threatening to become.

We meet some of these sensitive, idealistic individuals in the pages of Steiner's autobiography, their portraits drawn in loving and deeply appreciative ways. For those who know the book, the names of Eugenia delle Grazie, Alfred Farmer, Marie Lang, Rosa Mayreder, and Friedrich Eckstein call up vivid impressions of truly remarkable human beings. And yet, inwardly, Steiner experienced it as a tragedy that they were unable to carry their idealism and aesthetic sensibility into a living experience of spiritual reality. He wrote:

> At the close of this first chapter of my life it became inwardly necessary for me to become very clear about certain orientations of the human soul. One of those was mysticism. As I reviewed it through the various epochs of humanity's development—in Eastern wisdom, in Neoplatonism, in the Christian Middle Ages, in the efforts of the Cabalists—it was difficult for me, because of my particular predisposition, to establish any relationship to it.
>
> The mystic seemed to me to be a person who could not come to terms with the world of ideas, in which for me the spiritual manifested itself. I felt that it was a lack of real spirituality when

someone, with the idea of attaining satisfaction in the soul, wanted to plunge into an inner world devoid of ideas. In doing this I could see no path leading toward the light, but only to spiritual darkness. To me it seemed to be a kind of cognitional impotence when the soul sought to reach spiritual reality by escaping from ideas in which, although the spirit itself does not actually live within them, human beings can experience spiritual reality.

And yet something drew me toward the mystical strivings of humanity; this was the *nature* of the inner experience of the mystics. What they are looking for is an inner, living union with the sources of human existence, not merely an external contemplation of them, through ideas. It was also clear to me that we arrive at the same kind of inner experience when, *with* the full, clear content of the world of ideas, we sink down into the depths of the soul, instead of stripping off this content when we sink into our depths. I wanted to lead the light of the idea-world into the warmth of inner experience. The mystic seemed to me to be a person who could not perceive the spirit within ideas, and who, therefore, was inwardly chilled by them. The coldness that the mystic experiences from ideas drives such a person to seek, by turning away from ideas, the warmth needed by the soul.

For me, the inner warmth of experience was kindled in my soul just at the moment when I could give a formed expression in ideas to experiences of the spiritual world that were initially indefinite. I often said to myself: "How these mystics fail to recognize the warmth, or inner intimacy, that we experience when we inwardly unite with ideas permeated by the spirit!" For me this intimate union had always been like a personal acquaintanceship with the spiritual world....

The difficulty lay in finding the appropriate forms for expressing my [supersensible] observations in writing.... I concluded that the forms of expression used for the natural sciences consisted of ideas imbued with factual content, even though the content was at first materialistically conceived. I wanted to form ideas that pointed to the spiritual, similar to the way in which the ideas of science pointed to what was sense-perceptible. In this way I could preserve the idea-character of what I had to say. It seemed impossible to me to use mystical forms for this task, since these do not refer to the spiritual reality outside of us, but only describe subjective experiences within us. I did not want to describe human experiences but show how a spiritual world reveals itself in us through spiritual organs.

Out of such fundamental considerations as these, the idea-forms gradually took shape from which my *Philosophy of Spiritual Activity* later evolved. I did not want any mystical influences to overcome me in the forming of these ideas, even though it was clear to me that the ultimate experience of what reveals itself in ideas must be of the same character within the soul as the inner perception of the mystic. Yet the difference was that, in my characterization of the matter, the human being opens through inner activity to the spirit and brings the external spiritual world to objective manifestation within. The mystic, however, strengthens the inner life and, in this way, extinguishes the true form of the objective spiritual. (*The Course of My Life*, chap. 11)

~

Throughout most of his years in Vienna, Steiner was occupied with his work on Goethe's scientific writings, which he edited and introduced for the Kuerschner series on German national literature (*Deutsche National Literatur*). The reputation gained through this work led to his being called to the Goethe-Schiller Archives in Weimar in 1890 to collaborate on the great *Sophia Edition*, commissioned by the Grandduchess Sophia of Sachsen-Weimar. The preoccupation with Goethe's scientific work, which extended over many years, led to an important enrichment of Steiner's contribution to contemporary thought, but it also represented a digression from his central spiritual-scientific research. In this regard he wrote:

Rudolf Steiner in 1882

My presentation of Goethe's ideas was a continual struggle over many years to come to a better understanding of Goethe with the help of his own ideas. When I look back upon this struggle, I have to admit that I largely owe the development of my spiritual experiences in the realm of knowledge to that experience. As a result, this development proceeded far more slowly than it would have if destiny had not set the Goethe work upon my life's path. I would then have pursued my own spiritual experiences and presented them as they occurred. I would have been swept into the spiritual world more quickly, but I would have had no inducement to plunge—wrestling my way down—into my own inner being.

I thus experienced, through my Goethe work, the difference between a state of soul in which the spiritual world reveals itself to a certain degree as an act of grace, and one in which the soul, step by step, first strives to make its own inner being like the spirit—so that, when the soul experiences itself as true spirit, it may then stand within what is spiritual in the world. But in *this* way of "standing within," we first realize that the human spirit and the spirituality in the world may grow into a union with one another within the human soul.

During the time I worked on my interpretation of Goethe, his admonishing spirit was always beside me, ceaselessly calling to me: "Those who stride forward too quickly on the spiritual path can indeed gain spiritual experience within a narrow limit, but they enter an impoverished reality, stripped of all the richness of life."

In my relation to the Goethe work, I could clearly observe how karma "works" in human life. Destiny is made up of two different sets of facts that grow together into a single unity within human life. One streams outward from inner soul struggles; the other moves toward us from the outer world. My soul's own impulses moved toward the perception of the spiritual; the outer spiritual life of the world brought the Goethe work to me. I had to bring the two streams, encountering one another in my consciousness, into conscious harmony. I spent the final years of this first phase of my life alternately justifying myself in my own eyes and in the eyes of Goethe. (*The Course of My Life*, chap. 12)

What was the "Goethe work," to which Rudolf Steiner devoted so many significant years? For a comprehensive answer, readers will want to consult Steiner's introductions to the four volumes of Goethe's scientific works that he edited for publication.[3] In addition, there are many references to Goethe and his work in Steiner's later lectures. These references show us that it was not only the *content* of Goethe's research in the organic sciences, particularly in the fields of botany and zoology, but very centrally Goethe's cognitive method that Steiner recognized as an essential contribution to the

---

3. See also Rudolf Steiner, *Goethean Science*, Mercury Press, Spring Valley, NY, 1988.

further evolution of science. This recognition led him to postpone the completion of his editorial work until he had succeeded in characterizing the method that Goethe used to approach phenomena. Steiner described the fruits of this exploration in his book *The Theory of Knowledge Implicit in Goethe's World Conception*, which he completed in 1886 at the age of twenty-five.[4] The following excerpt from his autobiography may indicate the direction he saw as significant for the future of the organic sciences, as well as for our understanding of nature and our relation to it:

> I saw in Goethe a personality who, because of the particular spiritual relationship in which he placed the human being and the world, was also in a position to place, in an appropriate form, the knowledge of nature into the totality of human achievement.... The details of what Goethe thought and elaborated concerning this or that field of natural science appeared to me less important than the *central* discovery that I had to attribute to him: he had discovered how one needed to think wherever the organic world was concerned, in order to come to terms with it.... For me, Goethe became the Galileo of the organic world.
>
> To understand the inorganic world, concept after concept is arrayed, so as to survey the relationships between the forces that are active in and affect nature. In the organic realm, on the other hand, we have to allow one concept to grow out of the other in such a way that, in the continuous, living, ever-changing concepts, pictures of what appears in nature arise as a being possessing form. Goethe practiced this by seeking to hold an inner image of a leaf in his mind that was not a fixed, lifeless concept, but rather one that could express itself in the most varied forms. When we let such idea-forms proceed one from another, we can eventually construct the whole plant. We recreate in the mind, in idea-form, the process through which nature forms the plant in reality.

---

4. Entitled *The Science of Knowing: Outline of an Epistemology Implicit in the Goethean World View*, Mercury Press, Spring Valley, NY, 1988.

In the introduction to Goethe's botanical writings, I wanted
to point out that, in his theory of metamorphosis, he was thinking about the workings of organic nature in a way that accords
with the spirit. (*The Course of My Life*, chap. 6)[5]

In his thorough study of Goethe, Steiner discovered a scientific
method that leads from the observation of organic nature to the perception of the creative spiritual principles at work within it.

~

Rudolf Steiner's final years in Vienna brought him rich and varied
human contacts. He was a keen, active observer of political life, in
which national groups were struggling for identity and for cultural
and political autonomy. If ever there was a living laboratory in which
to get to know the forces working below the surface of the old social
forms, it was the Austro-Hungarian Empire in the late nineteenth
century, and Steiner was aware of much that his contemporaries
missed. He wrote:

I think back often on the sometimes endless conversations held
at that time in a well-known coffee house on the Michaelerplatz
in Vienna. I especially remembered them after the World War
when the old Austria was falling to pieces. The conditions that
led to this disintegration were even then clearly present everywhere. But no one wanted to admit it. Everyone had different
ideas about how to improve the situation, each according to the
person's particular national or cultural leanings. If the ideals that
live and flow on the rising tide are uplifting, no less great are
those that are born out of decline, out of the desire to reverse it,
though they are tragic. Tragic ideals, indeed, stirred in the
hearts of Vienna's finest citizens, and of all Austrians.

---

5. For an in-depth study of Goethe's approach to nature, see Henri Bortoft,
*The Wholeness of Nature: Goethe's Way toward a Science of Conscious Participation
in Nature*, Lindisfarne Press, 1996.

I often made these idealists unhappy when I expressed something of which I had become convinced through my absorption with Goethe's lifetime. I said that Western culture had reached a peak during that time, and that this level could not be maintained. The scientific age, with its consequences for both individual and community life, signified a decline. If there was to be any further progress, a totally new impulse — a spiritual impulse — was essential. The old trends and ways, the spiritual impulses that have guided us until now, could not be further pursued without falling into a decline. Goethe represents a high point, a culmination — not the beginning of something but the end of something. He reaps the harvest of a cultural evolution that leads up to him, as its highest expression; this development can go no further, however, without turning to far deeper sources of spiritual experience than any to which this evolution has had access. This was my mood when I wrote the last part of my presentation on Goethe.

I was still in this mood when I first met Nietzsche's writings. *Beyond Good and Evil* was the first book by him that I read. I was fascinated by his way of viewing things, and yet at the same time repelled. I found it hard to come to terms with Nietzsche. I loved his style, I loved his boldness; but I did not at all love the way he spoke about the most profound problems without intimately knowing them through fully conscious spiritual experience. I also saw that he said many things that were extremely close to my own spiritual experiences. I could intimately relate to his struggle and sensed that I must find some way to express the closeness that I felt to it. Nietzsche seemed to me one of the most tragic figures of that time. And this tragedy, I believed, arose for human souls of more than ordinary depth and sensitivity out of the nature of the spiritual and cultural outlook of the scientific age. I passed my last years in Vienna living with such feelings as these. (*The Course of My Life*, chap. 13)

~

From these excerpts we can glimpse a web of rich personal and cultural exchange. Through it all, a mind was ripening and coming to know itself. An important milestone in this process was Steiner's doctoral dissertation, published in 1892 under the title *Truth and Science* (*Wahrheit und Wissenschaft*).[6] Barred from taking a Ph.D. in Austria because he had attended the *Realschule* rather than the humanistic *Gymnasium* (even though he had privately completed that course and had tutored others in it), Steiner submitted his dissertation to Heinrich von Stein, then teaching philosophy at the University of Rostock in Germany. Steiner was attracted to von Stein because of his *Seven Books of Platonism*. "In the first chapters of von Stein's book," Steiner wrote in his autobiography, "the reader completely and vitally enters the Platonic worldview. Stein then goes on to describe how the revelation of Christ breaks into human evolution. He places the actuality of this spiritual reality breaking in— the spiritual life—higher than the elaboration of ideas through mere philosophy. Stein's thesis regards the development from Plato to Christ as the fulfillment of what human beings have striven for" (*The Course of My Life*, chap. 14). It was not only the content of the book but the warmth and deep religious feeling of its author showing through it that drew Steiner to him:

> I have always carried Heinrich von Stein's image deeply engraved on my heart. It would have given me boundless pleasure to meet the man again, but destiny did not bring us together after that. My doctoral examination is one of my happiest memories because the impression of Stein's personality outshines everything else connected with it.
>
> When I arrived in Weimar, my mood was still colored by the intensity of all the work I had been doing on Platonism. I think that this mood greatly helped me find my way into my assignment at the Goethe and Schiller Archives. How did Plato live in

---

6. *Truth and Knowledge: Introduction to "Philosophy of Spiritual Activity,"* Steinerbooks, Blauvelt, NY, 1981; also *Truth and Science: Prelude to a "Philosophy of Spiritual Activity,"* Mercury Press, Spring Valley, NY, 1993.

the world of ideas? How did Goethe? These thoughts occupied
me as I walked to and from the Archives; they also occupied me
as I went over the manuscripts of Goethe's literary estate. (ibid.)

The Vienna years closed with Steiner's submission of his doctoral
dissertation, which he himself characterized by the question: "How
can human consciousness come to understand itself?" Steiner's hard-
won accomplishments during this period included the work on his
dissertation; forging an epistemology (an understanding of the process of knowing) that would underlie Goethe's scientific work; the
struggle to understand and transcend mysticism as a deeply rooted,
but one-sided striving for reality; and a recognition of the greatness
and the tragedy inherent in Nietzsche's work and in Nietzsche himself. All these achievements and insights were the outer expressions
of Steiner's commitment to building a bridge of knowledge, so that
those who lived in a scientific, intellectual age could progress in freedom from sense-bound cognition to a conscious, self-sustaining
experience of spiritual reality. His central discovery was that human
thinking is *itself* that bridge, when it awakens through inner initiative to knowing itself as a free spiritual activity. *The Theory of Knowledge Implicit in Goethe's World Conception* and *Truth and Science*
documented his inner journey along this path, which was to lead him
directly to his fundamental philosophical work, *Die Philosophie der
Freiheit* (*The Philosophy of Freedom*), published in 1894.[7]

In 1889, at the age of 28, Rudolf Steiner made his first trip to Germany. He did so both to respond to an invitation to join the staff of
the Goethe-Schiller Archives in Weimar and also to take his doctoral examination with Heinrich von Stein in Rostock. He returned
to Vienna for a final, intensive six months, and in the autumn of
1890 moved to Weimar, leaving Vienna for good.

---

7. To avoid confusion, hereafter, *Die Philosophie der Freiheit* will be referred to by
its German title, since there have been several different English titles. Current
editions include *Intuitive Thinking As a Spiritual Path: A Philosophy of Freedom*
(Anthroposophic Press, Hudson, NY, 1995) and *The Philosophy of Spiritual
Activity: A Philosophy of Freedom* (Rudolf Steiner Press, Bristol, 1992). Steiner
himself suggested *Philosophy of Spiritual Activity* for the English translation.

3

The
Weimar Years

Nietzsche, Steiner and the Redemption of Thinking

Rudolf Steiner's autobiography introduces his Weimar period in a chapter devoted to the leading personalities at the Goethe- Schiller Archives. Through Steiner's descriptions we not only gain insight into a group of remarkably cultivated scholars but also glimpse two very different attitudes toward the task in which they were all engaged. One approach was anchored in philological scholarship and strove above all to be scientifically objective. The other was represented by scholars who allowed themselves to be filled with the soul and spirit of Goethe's creative personality. An outstanding member of this second group was Herman Grimm. "Whenever Herman Grimm appeared in Weimar, and at the Institute," Steiner wrote, "one felt that the place where Goethe's legacy was housed was somehow united with him by secret spiritual threads." Of interest to American readers is the relationship between Ralph Waldo Emerson and Herman Grimm; their correspondence spanned fifteen years, from 1856 to 1871.[1]

We meet these individuals in Steiner's autobiography through his refreshingly positive portrayals, which nevertheless allow clear, discriminating characterizations to shine through. As always, we are also given glimpses into the inner perceptions of the one who writes. Of Herman Grimm, whom he greatly admired, he said:

---

1. See Note C in Appendix, page 266.

Here was a man whose inner vision reached as far as the creative spiritual but who would not take hold of this spirituality for his own life of conscious cognition; he remained in the region where the spiritual expresses itself in human beings as imagination." (*The Course of My Life*, chap. 14)

This chapter, like so many in Steiner's autobiography, is worthwhile reading on its own.

Although many of the intensely interesting personalities who live in the autobiography's pages are virtually unknown to contemporary readers, there are several who were known far beyond the limits of Middle Europe and of the German language. Outstanding among these are Ernst Haeckel, Heinrich von Treitschke, the historian, Gabrielle Reuter, who wrote *Of a Good Family*, as well as Grimm. But unquestionably, the person who stirred the deepest response in Steiner during his Weimar years was Friedrich Nietzsche himself. Chapter 18 of Steiner's autobiography is devoted entirely to his encounter with Nietzsche.

As mentioned, Steiner first met Nietzsche's work during 1889, his last year in Vienna. This work impressed Steiner so deeply that, at the age of twenty-eight, he felt impelled to read virtually everything Nietzsche had written. After Steiner moved to Weimar, he absorbed himself in Nietzsche's tragic destiny, which was symptomatic of the spiritual drama of the late nineteenth century. After long immersion in Nietzsche's work, Steiner was finally able to stand in the physical presence of the man himself. In his opening essay on Nietzsche's character in his book, *Friedrich Nietzsche, Fighter for Freedom* (1895), Steiner characterized his relationship to Nietzsche by paraphrasing Nietzsche's own characterization of his relationship to Schopenhauer:

I am one of those readers of Nietzsche who, after they have read the first page, know with certainty that they will read every page and listen to every word he has said. My confidence in him was there immediately.... I understood him as if he had written just for me in order to express all that I would say intelligibly, but immodestly and foolishly. One can speak this way and still be far from acknowledging oneself as a "believer" in Nietzsche's worldview. But Nietzsche himself could not be farther from wishing to have such "believers."[2]

Nietzsche's sister, Elizabeth Foerster-Nietzsche (herself destined to play a tragic role), tried hard to convince Steiner to take over the directorship of the Nietzsche archives, which she hoped to establish on a basis similar to that of the Goethe-Schiller Archives in Weimar. Although her attempt was unsuccessful, Steiner did agree to organize Nietzsche's personal library. During one of Steiner's frequent visits to Nietzsche's house in Naumburg, Elizabeth Foerster-Nietzsche finally brought him into the room where the great thinker lay, totally disconnected in spirit from his immediate physical environment. Steiner described his experience:

He lay on a couch in mental darkness. His extraordinarily beautiful forehead was both that of an artist and a thinker in one. It was early afternoon. His eyes, though nearly extinguished, still actively revealed his soul, but now they merely pictured his surroundings, and the picture no longer reached his mind, his soul. One stood there, but Nietzsche was unaware of it. And yet one could have believed, from that spiritual, intelligent countenance, that it belonged to someone who had spent the entire morning in serious thought and now wished to rest awhile. The inner shock that gripped me was somehow transformed into a deep sympathy and understanding for the genius whose gaze was fixed on me and yet did not meet mine. The passivity of this gaze, which remained fixed on me for a long time, freed the understanding of my own gaze, allowing the power of eye contact to become active, even though my eyes were not met.

---

2. *Friedrich Nietzsche: Fighter for Freedom*, Spiritual Science Library, Blauvelt, NY, 1985, pp. 42–43.

I stood there and observed Nietzsche's soul, as though it hovered above his head, infinitely beautiful in its spirit light, freely surrendered to the spiritual worlds, which it had longed for but never found before illness clouded his mind. This soul was still bound to his physical body, which was only aware of it when the soul's longing was directed to the daily, physical world. Nietzsche's soul was still present, but it could maintain itself against the body only from outside, the body that had resisted the full unfolding of the soul's light as long as the soul remained within it.

Until now I had only *read* the words Nietzsche had written; now I *observed* the man who, within his body, actually bore ideas drawn from the most distant spiritual realms—ideas that still sparkled in their beauty, despite having lost their original radiance on the way. A soul that brought golden riches of light from previous lives on earth, but was not quite able to let it all shine in this life. I admired what Nietzsche had written; but now I saw a luminous form behind all that I had admired.

In my thoughts I could only stammer over what I had seen; and this stammering is in effect my book *Friedrich Nietzsche: Fighter for Freedom* [*Friedrich Nietzsche, Ein Kampfer gegen seine Zeit*, literally "Friedrich Nietzsche: A Fighter against His Time"]. That the book is no more than a stammering nevertheless conceals what is true, that the form of Nietzsche I beheld inspired the book.

Frau Foerster-Nietzsche then asked me to put Nietzsche's library in order. Doing this gave me the opportunity to spend several weeks in the Nietzsche archives at Naumburg. It also led to a closer friendship with Fritz Koegel. The task was a wonderful one, allowing me to see the books that Nietzsche himself had studied. His spiritual presence was alive in all the impressions that emanated from these volumes; a volume of Emerson, filled with notes written in the margins and bearing all the signs of devoted study. It was the same for Guyau's writings. There were pages of passionately critical comments in Nietzsche's handwriting, and a great many marginal notes in which one could see the germs of Nietzsche's ideas taking form.

Friedrich Nietzsche

One of Nietzsche's penetrating ideas from his final creative period lit up for me as I read the marginal comments he had made in Eugen Duehring's major philosophical work. In this book, Duehring develops the idea that one can picture the cosmos at any given moment as a combination of basic, fundamental components. Thus the evolution of the world would be a succession of all the possible combinations of these factors. When these had been exhausted, the original combination would take place again, and the whole series would repeat itself. If such a possibility were the true reality, it must already have occurred countless times in the past and would continue on again countless times in the future. We would thus come to the idea of an eternal repetition of the same conditions of the universe. Duehring rejects this thought as an impossibility. Nietzsche reads this; it impresses itself upon him and works on in the depths of his soul, and finally takes form within him as "the eternal return of the same," which, together with the idea of the *Übermensch* (the superhuman) dominates his final creative period.

I was profoundly impressed—even shocked—by the impression I received from thus accompanying Nietzsche in his reading; for I saw what a contrast there was between Nietzsche's spirituality and that of his contemporaries. Duehring, the extreme positivist, who rejects everything that does not arise out of a system based on a totally rational, mathematical approach, considers "the eternal return of the same" an absurd idea and only constructs it to demonstrate its impossibility. Nietzsche, on the other hand, is compelled to take it up, as though it were an intuition arising from the depths of his own soul, as *his* solution to the great, universal riddle.

Thus Nietzsche absolutely opposed much that assaulted him as the thought and feeling content of his own time. He took the brunt of this assault in such a way that it caused him intense sorrow, and out of sorrow and unspeakable pain, he created the inner world of his own soul. This was the tragedy of his creative work. (*The Course of My Life*, chap. 18)

That Steiner could enter so deeply and sympathetically into another's perspective while holding radically different views and conceptions, was something his contemporaries found almost impossible to understand. This limited view led many at the time to see Steiner as a "Nietzschean," an opponent of Christianity, and a dangerous challenger of the established, liberal, conventional, materialistic views.

Steiner concluded his chapter on Nietzsche:

It was clear to me that in certain of Nietzsche's thoughts, which strove to reach the realm of spirit, he was a prisoner of his own view of nature. This was why I was strongly opposed to a mystical interpretation of his idea of "the eternal return".... Nietzsche believed that lofty thought could be erected only on the basis of a scientific point of view. This was how he had to suffer the consequences of the age in which he lived.

My glimpse of Nietzsche's soul in 1896 thus showed me a man who looked toward the spirit and had to suffer because of the way that nature and the world were perceived and conceived at the end of the nineteenth century. (ibid.)

~

The main achievement of Steiner's Weimar years was the completion in 1894 of his book *Die Philosophie der Freiheit* (*The Philosophy of Freedom*).[3] This volume—which carried the subtitle *Results of Soul Observations Arrived at by the Scientific Method*—begins with the sentence, "Is a human being spiritually *free*, or subject to the iron necessity of purely natural law?" The search for an answer to this question lies at the heart of what it means to be, or to become, a moral human being. In our present time, it is precisely in the struggle to find that place in ourselves where we can experience freedom that we first become truly human. In the first part of *Die Philosophie der Freiheit*, we are led to discover that we forge, in the innermost activity of the self in thinking, the instrument that enables us to become free. If we can awaken to ourselves in the experience of thinking, the way is open for actions that are potentially free.

For the student of Steiner's *Die Philosophie der Freiheit* the question arises: Who is it, actually, who thinks in me? Is it this miraculous brain with its countless neural connections? And what is the real nature of the thoughts that light up so astonishingly in my consciousness? Whatever their ultimate nature may prove to be, and whoever this being is, who thinks in me, I know to begin with that I am the one who brings concepts to bear on perceptions from the outside world. I see a tree in a meadow, for example. Its leaves and branches are still. Then they begin to move, to toss, quiver, and shake. With no visible perception of the cause of such sudden motion, I know that a breeze has begun to blow. I am the one who unites the concept "breeze" with the phenomenon of moving leaves and branches. This act of uniting an idea, or concept, with a perception—this process of thinking—is how I have come to understand the world around me. By its means I have gained knowledge of the laws that govern the phenomena I observe.

If I now do not direct this activity toward the outer objects of perception, but instead place the activity of my own thinking itself at the

---

3. See footnote, page 45.

center of my consciousness, I find myself in a new and unique situation. I now focus my own self-generated thinking on an object that I have brought about myself—that is, I observe and think about my own process of thought.

I may, at first, be able to sustain this act of consciousness for only a split second. But if I work at it and practice it as a cognitional skill, I discover that my thinking begins to take on a new quality. I experience a sense of "muscle," I begin to be able to "feel out," or "touch," the object of thought, and I am able to direct this newly awakened organ of "thinking perception" toward an inner realm of experience in which ideas "light up" in a new and more conscious way. I gain the capacity to receive and select the ideas that come to me with greater consciousness and, as a result, also with a greater inner freedom. With continuous exercise I find myself more and more able to bring to bear on any particular situation, outer or inner, the particular concept that is uniquely related to the given object of perception. No matter how clumsy I may be at this exercise, I sense that I have set foot on a path that can lead me toward freedom.

As modern self-conscious human beings, we are born into a condition of consciousness in which the world confronts us as a "given" object of experience; we stand apart and observe this given world. But our everyday consciousness—like the prow of a ship cutting through the waves—divides the waters of the single ocean of experience into two separate streams that flow past and through us as percepts from without and as concepts from within. (It should be noted that what rise from the subconscious as memories, feelings, mental pictures, and so on, belong also to the world of the given.) We do not know whether concept and percept really belong together. We know only that one concept appears to explain a given percept, that one "works," and another doesn't.

If, however, I can find my way to the bow of the ship of human consciousness and, standing at the prow, see the single ocean ahead and, thus, also know that the water to starboard was an instant ago mingled with the water to the port side and that it will mingle again the moment the ship has passed, then I can know with confidence that percept and concept are two aspects of a single whole. One way to characterize Steiner's *Die Philosophie der Freiheit* is to say that it can lead us to the "prow of the ship" where we can see that percept and concept are indeed two aspects of a single reality that we reunite through the act of cognition. Thinking can thus come to know itself as the activity that reunites the outer world of perception with the inner world of human experience.

The knowledge of freedom makes possible the reality of freedom in human actions. Correspondingly, the first part of this book deals with moral insight, and the second part with moral action. In the awakening of the individual to the experience of thinking, to its innermost activity as ideal yet direct perception of spiritual reality, Steiner found the bridge that can, in free cognition, lead modern human beings from the world of sense experience to the realm of supersensible perception, from the world that we "see" to the world that, initially, we "do not see." Published when Steiner was thirty-three, *Die Philosophie der Freiheit* provided the cognitive cornerstone on which to build the structure of a spiritual science—*Anthroposophy*—when the time became ripe.

~

Another circumstance of his life in Weimar, for which Steiner expressed tremendous gratitude, occurred after nearly two years of unsatisfactory bachelor life. He found a congenial home amid the family of Anna Eunicke, whose husband had recently died, leaving her with the responsibility of raising five children—four daughters and a son. Frau Eunicke offered Rudolf Steiner an apartment in her house with the understanding that he would help with her children's education, which he was glad to do. This provided Steiner with the living situation he needed and with the freedom to devote himself to his work. He became thoroughly at home in the Eunicke family, where he and Anna Eunicke developed a warm friendship. They were subsequently married during October 1899 in Berlin; the Eunicke family had moved there a short while before Steiner's own move to that city. Anna Steiner-Eunicke died in March 1911. She had separated from Rudolf Steiner several years before her death, as his life became increasingly absorbed in the activities that arose from his spiritual-scientific work. Shortly before her death, she spoke to her daughter Wilhelmine, saying that her time with Rudolf Steiner was the most beautiful period of her life.

~

The close of Rudolf Steiner's Weimar years coincided with a powerful inner transition that began as he turned thirty-five. He wrote:

> Understanding what can be experienced in the spiritual world was always second nature to me; but to grasp the sense world in fully aware perception had always been extremely difficult. It was as though I could not pour my soul's experience deeply enough into my sense organs to connect the full extent of what *they* experienced with my soul. (*The Course of My Life*, chap. 22)

Until the age of 35, Steiner had experienced no difficulty in grasping wide-ranging scientific and philosophical concepts. He had firmly grasped them in his mind just as he had made spiritual realities his own. But to perceive outer objects in an exact and detailed way, and to remember those perceptions, had required enormous concentration and effort on his part. This now changed; a new capacity of attentiveness awoke in him. Physical details became important. It was as though the sense world had something to reveal that could be revealed in no other way:

> I realized that I was experiencing a major developmental change at a much later age than was usual for other people. I also saw that this had very specific consequences for my inner life. I saw that, because at an early age people leave the stage behind where the soul weaves within the spiritual world and pass on to an experience of the physical, they do not achieve a pure grasp of either the spiritual or the physical world. They continually mix up, completely unconsciously and instinctively, what *things* say to their senses and what the mind experiences from the spirit and then uses to "conceive" things and to make mental pictures.

In the exactness and thoroughness of sense perception, I experienced a doorway into a whole new world. To free oneself from all subjectivity, and confront the sense world in a totally objective way, revealed something to which a spiritual outlook had nothing to say. (*The Course of My Life*, chap. 22)

Steiner discovered that this new ability to penetrate sense perceptions with the fullest activity of his soul also intensified his capacity for pure soul-spiritual experience. It was as if the outward grasp now freed a force for inner observation that brought new clarity, unintruded upon by the physical.

This revolution in consciousness had even further consequences. Steiner's newly intensified sense activity brought with it an enhanced power for observation in the human realm. He expressed this as an ability to "take in quite objectively, purely through perception, what lives in a human being" (ibid.). To observe uncritically, free from any sympathy or antipathy, became his ideal.

As never before, the experience of the sense world on the one hand, and of the spiritual world on the other, confronted him in full opposition. But it was not a gray or lifeless equalizing of the two worlds that he was seeking:

Rather, I felt that, to stand fully amid this confrontation of opposites was necessary to "an understanding for life." Wherever contrasts *appear* to have been smoothed over, there the force of death, of lifelessness, has taken over. Wherever there is life, unresolved opposites are actively working. Life itself is the continuous overcoming and, at the same time, the new creation of opposing forces. (ibid.)

What now ensued for Steiner was a strengthening of all he had struggled for in his attempt to understand how spiritual reality can pass over into human conscious experience through the mediation of thought. It had become clear to him that the world presents itself to us as a riddle, and we must look for the solution in our own being:

"The human being *is* the solution to this riddle." Seen in this light, knowledge is not merely incidental to world reality; it is a real event in the world, an active, co-creative force:

> We are not beings who produce what we know and understand just for ourselves. No, we provide through our own souls the stage on which the world first comes to experience some of its existence and becoming. If there were no [human] knowledge and understanding, the world would remain incomplete.... In my concept of knowing, we ourselves are co-creators of the world and not mere copiers of something that could be taken away from the world without lessening its completeness. (ibid.)

Along with this inner change, Steiner experienced meditation in a new way. It was no longer an activity that he recognized as important for his mental life in terms of ideas, but it became "a living necessity" for his inner life: "The life of the soul that had been developed needed meditation just as an organism at a certain stage in its development [that is, at birth] needs to breathe through its own lungs" (ibid.).

To the knowing based on sense perception, and the spiritual knowing through ideas gained through the thinker's grasp of his or her own thought activity (as developed in *Die Philosophie der Freiheit*), a third level of cognition now opened up for Steiner: a form of knowing in which the knower could become "as free of the physical organism as if it were not there at all."

With this achievement we could say that Steiner's preparation time was over. He was now ready to assume his rightful place as a master. His inborn gift of spiritual perception had been tested and transformed and was now a fully disciplined and conscious instrument for knowledge. Spiritual science and the possibility for genuine spiritual-scientific research were now potentially available, even though it was the inner achievement of only a single individual. For him the burning question was: "How can a way be found to bring what is inwardly perceived as true into forms of expression that can be understood by this age?" Had the time finally come? Was he at last ready? Were there human beings who wanted to hear what he had to say? These were the questions that he carried with him when, in 1897, he left Weimar and moved to Berlin.

Rudolf Steiner in 1901

4

The Years
of Inner Testing

Berlin

During the years in Vienna and Weimar, Rudolf Steiner had experienced many wonderful friendships and made significant acquaintances. The pages of his autobiography are filled with descriptions of these men and women. In these people, he had seen a great deal of idealism, many hopes and strivings, and abundant gifts and talents. Yet, inwardly, he remained alone. Steiner found it possible with only very few to go beyond a world of subjective soul experience and enter the realm of spiritual reality, though friendships remained heartfelt and often deeply personal. Even with those who directly experienced the spirit, there was never the awareness that such experience might lead one into disciplined, objective spiritual research. Steiner remained silent, therefore, about the questions that concerned him most deeply. And yet he felt increasingly that the day must come when he would be free to speak, because he had been asked. He saw that human and earthly needs were growing constantly.

Behind the scenes of the complex events taking place in the outer world, momentous things were happening. In his later work, Steiner spoke about them on many occasions. In 1879, he said, a guiding spiritual power began its rise to leadership in a world invisibly adjacent to sense-perceptible existence, and this being's leadership will continue for the next three to four hundred years. Steiner identified this guiding power as the spiritual being (known by various names) referred to in the Bible as *Michael*. Traditional Christianity knows him as the Archangel Michael, or as Saint Michael. Saint George is a human and earthly reflection of this being. Steiner characterized this Michaelic power as one of cosmic intelligence, one that will not intervene directly in human affairs, but waits for human beings to initiate spiritual matters.

The second event—a significant milestone in spiritual history—was the transition from what ancient wisdom knew as the Age of Darkness, the Iron Age, to the dawning new age, the Age of Light. The Vedas say that the Kali Yuga, the Age of Darkness, will last for 5,000 years. Rudolf Steiner confirmed this tradition, adding that the Dark Age ended in 1899.

~

Steiner's Weimar assignment was concluded when he published his book on the epistemology underlying Goethe's approach to nature. The book appeared in 1897 under the title *The Theory of Knowledge Implicit in Goethe's World Conception*. With this achievement behind him, Steiner seized an opportunity to gauge and "sound out" the souls of his contemporaries by accepting an offer to take over as editor of a weekly journal in Berlin.

The *Magazin für Literatur* was founded in 1832, the year of Goethe's death, and went through various phases in the following years. In the eighties and nineties, it was swept into the currents of change that were seeking literary and artistic expression. To keep its readership, the magazine had become a vehicle for the Independent Literary Society, headquartered in Berlin with branches in various German cities. As its editor, Steiner was required to engage with the Society as well:

> This gave me a ready-made circle of readers for the magazine, and now I had to find my way into their intellectual and spiritual needs. The Independent Literary Society gave me a membership who expected something very specific, because something very specific had been offered to them until now. In any case, they were not expecting the kind of thing that I would have liked most to give them out of my own heart. The characteristic

stamp of the Independent Literary Society was created by its desire to form a sort of opposite pole to the *Literarische Gesellschaft* (Literary Society), which received its predominant tone from individuals such as Spielhagen.

My position within the spiritual world called for me to enter into this new situation as intimately as possible. I made every effort to transpose myself into the minds and hearts of my readers, and into the membership of the Society, in order to find, out of their spiritual makeup, the forms into which I could pour what I wanted to give them.

I cannot say that, at the beginning of this activity, I succumbed to illusions that were gradually destroyed. But this kind of working outward from the circle of readers and listeners, according to the possibilities given to me, met with increasingly greater obstacles. You could not count on any serious or penetrating spiritual motives from the people who had been attracted to the magazine before I took it over. Only in a few cases were their interests very deeply rooted. And even in these few cases, there were no strong, clear underlying forces arising from the human spirit, but more of a general desire seeking expression in a medley of artistic and other intellectual forms.

So I soon had to question whether or not I could justify—either to myself or to the spiritual world—working within this circle of people. Even though many of those concerned were very dear to me, and I felt connected with them through ties of friendship, yet even they were among the ones who led me—as I confronted what lived so vitally in me—to ask myself: Must I continue to keep silent? (*The Course of My Life*, chap. 24)

It was characteristic of countless personal relationships that Steiner had formed in both Weimar and Vienna that there was always a purely human element that went beyond the literary or scholarly countenance of a given personality. However, at that time in Berlin, a person's outer attributes (one might call them the stamp of a given trade or calling) were so deeply embedded that the purely human qualities were pushed into the background. Thus, because of the prevailing social circumstances, it was difficult for Steiner to mingle freely in a simple, human way in the strongly contrasting realms of social life characteristic of life in Berlin at this time. Destiny cast him, through the *Magazin für Literatur* and the Independent Literary Society, into the avant-garde stream of life among the writers, dramatists, and artistic personalities who studded the last years of the century in the cosmopolitan capital of the new Germany. He found himself isolated from the more traditional and "respectable" circle of friends, whom he had also delighted in knowing in Weimar.

Rather than lessening Steiner's interest in individual human qualities, these circumstances seemed to intensify it. He observed his contemporaries objectively and compassionately, perceiving indications about their karma in the outer physical details of their bodily structure and in their characteristic gestures. This interest is expressed particularly in his autobiography, as, for example, when he describes his impressions of the playwright Frank Wedekind, whom he met at a literary gathering in Leipzig. The delicacy of Steiner's sensible and supersensible perceptions requires an inner mobility of vision on the part of the reader:

> Once, after I had given a lecture and O. J. Bierbaum had given a reading at the Independent Literary Society in Leipzig, I was sitting with a group that also included Frank Wedekind. I could not take my eyes away from this truly rare figure of a man. I mean "figure" here in a purely physical sense. Such hands! They were as though from a previous earthly life in which they had done things that can only be done by people who let the spirit flow right down through the branching fingers into each fingertip. Perhaps this could have given an impression of brutality, because energy had been expended, yet what streamed from those hands attracted the greatest interest. And that expressive head—it was altogether like a gift from that characteristic will gesture of the hands. There was something in his glance and the play of his features that voluntarily gave itself to the world, but could also retreat again at will, just

as the gestures of the arms give themselves to expressing what the hands experience.

A spirit at odds with the present time spoke from that head—a spirit that really placed itself apart from the human impulses of the present, a spirit that could not be inwardly clear about *which* world of the past it belonged to. As a writer (and I am only stating what I perceived in him and not making a literary judgment) Frank Wedekind was like a chemist who utterly rejects contemporary views about chemistry and practices alchemy, but even so, in a cynical way, without an inner commitment to it. One could learn a great deal about the working of the spirit on the [human] form by taking the outer appearance of Frank Wedekind into the soul's vision—not staring like one of those psychologists who wants to "look at people," but looking in a way that shows the purely human against the background of the spiritual world through an inner dispensation of destiny, which one does not seek but simply comes.

Someone who becomes aware of being observed by a psychologist may justly be annoyed; but moving from a purely human circumstance to "perceiving the spiritual background" is also purely human, somewhat like passing from a casual to an intimate friendship. (*The Course of My Life*, chap. 24)[1]

Two important points are indicated here. One is the significance of the physical form as an expression of the spirit's formative role in the building of the body. Of equal importance is the attitude of the observer, of the one qualified to conduct "karmic research." For anyone endowed with the capacity for spiritual-scientific research, objectivity and true selflessness are decisive factors. The researcher must be able to observe without triggering the slightest personal sympathy or antipathy.

---

1. Steiner further commented on Wedekind in *Karmic Relationships: Esoteric Studies*, vol. 2, Rudolf Steiner Press, London, 1996 (lecture of Apr. 26, 1924; see Note D page 267 in Appendix.

In practicing such observations, it became clear to Steiner that these men, with whom he was associated through the magazine and the Society, were woven into his destiny, yet he also had to recognize that he was "in no way woven into theirs." He wrote: "My position within this group became inwardly unbearable because of the feeling that I knew why I was there, but they did not" (ibid.).

~

Yet another initiative was linked with Steiner's work as editor of the *Magazin für Literatur* and his contributions to the Independent Literary Society: he actively involved himself with a dramatic society dedicated to producing contemporary plays that never would have been produced in the established theaters of the day. Steiner especially enjoyed staging the plays, and he and Hartleben—the lovable, but unpredictable coeditor of the *Magazin*—worked together in this. Steiner was intensely interested in how to work so as to evoke a feeling of participation and of freedom in the actors and the audience. He made these observations:

> We saw that all theorizing and dogmatizing were useless if they did not emerge from a living artistic sense that intuitively grasped, in each detail, the general requirement of the overall style or quality called for. We had to work at avoiding any general rules. Anything that a person's talent might bring to such an effort had to be sacrificed at any moment, out of a sure sense of style and gesture, to the way the scenes were directed. When you work in this way, what you create brings—without any intellectual consideration, but out of an active sense for style— a feeling of satisfaction to every artist in the cast, whereas an arbitrary rule stemming from the intellect gives them the feeling that their inner freedom is being infringed upon.
>
> I looked back again and again with great satisfaction to the experiences I had in this field. (*The Course of My Life*, chap. 25)

Steiner was often called on to introduce a production with a "few words" if the play expressed an artistic purpose unfamiliar to the audience. Especially satisfying to Rudolf Steiner in this role was the opportunity it gave him to allow a certain mood, a certain soul quality, to come to expression. For Steiner, a mood that flowed from the spirit was thus given a voice and an entry into an environment that otherwise had no ear for the spirit.

This active life in the theater also led Steiner to write dramatic criticisms for the magazine, a task for which he developed his own approach. His goal was to write about a play, and a production, in a way that offered the reader an in-depth experience of the "living, though unconscious, spiritual gesture that inspired the actor, the director, or the playwright," rather than simply making a subjective critic's "judgment." As Steiner describes it, when this ideal is practiced for all branches of art, "a literary-artistic periodical can stand in the midst of real life." This was the goal he strove for as long as he edited the *Magazin für Literatur*.

~

In the very last years of the nineteenth century and the first of the twentieth, Rudolf Steiner experienced what he spoke of as a time of great inner testing. Such testing is given to each of us by destiny and has to be experienced and transformed through our spiritual development. It is most significant that Steiner's testing was intimately connected with his relationship to the essence of Christianity.

Rudolf Steiner had been accused earlier of being anti-Christian. It was subsequently said that his statements around the turn of the century were inconsistent with what he wrote later. He deals with this criticism in one of the shortest chapters in his autobiography. There he points out that it is the concept relegating Christianity to the "beyond" that he opposed. For him, the view of Christianity as a revelation that comes to the human being from without—from a realm we may believe in but cannot know—was at odds with his awareness of a world of spirit that could be experienced and known directly through an act of free cognition. The "ethical individualism" whose cognitive foundations he had developed in *Die Philosophie der Freiheit* (*The Philosophy of Freedom*) also opposed a system of ethical conduct based on precepts coming to humanity from an outer authority. In

Die Philosophie der Freiheit he had worked his way to a concept of moral guidance coming "not from without by way of commandments to be obeyed, but out of the unfolding of the human soul and spirit, in which the divine lives" (*The Course of My Life*. chap. 26).

For us today, living more than one hundred years after the time referred to in Steiner's autobiography, the existential question might be expressed as follows: How will human beings come to experience their own thinking? Can we learn to think in a new way, a way that is truly alive and springs from the creative forces of the cosmos? Our faculty of thought has been gained over the course of centuries through the struggle to wrest knowledge from the natural world. Knowledge has been attained through an objective, disciplined sense perception that is digested, analyzed, and penetrated by impersonal, scientific thinking. Do we have the inner energy and activity of soul to transform it into knowledge of experienced spiritual reality, or will we yield to forces that would reduce all knowledge to what is mechanistic and quantifiable? Steiner fought this battle in his own soul; as one who lived within supersensible reality, his struggle was not against abstractions, but with actual beings. He writes:

> What went on at that time within my soul as I stood face to face with the experience of Christianity was for me a powerful testing. The time between leaving Weimar up until the time when I was working on my book *Christianity as Mystical Fact* was filled with testing. Such soul challenges are the resistance given us by destiny, by karma, which we have to overcome through our spiritual development.
>
> I saw in the thinking that can follow from knowledge of nature, or true natural science—which did not then, however, actually follow from it—I saw in this thinking the foundation on which human beings can achieve insight into the world of spirit. I therefore sharply emphasized the knowledge of the natural foundation that must lead to spirit knowledge. For the one who is unable to stand in inner experience within the spiritual world, as I did at that time, such a submerging of oneself into a direction of thought is merely a mental exercise. For the one, however,

who experiences the spiritual world, it signifies something very different. Such a one is brought into the presence of beings in the spiritual world who wish to make the physical-material direction of thought exclusively dominant. In such a situation, one-sidedness in knowledge is not merely the cause of abstract error; for then, what is merely error in the human realm is living spiritual interaction with beings. I later spoke of ahrimanic beings when I wanted to indicate this realm of experience. For these beings it is an absolute truth that the world must be a machine. They live in a sphere that borders directly on the sense-perceptible world.

In my own thinking, I did not fall prey to these beings, even for a moment. Also, not in the subconscious, for I gave the closest attention to be sure that all my knowledge was gained in clearest, most awake experience. In consequence, my inner battle was all the more conscious against these demonic powers whose will it was that a mechanical-materialistic way of thinking should arise from the knowledge of nature, rather than perception of spirit.

The one who seeks knowledge of spirit must *experience* these worlds; for such a person, merely theoretical thinking about them does not suffice. I had to rescue my spirit perception in inner storms of battle. These storms stood behind my outer experiences.

I was only able to make progress in this time of testing when I was able to bring the evolution of Christianity, in spirit perception, before my soul. This led to knowledge that came to expression in the book *Christianity as Mystical Fact.*... Nowhere in the existing Christian religious denominations had I found the Christianity that I felt the need to seek. After I had been forced to undergo the hard soul battles to which this time of testing subjected me, I found it necessary to steep myself in Christianity—indeed, to do so in that realm in which Christianity appears to spiritual perception. (*The Course of My Life*, chap. 28)

In the midst of describing his struggle with the essence of Christianity, Steiner refers to a much earlier experience that contributed to his questioning the existing exoteric religious confessions.

During his Vienna years, Steiner came into contact with a number of professors in the theological faculty of the University of Vienna, Catholic priests of the finest intellectual learning. Outstanding among them was Wilhelm Neumann, a Cistercian priest of the Order of the Holy Cross. Steiner, who was then in his twenties, gladly accompanied Neumann as they left the stimulating gatherings in the home of the poet Eugenia delle Grazie. Steiner recounts his experience of two conversations with Neumann. The first concerned the Christ Being. Steiner described in this conversation how Jesus of Nazareth received the Christ Being into himself and how Christ then lives within human evolution as a spiritual entity since His death and resurrection, the event that Steiner almost always refers to as the "Mystery of Golgotha."

> This conversation remained deeply impressed within my soul, from which it arose again and again in memory. It had deep significance for me. In this conversation, three persons actually spoke together: Professor Neumann and myself and a third, invisible presence, the personification of Catholic dogma, who revealed himself to supersensible observation behind professor Neumann. Whenever the finely-tuned logic of the learned man tended to agree with me too readily, the invisible presence tapped him admonishingly on the shoulder to set him right. In this encounter it was curious how often the opening part of the sentence reversed itself in the conclusion. On such occasions, I stood in the presence of one of the finest representatives of the Catholic way of life; just through this experience I learned to respect it, but also learned to know it in a truly well-grounded way. (*The Course of My Life*, chap. 7)

In this passage, we glimpse Rudolf Steiner in his early adult years, searching the finest, most subtle thinking of representatives of Christian tradition, for the echoes of the realities that lived within him as direct supersensible experience. He writes at the close of this chapter:

At the time when I made the statements about Christianity, which in their literal content were so contradictory to what I later said, it was also true that the real content of Christianity was beginning to unfold within me like an inner seed-germ of knowledge. Around the turn of the century this seed-germ was in a continual state of unfolding. The testing of my soul that was described above ushered in the turn of the century. The development of my soul was achieved through having stood spiritually before the Mystery of Golgotha in a most inward, most solemn festival of knowledge. (ibid.)

The following chapter begins:

The thought then hovered before me that the turn of the century must bring a new spiritual light to humanity. It seemed to me that the closing off of human thinking and willing from the spirit had reached its peak. A revolutionary change in the process of human development seemed to me an absolute necessity. (*The Course of My Life*, chap. 27)

~

During these years Steiner was asked to give courses in history and public speaking at the Berlin Workers' School, founded by Karl Liebknecht in 1891. Steiner's view of history directly contradicted the Marxist view that dominated the Workers' School. To Marx, economic and material forces were the only realities involved in shaping the historical process. Cultural ideals, as expressed through intellectual life, art, and religion were only froth on the surface of historical reality; they were, in his view, unrealistic ideologies—merely bourgeois self-indulgences. Steiner made it clear to the school's executive committee that he had to lecture and teach entirely in accordance with his own views. The committee made no objection to this, and Steiner began an activity that gave him great satisfaction. In many of his pupils—mostly working men and women of mature years—he experienced a yearning for knowledge and an untapped vigor of soul that lived beneath the surface of their

William Liebnecht

social-democratic, Marxist indoctrination. Steiner experienced the immense tragedy that the so-called educated classes offered only a materialistic worldview to the proletarians, who formed such a reservoir of human intelligence and potential idealism. He saw how these fresh human forces were gradually being trapped within the dogmatic, one-sided intellectual materialism expressed in the works of Marx, Engels, and others.

In his presentations on history, Steiner showed his Workers' School pupils how the materialistic view of history had gradually emerged out of an older idea that had recognized spirit. The socialist view was only valid for recent history—basically since the sixteenth century—and had reached its climax only during the time in which they were living. "In this way," Steiner wrote, "the workers got the idea of different capacities for knowledge, and of religious, artistic, and moral impulses in history, and thus got away from regarding these as mere 'ideology.' It would have been senseless to rail against materialism; I had to allow idealism to arise out of materialism" (*The Course of My Life*, chap. 28).

That his teaching was very welcome is shown by the students' request that, in addition to his history and public speaking courses, he speak to them about the sciences as well. Steiner was eventually speaking to groups within and outside the school every night of the week. He was asked by the Berlin printers' union to give the festival address on June 17, 1900 in honor of the Gutenberg Centennial Jubilee before 7,000 typesetters and printers in a large auditorium. Of this occasion Rudolf Steiner observed dryly: "The workers seemed to like the way I spoke to them" (ibid.).

Insights into what lay behind the social struggles just beginning to engage the minds and wills of the workers led Steiner to foresee the coming social cataclysms for Europe and the world in the twentieth century. After describing his activities at the Workers' School, he writes:

Destiny had once again thrust me into a segment of life in which I had to submerge myself. I came to see how individual souls within this workers' group slumbered and dreamed, and how a sort of "mass-soul" gripped them, encompassing their views, judgment, and bearing.

But, you must not imagine that those individual souls were completely dead, for I was able to look deeply into the souls of my pupils, into the souls of the whole workers' group. This brought me to the task that I set for myself in all this activity. The attitude toward Marxism was not yet what it became two decades later; it was still something that they took in as a sort of economic gospel and thoroughly deliberated. Later it became something that, like a possession, seemed to take hold of the mass of the proletariat.

The proletariat consciousness then consisted of feelings that manifested as the effects of mass suggestion. Many of the individuals said again and again: "A time must come when the world will develop spiritual interests again; but for the moment, the proletariat has to be freed in a purely economic way."

I found that my lectures did their souls some good. They even took in things that went against materialism and the Marxist view of history. Later, when the leaders discovered the way I was working, they fought it. One of these "minor leaders" spoke to a group of my students and said: "Freedom is not what we want in the proletarian movement; what we want is reasonable compulsion." As a result, they wanted to get me out of the school, against the wishes of my students. This gradually made my work so difficult that I dropped it soon after I began my anthroposophical work.

My impression is that, if the workers' movement had been pursued with interest by a greater number of unbiased people, and if the proletariat had been better understood, this movement could have developed in a very different way. But we left the people to live their lives within their own class, and we lived in ours. Each class held views of the other that were merely theoretical. They dealt with one another in matters of wages and whenever strikes and the like required it; all kinds of welfare movements were established. Such efforts were exceedingly worthy.

But these world-shaking questions were simply not brought together with a spiritual viewpoint—this was completely lacking. Yet only such a direction could have removed the destructive forces from this movement. It was a time when the upper classes were losing their sense of community, when egoism, with its fierce competitive struggles, was becoming widespread. This was when the worldwide catastrophe of the twentieth century's second decade was already being prepared. Along with this, the proletariat was developing, in its own way, a sense for community as the proletarian class-consciousness. It took part in the culture developed by the upper classes only insofar as it provided a means for justifying a working-class consciousness. Gradually, there ceased to be any bridge at all between the various classes.

And so, because of my involvement with the magazine, I had to merge myself into the being of the middle-class bourgeoisie, and through my activity among the workers, with the proletariat. This was a rich field, in which one could consciously experience the driving forces active at that time. (ibid.)

~

As Rudolf Steiner entered the final years of the nineteenth century, he was forced to wrestle more and more concretely with the question that had already occupied him for so long: "Must I remain silent?" By even asking this question, he came into conflict with those who considered themselves the guardians of esoteric wisdom as handed down from the past. In their view it would constitute a betrayal of the mysteries if this knowledge were made public. Humankind, in their opinion, was not yet ready to receive what mystery wisdom could reveal. On the other hand, the conviction was ripening in Steiner's soul that such secrecy was directly opposed to the deepest needs of the modern age. In his view, humanity was entering a time when esoteric matters needed to be made fully public; continued secrecy was incompatible with individual spiritual freedom. In this regard Steiner was under no occult "obligation" to remain silent, since his insights came out of his own research, and he could stand unequivocally behind them.

> I was under no obligation to anyone to guard the mysteries, for I was receiving nothing from the "ancient wisdom"; my spiritual knowledge was entirely the result of my own research. When any knowledge came to me, only then did I place beside it—from whatever side—the "ancient knowledge" already made public, in order to indicate the harmony between the two and, at the same time, to show the advances possible through contemporary research.
>
> Thus, after a certain point in time, it became very clear to me that I would be doing the right thing by making this knowledge public. (*The Course of My Life*, chap. 29)

In the issue of the *Magazin für Literatur* of August 28, 1899 (the 150th anniversary of Goethe's birth) Steiner published an article on Goethe's fairy tale *The Green Snake and the Beautiful Lily* entitled "Goethe's Secret Revelation."

> Since the 1880s I had been occupied with imaginations that, for me, became connected with this fairy tale. Goethe's way of

moving from the observation of outer nature into the innermost
recesses of the human soul, and the way he placed this before the
spirit—not in concepts, but in pictures—all of this I found expressed in the fairy tale. Concepts seemed to Goethe far too
poor, too dead, to represent the living, working forces of the
soul. (*The Course of My Life*, chap. 30)

It was clear to Steiner that with this fairy tale, one "had entered the
outer courtyard of the esoteric."

Exactly one year later, destiny offered Rudolf Steiner an opportunity to speak more specifically from the experiences of his spiritual-
scientific research. Friedrich Nietzsche died in August 1900, and in
September Steiner was invited by the Count and Countess Brockdorff to speak about Nietzsche at one of their weekly gatherings.
This lecture was evidently well received, since Steiner was immediately invited to return the following week to speak on a theme of his
own choosing. Thus, on September 29, 1900, Steiner decided to
speak about Goethe's fairy tale. We can imagine what it must have
meant to him to be free at last to speak from his own esoteric
research. He wrote:

It was an important experience for me to be able to use words
stamped by the world of spirit, since until now I had been
forced by circumstances, throughout my Berlin period, to allow
the spiritual only to shine through my presentations. (ibid.)

The Brockdorffs were leading members of the Theosophical Society in Berlin, and it was due to them that Steiner was invited during
the winter of 1900–1901 to hold a series of lectures before a theosophical audience. The subject he chose for this first cycle of lectures
on a spiritual theme was both Western and Christian, whereas the
theosophical movement drew more heavily upon Eastern spiritual
tradition. Steiner spoke about the great German mystics of the late
Middle Ages and of the Renaissance, and a book based on these lectures was later published as *Mysticism at the Dawn of the Modern Age*.[2]

2. Steinerbooks, Blauvelt, NY, 1980.

This course of lectures was followed by a second, also at the invitation of the Brockdorffs, during the winter of 1901–1902. In these lectures Steiner developed an outlook on Christianity as related to the mysteries of earlier times. He showed how the cultic rituals of a pre-Christian era—for example, the Adonis mysteries of the Near East, in which the death and resurrection of a divine being are presented in symbolic, dramatic images—culminated as earthly fact with the death and resurrection of the Christ Being in the event of Golgotha. Steiner wrote the book *Christianity as Mystical Fact* based on these lectures.[3]

> From the very beginning I let it be known that the choice of the words "as mystical fact" in the title is important. I did not want to represent only the mystical content of Christianity; my object was to show the progression from the ancient mysteries to the Mystery of Golgotha in such a way that not only earthly, historical forces were seen to be at work in this development but also spiritual, super-earthly impulses. And I wanted to show that, in the ancient mysteries, ritual images of cosmic events were presented that were fulfilled in the Mystery of Golgotha as *facts*, transposed from the cosmos to the earthly historical plane. (ibid.)

Prior to the two courses that were held within the circle of theosophists, Rudolf Steiner had written the two-volume work, *Conceptions of the World and of Life in the Nineteenth Century*, which he later revised and extended under the title, *Riddles of Philosophy*.[4] In this work he traces the direction of philosophic thinking as taken by Kant, on the one hand, and Goethe, on the other, and shows how Goethe can become the basis for the further unfolding of science, especially the concept of evolution as presented by Darwin and Ernst Haeckel during the nineteenth century. Steiner recognized Darwin

---

3. Anthroposophic Press, Hudson, NY, 1997.
4. Anthroposophic Press, Spring Valley, NY, 1973.

as an observer who saw how organic form emerges from organic form in an evolutionary metamorphosis. Steiner said of Haeckel:

> In Haeckel I saw a person who courageously took the thinker's point of view in science, whereas the rest of the scientific community excluded thought and wanted only to recognize the results of observation using the senses. The fact that Haeckel valued creative thought in establishing the basis for reality drew me to him again and again. Thus, I dedicated my book to him in spite of the fact that its content—even in its earlier form— was not at all conceived in his sense of things. (ibid.)

Haeckel was passionately attacked from many quarters for being "anti-spiritual," and the fact that Steiner dedicated his *Conceptions of the World* to him led to much criticism and misunderstanding. In this regard, a conversation between Steiner and Haeckel in Leipzig is of special interest. Steiner quotes Haeckel as saying, "People say that I deny the spirit. I wish they could see how various materials shape themselves through their own forces; then they would perceive "spirit' in everything that happens in a laboratory retort. Spirit is everywhere." Steiner continues:

> Haeckel actually knew absolutely nothing about what spirit really is. The forces of nature themselves were for him the "spirit."... It was unnecessary to criticize such blindness to the spirit with philosophically dead concepts; one had to see how far the age itself was removed from spiritual experience and seek, out of the foundations that the age afforded, the biological explanation of nature that could create spiritual sparks.
>
> This was my opinion at the time. On that basis I wrote my *Conceptions of the World and of Life in the Nineteenth Century*. (ibid.)

~

The invitation to speak to an audience on a topic of his own choosing and out of his own research and experience marked the beginning of Steiner's years as a spiritual teacher. At last, he was free to speak, because he had been asked. This reticence—or one might say, this unending patience and willingness to wait until destiny had spoken—is a characteristic gesture of Steiner's whole life. Behind it stands his fundamental respect for human freedom. Answering questions that have not been asked leads to narrow, by-the-book sectarianism. For Steiner, freedom must be the basis of all spiritual life.

This fundamental respect for the freedom of others was not accompanied by any uncertainty about his own direction. In 1902, when Steiner was asked to lead the budding German section of the International Theosophical Society, he made it clear that he could do so only if he were free to give nothing but what he could stand behind through his own insight and experience. In this connection it is interesting to note that it was right at this time that Steiner first used the word *anthroposophy* in the title of a series of lectures in Berlin for a group called *The Coming Ones* (*Die Kommenden*). The first lecture was on October 6, 1902, titled "From Zarathustra to Nietzsche: The History of Human Evolution in Relation to the Worldviews of Earliest Oriental Times to the Present; or Anthroposophy." Steiner characterized his inner relationship to the traditional teachings that provided the primary content for the Theosophical Society:

> When I went to London to attend a theosophical congress, one of the leading personalities said to me that true theosophy was found in my book *Mysticism at the Dawn of the Modern Age*. I was satisfied with this, since I had given only the results of my own spiritual observation, and this was accepted within the Theosophical Society. There was now no longer any reason why I should not present this spiritual knowledge to theosophical audiences—who at first were the only ones actively seeking spiritual knowledge and understanding—*in my own way*. I subscribed to no sectarian dogmatics; I was a man who said what he believed he could say, based entirely on what he himself experienced as the spiritual world. (ibid.)

Rudolf Steiner had been connected with hundreds of people during the early years of his life, but not one of these accompanied him
into his public activity when he began to speak from his own spiritual-scientific research and experience. In many cases the personal
contacts remained alive; correspondence continued, meetings
occurred, and Steiner often followed their careers and achievements
with interest. Only in the rarest instances, however, did they recognize that their earlier colleague, friend, or acquaintance now spoke
and wrote out of a new dimension of human experience. In some
cases, when they *did* recognize that Steiner was speaking from a new
level of cognition, it led to their estrangement. Yet just at this time,
new individuals also came forward. This new dimension of knowledge was precisely what drew them toward Steiner, and toward the
sources of his research.

Among these individuals was a young and gifted woman who had
grown up in a German-speaking family in the area of St. Petersburg
and the Gulf of Finland. Marie von Sivers appeared one day in the
late autumn of 1900 at a lecture on the German mysteries of the late
Middle Ages and the Renaissance. Steiner said, "She was chosen by
destiny at that time to take the German Section of the Theosophical
Society into strong hands; the Section was founded soon after my
lecturing began. Within this Section I was now able to develop my
anthroposophical activity before a continually increasing audience"
(ibid.).

Marie von Sivers was not alone in recognizing Steiner as a great
esoteric teacher, but her capacities and her commitment were decisive, and they made the next steps possible for Rudolf Steiner.

In 1902, Marie von Sivers and I took on the leadership of the
German section of the Theosophical Society. Marie von Sivers
was *the* person who, thanks to her whole being, made it possible to avoid anything sectarian in what came about through us,
and to give it a character that won a place within the general
intellectual and educational culture. She was deeply interested
in drama and the spoken arts and had completed studies in
these disciplines at the very best institutions in Paris, which

had given a beautiful refinement to her talents. She was still involved in these studies, pursuing various methods of artistic speech, when I became acquainted with her in Berlin.

Marie von Sivers and I soon became great friends. On the basis of our friendship, we began to work together in the most varied intellectual and spiritual spheres, over a very wide area. Not only anthroposophy, but also a shared cultivation of the arts of poetry and speech, soon became an essential part of our lives. It was only in this spiritual work that we pursued together that the central point could be found from which anthroposophy—at first within the framework of the Theosophical Society—could be carried out into the world.

During our first visit to London together, Marie von Sivers heard much about H. P. Blavatsky from Countess Wachtmeister, who had been an intimate friend of Blavatsky, as well as about the tendencies and development of the Theosophical Society. Marie von Sivers was entrusted to the highest degree with the spiritual content that had been revealed to the society and with how this content had been developed and fostered.

When I said that within the framework of the Theosophical Society it was possible to find the people who wanted knowledge of the spiritual world, I did not mean that those who were members of the Theosophical Society were the best possible candidates. Many of them, however, very soon proved receptive to my kind of spiritual knowledge. But a large number of the members were fanatical followers of individual leaders within the Theosophical Society. They swore by the dogmas given out by these leaders, who acted in a strongly sectarian spirit.

The triviality and dilettantism inherent in this kind of activity within the Theosophical Society repelled me. Only among the English theosophists did I find an inner content that still flowed from Blavatsky and was being further cultivated by Annie Besant and others in a pertinent way. I myself could never have worked as these theosophists were working, but I observed what was living among them as a spiritual center, which one could unite well with in a deep and serious desire to spread spiritual knowledge as widely as possible. So it was not the membership of the Theosophical Society as a whole that Marie von Sivers and I counted on; we mainly counted on the hearts and minds of those who appeared whenever spiritual knowledge was being seriously pursued.

Working within the existing branches of the Theosophical Society, which was necessary as a starting point, comprised only a part of our activity. The biggest task was arranging public lectures in which I spoke to audiences not connected with the Theosophical Society at all and who came to my lectures only because of the subject matter.

What later became the Anthroposophical Society arose within the framework of the Theosophical Society from both these people who met what I had to say about the spiritual world through such lectures, and from those who were involved in various theosophical activities and found their way into my manner of working. (*The Course of My Life*, chap. 31)

A clear understanding of Steiner's relationship with the Theosophical Society—which he faithfully served as General Secretary of the German section for several years—is essential for an understanding of the anthroposophical movement itself, which emerged from the theosophical movement and its society. This subject will be returned to later.

~

Steiner begins the final chapter of his autobiography with the words, "In the following pages, it will be difficult to separate the story of my life from the history of the Anthroposophical Society" (*The Course of My Life*, chap. 37). He intended to continue his life story, but his death on March 30, 1925, ended the narrative: it closed with the events of 1906–1907. Had Steiner been allowed to do what he intended, it would not be necessary for this writer to go any further, because Steiner's biography, and his presentation of anthroposophy would have been virtually synonymous.

Marie von Sivers in 1901

Rudolf Steiner and Annie Besant

5

The
Work Unfolds

On February 27, 1902, Rudolf Steiner entered his forty-second year—a year that proved to be a watershed both in his own life and in the anthroposophical movement. It has already been mentioned that, behind the scenes of history, mighty, far-reaching spiritual events were occurring, virtually unobserved by contemporary humanity. The year 1879 had marked the dawn of a new age of spiritual consciousness, and in 1899 the age of darkness, the Kali Yuga, finally came to an end, giving way to the first glimmering of an age of new spiritual light.

It was during this time that Steiner was invited to speak to the circle of people around Count and Countess Brockdorff in Berlin. Their recognition of him and their confidence in the authenticity and integrity of his research led naturally to the desire to establish a forum for this work in Germany and to the conviction that Steiner was the person to lead it.

In July, 1902, he and his closest coworker, Marie von Sivers, were called to London, where the International Theosophical Society had its headquarters. It was decided in London to establish a German section of the Society, with Steiner as General Secretary. The festive founding of the new section occurred the following October in Berlin, where Mrs. Annie Besant, president of the international society, actively participated in the proceedings. How this occurred, and how Steiner maintained his spiritual independence while accepting the obligations of his position, have already been briefly explained and are described more fully toward the end of his autobiography.

What came into being through Steiner's initiative and activity during the less than twenty-three years that followed resembled the emergence and growth of a living organism. It was as though the "Being of Anthroposophy" itself was gradually growing into the cultural life of the twentieth century in order to eventually take firm root there. This entry into life appears to have unfolded in sequences of about seven years each, comparable to the stages through which the human organism develops.

During the first phase—which lasted from around 1902 to 1909—anthroposophy made its entrance in the only way that does not intrude on individual freedom—that is, through the narrowest of all doorways, the door of insight and understanding. During these years, anthroposophy was able to speak to the contemporary world through the activity of Rudolf Steiner, who worked primarily as a teacher, communicating the insights he had won through spiritual-scientific research. Despite the growing demand for his lectures, it was primarily through the written word that anthroposophy—though still expressed largely through the vocabulary of the theosophical movement—first reached a wider public.

Following the publication of *Mysticism at the Dawn of the Modern Age* and *Christianity as Mystical Fact*, which were both revisions of lectures, Steiner published *Theosophy* in 1904.[1] There he introduced a new understanding of the total human being based on a clear and disciplined knowledge of the realms of soul and spirit, including the working of the laws of karma within the sequence of human lives on earth. In chapter 33 of his autobiography, Steiner explains that his intention in writing *Theosophy* was to awaken the cognitive activity and understanding of his readers through descriptions actually drawn from supersensible experience. The language used, nevertheless, had to be taken from the world of sense perception and the intellect.

---

1. *Theosophy: An Introduction to the Spiritual Processes in Human Life and in the Cosmos (Theosophie, Einführung in übersinnliche Welterkenntnis und Menschenbestimmung)*, Anthroposophic Press, Hudson, NY, 1994.

Rudolf Steiner in 1904

It is important to note that the closing chapter of *Theosophy* is devoted to the path of knowledge that modern individuals may follow and may develop the faculties to transcend the limited experience of the senses. By including in his book this introduction to a practical path of self-development, Steiner satisfied one of the fundamental demands of the scientific method—that the same or equivalent results must be attainable by others, and the steps leading to this attainment must be clearly presented and open to scrutiny.

Steiner presented this practical path in a general, introductory form in *Theosophy*. He later took it up in more detail and depth in a series of articles that appeared in the magazine *Luzifer*, later entitled *Lucifer-Gnosis*. In 1904 these articles were collected and published as *How to Know Higher Worlds* and *The Stages of Higher Knowledge*.[2] In

---

2. *How to Know Higher Worlds: A Modern Path of Initiation* (*Wie erlangt man Erkenntnisse der höheren Welten?*), Anthroposophic Press, Hudson, NY, 1994; *The Stages of Higher Knowledge* (*Die Stufen der höheren Erkenntnis*), Anthroposophic Press, Hudson, NY, 1967.

1909 he published *An Outline of Occult Science*, which presents a spiritual cosmogony.[3] It describes a grand panorama of the stages of the earth's evolution and includes a detailed chapter on the path of knowledge that led to the research results.

In personal conversations Steiner mentioned that knowledge of planetary and cultural evolution had not been achieved in chronological sequence, but had been researched by beginning with present conditions and working back. Steiner had also spoken of the immense double nature of the task: first, the research itself, which required years of developing and training his cognitive powers for spiritual science; and second, the creative search for the right words to express the achievements of occult investigation. He had to find language that could present these experiences in a way that is comprehensible and provides modern, genuinely open-minded people full access to them.

We should remember also that the body of Steiner's anthroposophical work is incomplete without the books he published before the turn of the century. These include his books on Goethe's methods of scientific inquiry and the cognitive foundations of Goethe's work, which lead from a science based entirely on sense-perception to a way of knowing that allows the living world to speak through phenomena. Above all, Steiner's *Die Philosophie der Freiheit* lays the foundation for recognizing the individual as the primary instrument—through the human capacity for thinking—for spiritual cognition.

~

The year 1909 was the culmination of the first phase of anthroposophy's gradual entry into contemporary human culture. That year saw the final separation of Steiner's work from that represented by Annie Besant. Mrs. Besant and Steiner shared the platform for the

---

3. *An Outline of Occult Science* (*Die Geheimwissenschaft im Umriss*), Anthroposophic Press, Hudson, NY, 1984. This book has been newly translated by Catherine Creeger as *An Outline of Esoteric Science*, Anthroposophic Press, Hudson, NY (fall 1997).

last time at the Theosophical Congress in Budapest at the end of May. Under Besant's leadership, the theosophical movement and its international society were turning more and more to the East for inspiration and authority, and thus denying the central evolutionary role of the Christ Event in human history. For Steiner, however, that event is at the very center of human existence.

On May 30, Besant, whose headquarters were already in India, spoke of the need to bring an Eastern, Buddhist wisdom into Western spirituality. On the following day, Steiner gave a lecture entitled "From Buddha to Christ."[4] In no way did he deny the greatness of the pre-Christian initiates or the profound nature of the mystery wisdom speaking through them. On the contrary, he attributed immense significance to the figures of Scythianus, Buddha, Zarathustra, Moses, and Manes within the stream of human evolution. He did point out, however, the decisive difference between the historically important teaching of such initiates and the act of Christ. As Guenther Wachsmuth, a younger colleague of Steiner, characterized it, "The former had taught the wisdom of the divine beings and their actions; Christ lived it out and made it a deed of redemption for the whole of humankind."[5]

During this same congress, Steiner had a final conversation with Besant; he made it clear that they were on different paths to the spirit. After they parted in Budapest, their destinies never brought them together again.

~

It was at this same time that occurrences within the supersensible realm immediately adjacent to the sense-perceptible world (referred to by Steiner as the *etheric world*) must have been experienced by Rudolf Steiner. In 1910 and in the years that followed, he spoke of

---

4. Contained in *From Buddha to Christ*, Anthroposophic Press, Hudson, NY, 1987.
5. Guenther Wachsmuth, *The Life and Work of Rudolf Steiner: From the Turn of the Century to His Death*, Spiritual Science Library, Garber Communications, Blauvelt, NY, 1989, p. 125.

this event as the appearance, or re-appearance, of Christ in the etheric world.[6]

Steiner's experience of the mystery of Christ's incarnation, which had ripened in his soul over many years, reached a certain culmination in 1909. He described it in writing and in many lectures, usually referring to it as the *Mystery of Golgotha*. How are we to understand this mysterious, world-transforming event; how are we to understand the Christ Himself?

Such questions could absorb one's whole lifetime. Nevertheless, we may see in the Christ a Being of divine, supra-earthly origin, deeply related to the spiritual, life-giving power of the Sun, which also gives us light and life on the physical earth. As the writer of the Gospel of John expressed it: "In Him was life, and the life was the light of human beings" (John 1:4).

His incarnation was foreshadowed in the earlier mysteries, which were fulfilled during the three years when this lofty spiritual being dwelt within the earthly, physical body of Jesus of Nazareth. Those three years spanned the period between the Baptism by John in the Jordan and the Crucifixion on Golgotha. Through His death and Resurrection, and in the subsequent events of Ascension and Whitsun (or Pentecost), Christ united His being with the earth and with the stream of human and earthly history. This sublime physical event, enacted within the earthly sphere, is unique and central to evolution. Spiritual science relates that the Christ Being, having united with humanity and with earth, continues to live within our earthly environment, invisibly present and spiritually active.

---

6. When Steiner uses the term *etheric world*, he is speaking of the supersensible forces that underlie all living organisms and distinguish the organic from the nonliving, inorganic world. We approach these living etheric forces most directly in the plant kingdom, where they bring about germination, growth, and the propagation of the species. We can observe their effects indirectly in all living phenomena, but they may also be studied directly when human beings have developed their thinking through the discipline described in *How to Know Higher Worlds* and similar works. Such development leads to the awakening of the cognitive faculty that spiritual science calls *Imagination*, which makes possible direct observation of the etheric realm.

It is of key significance for modern human beings that it is now possible for us on earth to experience the Christ. He is, since the early twentieth century, in the realm of those life forces, or etheric forces, that form a sheath around the physical earth. Speaking of this new possibility, Steiner referred to a new clairvoyance that would awaken in humanity and enable human beings to experience the Christ in the etheric sphere, the sphere of life. He first spoke of this event in 1910 and later pointed to the 1930s as the time when this new clairvoyance would begin to manifest in certain individuals, often in unexpected and perhaps confusing ways. He pointed out that it would be tremendously important that a certain number of people be inwardly prepared to understand and support this experience when it occurred.

In a 1917 lecture cycle in Berlin, when people were in the middle of war and intense suffering, Steiner characterized the dawning of this new experience:

> As far removed in conduct as humankind seems today from being permeated with the Christ Spirit on the physical plane, just as near to human souls is the Christ, who is coming—if only they will open themselves to Him. And, since around 1909, the seer is even able to indicate how, in a distinctly recognizable way, what will come has been in preparation—that, since 1909, we live inwardly in a very special time. Moreover, it is possible today, if we only seek Him, to be very close to Christ, to find Him in a very different way from that of previous times.[7]

Steiner shared his profoundly intimate perception of the dawn of the possibility of a new Christ experience with those theosophists who had united their work and striving with the German Section. Beginning with a lecture to members in Stockholm on January 12, 1910, he carried the message of the Christ's reappearance the length of Europe, traveling as far south as Palermo in Sicily. Closely linked

---

7. Lecture of February 6, 1917, in *Cosmic and Human Metamorphoses*, Spiritual Research Editions, Blauvelt, NY, 1989, p. 8.

with these lectures were the extensive lecture cycles on the Gospels. Beginning with a cycle of eight lectures on the John Gospel in November, 1907 Steiner held no less than ten cycles directly related with the Gospels, culminating in 1909 and 1910 in six cycles of nearly seventy lectures in Christiania (Oslo), Norway; Kassel, Germany; Basel, Switzerland; Stockholm, Sweden; Bern Switzerland; and ending with a series of ten lectures in Berlin on the background of the Mark Gospel from October, 1910 until June, 1911. In addition to these lecture cycles, which dealt directly with an esoteric understanding of the Gospels, there were many lectures that addressed the mission of a spiritual Christianity for our time.[8]

The impulse of anthroposophy—which twentieth-century human souls first met as a path of scientifically disciplined cognition, with clear conceptual forms that left the recipient inwardly free—began to take on life and breath. It began to find a place in the human heart. This movement from head to heart characterized the gradual penetration of spiritual science into contemporary culture as anthroposophy entered its second phase. What had been given as ideas, as clear concepts, was taken into everyday individual experience, digested, and transformed until these concepts began to live in the people who had made them their own in a new and vital way. Now these transformed ideas could awaken as nuances of feeling in new depths of experience, as creative impulses in the warmth of individual human hearts. This step opened the way to new dimensions of artistic expression.

The dawn of this second, artistic phase of what might be called the "biography" of anthroposophy was thus heralded by the intensifying message that the Christ Impulse is the central, transformative event in earthly evolution. This *Christological* phase was accompanied by a flowering of artistic creativity in Rudolf Steiner's own life.

~

8. *The Gospel of St. John and Its Relation to the Other Gospels*, Anthroposophic Press, Spring Valley, NY, 1982; *The Gospel of St. John*, Anthroposophic Press, Hudson, NY, 1962; *The Gospel of St. Luke*, Rudolf Steiner Press, London, 1988; *Background to the Gospel of St. Mark*, Rudolf Steiner Press, London, 1985; *The Gospel of St. Mark*, Anthroposophic Press, Hudson, NY, 1986; *The Gospel of St. Matthew*, Rudolf Steiner Press, London, 1985.

On November 25, 1905, Rudolf Steiner wrote to Marie von Sivers:

> This should be our ideal: to create *forms* that express the inner life. For an era that cannot see forms nor create them with inner sight, must necessarily reduce the spirit to an inessential abstraction, and in the face of this merely abstract spirit, reality must appear as an aggregation of matter devoid of spirit.[9]

Since his early years in Vienna, Weimar, and Berlin, Steiner had been intensely interested in the questions of artistic creation that moved the artists of his time. His work had led him deeply into Goethe's creative, artistic approach to the phenomena presented by the world. Goethe's recognition of the role of metamorphosis in the living world, as each form grows organically out of a preceding form, as well as in his discoveries about light and color, showed Steiner the cognitive foundations for a new understanding of nature that could also become the foundation for a new understanding of art and aesthetics. His 1888 lecture in Vienna on this subject was later published under the title "Goethe as the Father of a New Aesthetics." Thus, we should not be surprised that in 1907 Steiner created a rich background of color and form for the Theosophical Congress in Munich. He wrote about this briefly, just before his death in March, 1925, in the last chapter of his autobiography:

> Because of the work in Munich, the theosophical conference, which was to be organized by the German Section in 1907, was held there. These conferences, previously held in London, Amsterdam, and Paris, included sessions in which theosophical problems were addressed in lectures and in discussions. They were modeled after the conferences held by academic societies. The Theosophical Society's administrative problems were also discussed.

---

9. *Correspondence and Documents: 1901–1925*, Rudolf Steiner Press, London, 1988, p. 69.

Some of this customary format was modified in Munich. We—the organizers—decorated the large concert hall where the conference was to take place. The forms and colors were intended to reflect artistically the prevailing mood of the spoken presentations. The surrounding artistic environment was to form a harmonious unity with the spiritual activity taking place there. To me it was of the greatest possible importance to allow the artistic mood to speak for itself and to avoid abstract, inartistic symbolism.

We also introduced an artistic presentation into the conference program. Marie von Sivers had long before translated Schuré's reconstruction of the Eleusinian drama. I adapted the language for a dramatic performance, and we included this play in the program. It established a connection with the ancient mysteries—even though in a small way. The important thing was that the conference was given an artistic element—one that showed our intention not to pursue the spiritual life of the Society without an artistic dimension. (*The Course of My Life*, chap. 38)

The congress was attended by about 600 delegates and participants from many countries. It was held in the Munich Concert Hall, which had been transformed under Steiner's direction. First, the walls were hung with material of a clear, strong, red color. Seven "columns" were placed against this background, each painted on a narrow board with its own unique capital. Each capital was inscribed with a different planetary sign, and between the columns were the seven apocalyptic seals from the Book of Revelation. Steiner had hoped to drape blue material across the ceiling to give the impression of arches, but limitations in the rental agreement prevented him from doing so. His intention "to imbue the hall with a polarity of red and blue" was accomplished in the colors of two columns placed at the front of the auditorium: "One, red, bore the letter *J*, and the other, blue, the letter *B*, the initials of Joachim and Boaz, the two pillars of Solomon's Temple."[10] Members of the audience thus

---

10. Hilde Raske, *The Language of Color in the First Goetheanum: A Study of Rudolf Steiner's Art*, Walter Keller Verlag, Dornach, 1987, p. 23.

found themselves "embedded" in color and surrounded by artistic representations of the planetary columns and the apocalyptic seals.

Within this setting, on Whitsun, May 19, Edouard Schuré's drama *The Mystery of Eleusis* was performed. This drama revealed the mystery of Demeter and Persephone with which, in ancient Greece, the great initiation festival at Eleusis had culminated on the ninth day. Marie von Sivers played Demeter, demonstrating the art of speech formation that she was developing in collaboration with Steiner. In this revival of the ancient art of recitation, it was their aim to free speech from its present-day confinement to intellectual communication and to allow consonants and vowels, rhythm and phrasing to become the bearers of a deeper, more comprehensive, and vital meaning. The costumes and scenery were also created according to Steiner's direction.

Marie von Sivers as Demeter in Schuré's Eleusis

The constraints of time and the awkwardness of having to rent the space restricted these artistic efforts to only the smallest of beginnings; nevertheless, it was very important to Steiner that the beginning was made. The living ideas of spiritual science ultimately demanded artistic expression, and this fact inevitably led to the separation of Steiner's work from the more traditional forms of the Theosophical Society. He expressed this predictable development in the final paragraph with which his autobiography abruptly closes:

> Many of the old members of the Theosophical Society from England, France, and especially from Holland were not at all pleased with the innovations introduced at the Munich conference. It would have been good if it could have been understood (though only a very few comprehended it at the time) that the anthroposophical stream brought something of an entirely different nature and inner direction from what the Theosophical Society had thus far brought. This inner attitude contained the *real reason* why the Anthroposophical Society could no longer exist as a *part* of the Theosophical Society. (*The Course of My Life*, chap. 38)

~

A young mathematics student who attended the Munich Congress was fired by the idea that what had been attempted there might be translated into an actual building. "Columns want to be built!" he thought when he saw the flat, painted planetary pillars in the concert hall. He asked Steiner how he would picture such a structure, and Steiner gave him several indications for a building of elliptical design. The young man was Karl Stockmeyer, who, together with his father, enthusiastically began to construct a small-scale building in Malsch, near Karlsruhe. In her book, *The Language of Color in the First Goetheanum*, painter Hilde Raske describes the Malsch structure:

The building, which still stands today, is about three and a half meters high. Two rows of seven columns, complete with capitals and pedestals, carved from oak, support the elliptically-arched ceiling. The entrance lies in the west; the speaker speaks from the east.

The apocalyptic seals have been painted directly upon the red-madder walls, with the signs of the zodiac painted in gold on the arched, indigo-blue ceiling.... The pairs of seals and columns mirror each other in succession from west to east. The colors of the seals shine between the wooden columns. Rudolf Steiner had suggested carving the columns out of Siberian syenite, which has a greenish hue. The green of the stone would have been magnificent against the red of the walls.

At the spring and autumn equinoxes, a ray of light passes through a small window in the ceiling and falls upon the first, or Saturn, column. All in all, the little building gives the impression of a strong, self-contained work of art and awakens a festive, sacred mood. (p. 24)

The model for the Malsch building

Definite steps had now been taken toward the desired creation of an architectural expression, in color and form, of the life of thought and feeling unfolding within the group around Rudolf Steiner. A further step was Steiner's interior design for an auditorium and festival hall in the building that housed the theosophical activities in Stuttgart, where a strong center was developing. In 1911, the Stuttgart members, with Steiner's guidance, began to transform the interior of their building into spaces that would reflect the life of soul and spirit that was awakening. Just over a year later, the Anthroposophical Movement emerged as a separate entity, inwardly independent as well as outwardly independent of the Theosophical Society. This final separation—which was the culmination of a long process of fundamental clarification—coincided with the growing resolve to create a home for anthroposophy and, above all, for the production of Steiner's mystery dramas, which were being performed each year in August—as they were written—in a rented theater in Munich.

~

The Hall in Stuttgart

Consideration of Rudolf Steiner's mystery dramas and the way in which they arose brings us to a special moment in his life, as well as in the development of the anthroposophical movement. We find ourselves looking into the inner creative process of a very great artist, who is nevertheless drawing on the broadest, most universally valid insights, gained through years of painstaking spiritual-scientific research. Steiner repeatedly emphasized that he had to establish the cognitive, scientific foundations for his spiritual-scientific research *before* he could share its concrete details in a responsible way. His four mystery dramas appear as milestones that mark this transition from the more general and scientific to the artistic and concrete.

In a lecture given in Berlin on October 31, 1910, Steiner speaks about this transition:

> There is no such thing as development per se, no such thing as common, ordinary, orthodox development. There is only the development of this or that person, of a third, fourth, or twentieth human being. For each individual in the world, there must be a different process of development.
>
> For this reason, the most honest description of the esoteric path of knowledge must have such a general character that it never in any way will coincide with an individual development.[11]

The Swiss poet, essayist, and dramatist Albert Steffen (later a younger colleague of Steiner in Dornach) experienced the four mystery dramas between 1910 and 1913 in Munich, where he was living and working. In his essay "On the Genesis of Rudolf Steiner's Mystery Dramas," he wrote:

> When, in 1910, Steiner's mystery drama *The Portal of Initiation* had its world premiere in Munich (still recognized then as a

---

11. *Three Lectures on the Mystery Dramas: The Portal of Initiation and The Soul's Probation*, Anthroposophic Press, Hudson, NY, 1983, p. 39.

cosmopolitan center for the arts), the participants, who streamed together from all the countries of Europe, from England to Russia, from Italy to Scandinavia—indeed, even from the American continent—were aware that, in this event, they were permitted to be in the presence of a renewal of an art as it arises from the mysteries. Not the renewal of a cultic-ritual, such as the Eleusinian mysteries or a medieval Passion Play, but the representation of a community of contemporary human beings who, in fulfillment of a task, find themselves searching for the spirit that belongs to humanity. This was a community consisting of individuals from the most varied professions— scientists, artists, technicians, directors, and employees of an industrial enterprise, women and men, with all their capacities and their mistakes—called together by destiny and determined to undergo and overcome the most varied tests of soul on their paths of life. All of the individuals in this "initiation drama" (as Rudolf Steiner once called it) find themselves on the threshold of the awakening to their higher humanity.[12]

Steffen recognized that such a community of individuals, striving out of their own free initiative toward common human ideals—ideals that can nevertheless be realized only along paths of completely individual development—had never existed before and was altogether new. As it gradually takes form, tempered in the fires of individual frustration and failure, this community creates an organism of human destiny that contains the potential for future capacities, just as the plant gives rise to new possibilities not apparent when it first sprouts. As individuals succeed in bringing order into their separate and collective destinies, only then can such a new social organ manifest.

The character in the mystery dramas named Benedictus—who is the spiritual teacher of the group that comes together in the first drama—addresses this process when he pronounces in the first

---

12. Albert Steffen, *Über den Keimgrund der Mysteriendramen Rudolf Steiners*, Verlag für Schöne Wissenschaften, Dornach, 1971.

scene: "Within this circle a knot [of destiny] now forms itself from the threads that karma spins in world becoming." After quoting these words, Steffen writes:

> This speech by Benedictus in the first drama, *The Portal of Initiation*, is the leading motif of the mystery dramas. Their author and poet [Steiner] makes the threads of destiny visible as they begin, and as they run their course. This is actually his artistic method, based on capacities that have thus far never been applied to dramatic art. Rudolf Steiner has described the path into the spiritual world in terms that are generally, humanly valid—especially, for example, in the second part of *An Outline of Occult Science* and in *How to Know Higher Worlds*. In his dramas he presents the way this path unfolds quite differently for each individual, so that one has to say that any course of development is valid only for the particular personality in question. This description of the spiritual path, Rudolf Steiner says, expresses itself more intensively, "in more living ways, and is therefore truer to life." (ibid.)

Steiner adds:

> The book *How to Know Higher Worlds* contains, to a certain extent, the beginning of the secrets of all human development. The Rosicrucian mystery drama [*The Portal of Initiation*] contains the secrets of the development of a single individual, Johannes Thomasius.[13]

The character Johannes Thomasius, a young painter, is in a particular sense the key figure in the "knot of destiny" that unfolds throughout the four dramas. Surrounding him, with their personal destinies linked and interwoven in many various ways, is a group of people who share a spiritual striving, though their individual paths in life are strikingly different, and at times directly conflict with each

---

13. *Three Lectures on the Mystery Dramas*, p. 39.

other. A prominent figure in the group is Maria, with whom Johannes is deeply connected through love and shared endeavor. In her house we meet Capesius, the brilliant professor and historian; Strader, the scientist and mechanical inventor; the "other Maria," a woman to whom life had brought great suffering, kindling in her a warmth of human wisdom; Felix Balde, a simple man who gathers wild herbs for a livelihood, and who is profoundly versed in the hidden realities of nature; his wife, Felicia, a teller of wondrous fairy tales; and Theodora, who through clairvoyant vision speaks of the coming of a new experience of the Christ. These individuals, as well as others, have gathered in Maria's home to hear Benedictus speak about his experience of spiritual realities.

Mieta Waller and Marie von Sivers
in a scene from The Souls' Probation

In the opening scene of the first play, this gathering is the germinal point from which we follow these characters through their experiences in supersensible realms, where they encounter beings who both help and hinder them on their life paths. We also observe their experiences in previous lives on earth, which shed light on trials and situations encountered in their present incarnations. To grasp the complex drama of human destiny portrayed in these plays, one must actually witness them, but the minimal indications given here show that this is a new kind of theater, one that widens perspectives and includes realms otherwise hidden until now.

The theater has of course seen flashes of dramatic fantasy, or of chaotic, subjective imagination, but these mystery dramas take us into new dimensions. One may judge these plays as one will from the viewpoint of yesterday's naturalism, or today's postmodern worldview, yet the individuals who gathered to stage these plays every summer in Munich—becoming amateur actors and actresses, stage and costume designers, and artisans—as well as the audiences, were very much aware that they were taking a new and revolutionary step in theater. This was expressed not only by the youthful Albert Steffen, but also by his much older, revered colleague, the poet Christian Morgenstern, who wrote to his friend and biographer, Michael Bauer, following the performance of the first drama in 1910:

> It is not a play, but mirrors worlds of the spirit and great truths. It introduces—perhaps burdened with the labor of a beginning work, of a pioneer first attempt—a new level, a new era of art. The era itself is still distant; it may well be hundreds of years before there are enough human beings who want this pure, spiritual art, so that in every city mystery [plays] of this kind may be worthily offered and received—but here, in the *Portal* ... is its historical point of origin, here we are present at its birth.[14]

~

---

14. Quoted in Albert Steffen's *Über den Keimgrund der Mysteriendramen Rudolf Steiners*. Regarding Christian Morgenstern see Note E in Appendix, page 268.

Those in the audience who were familiar with Goethe's fairy tale, *The Green Snake and the Beautiful Lily*, might have noticed a resemblance between certain figures in the play and the fairy tale. They may have sensed that the fairy tale itself had undergone a metamorphosis and come to life again in Steiner's drama.

Steiner had turned to the fairy tale to commemorate the 150th anniversary of Goethe's birth on August 28, 1899. When invited by the Brockdorffs to speak to their theosophical group, he again chose the fairy tale. Now it appears again, metamorphosed from the language of imaginative pictures into dramatic form. We can try to accompany this process as Steiner described it.

He first experienced the fairy tale in its fullness in 1889. This experience, he said, had to sink into his subconscious and be digested for many years. In 1896, seven years later, the tale might have been newly expressed, Steiner said, but the transformation still would have been incomplete. By 1903 it was digested but still tied to his own personality; in order to gain its own life, it needed to be "given away" and freed from all subjective interpretation. He had to hand it over to the spiritual world and again wait. In 1910, after another seven years, Steiner could receive it back in its final objective form as the first mystery play, *The Portal of Initiation*.

That creative process took twenty-one years to ripen and produce its fruit. Not every creation must take so long, but in every truly creative act there is always a "giving away" and a waiting to see what "comes back." This is the unavoidable risk, this death and resurrection, that distinguishes what is deeply creative from mere superficial manipulation. The latter may be brilliant and stimulating, but it has not been transformed. Behind the writing of *The Portal of Initiation*, as well as Steiner's other plays, was a process of archetypal creation.

In Steiner's biography we discover that those twenty-one years of living and working with Goethe's fairy tale paralleled his innermost struggle to experience and understand the meaning and reality of Christianity for our time. In 1889 he was deeply occupied with Nietzsche's work in its inner relationship to Christianity. In 1896, when Nietzsche had become ill, Steiner described him as a heroic, defeated warrior, crushed under his failure to break through the barrier of scientific materialism to a knowledge of the spirit. Seven years later, in 1903, Steiner revised his lectures to the theosophists in Berlin and published them as *Christianity as Mystical Fact*. There he developed the thought that in the life, death, and resurrection of Christ Jesus, the pre-Christian mysteries (with which Nietzsche was deeply connected) were enacted as a physical reality. What had been given in pre-Christian times as symbolic representations, to be experienced meditatively within the souls of those prepared to receive them, became through the Mystery of Golgotha, *mystical fact*.

During the succeeding seven years, Steiner came to realize that humanity will gain access, through a new quality of clairvoyance, to the reality of the living Christ in the etheric realm, just beyond the world of the physical senses. This dawning faculty for a new Christ vision is, in the opening scene of the first mystery play, dramatized by Theodora, who, like the hawk in Goethe's fairy tale, can reflect, in the clear mirror of her clairvoyant soul, the rays of the spiritual sunrise dawning for modern humanity. Her closing words are:

> But now the future nears,
> When with new powers of sight
> Humanity on earth will be endowed.
> What once the senses saw
> When Christ walked the earth
> Will human souls one day behold,
> When soon the time shall be fulfilled.[15]

~

---

15. *The Portal of Initiation: A Rosicrucian Mystery Drama & Fairy Tale of the Green Snake and the Beautiful Lily,* Spiritual Science Library, Blauvelt, NY, 1981, p. 71.

In Rudolf Steiner's biography, which, toward the end of his life, increasingly coincided with the biography of the anthroposophical movement, certain years seem to carry the signature of a special concentration of creative forces. One such year was 1912, when the third mystery drama, *The Guardian of the Threshold*, was written and performed. In this play we meet the being who, according to spiritual science, protects us from consciously experiencing the spiritual world—and suffering serious harm—before we are inwardly prepared to meet it. He is thus the guardian of the threshold that we cross unconsciously every night when our soul and spirit leave the physical body, and we fall asleep. We also meet him at the threshold where we completely separate from the physical body at death.

We can meet the guardian, however, on the path of inner spiritual development as a first step in supersensible experience. We meet him when we have achieved the strength to free ourselves, in full consciousness, from our dependence on the physical organism, and when we have come to know ourselves as we really are, with all the "unfinished business" of our everyday human nature. In this sense, the guardian is both protector and guide as we prepare to enter the realm of spiritual experience, where we are required to transform earthbound thinking, feeling, and willing into their cosmic counterparts. Johannes Thomasius comes face to face with this experience in the seventh scene of *The Guardian of the Threshold*.

In addition to this remarkable play, 1912 also brought two other singularly creative events. Steiner published a poetic meditation of fifty-two verses, which helps us to experience, week by week, the dynamic inner relationship we have with the changing seasons in nature. With a poetic mastery of the German language, Steiner wove a wreath of verses that allows the human soul to accompany the outbreath of earth's being during spring and summer, and its inbreath during autumn and winter.

In the crescendo of light and warmth that accompanies the earth's outbreathing, the human soul can experience a cosmic kindling, which can then be transformed, as the world again draws inward, into the birth of inner, spiritual selfhood as the darkest time of the winter nears. This *Calendar of the Soul* has been translated into many languages.[16] It has accompanied and sustained many people in their search to connect with the world of nature, from which modern human beings have become more and more estranged.

The name of Christ does not appear in the verses themselves, and yet they have become for many a living path into an expanded, cosmic Christianity. Steiner dated the original edition "1879 years after the birth of the I Am," linking it with the death and Resurrection of Christ at Easter in 33 A.D. The *Calendar* begins and ends at Easter, the turning point. Later, Steiner spoke of the thirty-three-year rhythm that can be discovered in human history since the event of Golgotha, when Christ united with the earth and with human evolution.

In a lecture on December 23, 1917, Steiner said that we can look for the "Easter" of events whose "Christmas" had taken place thirty-three years before. The significance of 1879, according to Steiner, is that during that year the being known as Michael assumed the spiritual regency of our modern era. The year 1879, and the spiritual significance of the advent of Michael, was "Christmas" in relation to 1912, when the *Calendar of the Soul* became an "Easter" fruit.

The third significant event of 1912 occurred in September, following the August festival in Munich where *The Guardian of the Threshold* was first performed. (That festival also included performances of Steiner's first and second mystery plays, as well as Edouard Schuré's drama, *The Mystery of Eleusis.*) Steiner was approached at that time by a woman who asked whether he had any thoughts on how the art of dance might be led back to its sacred, temple origins, but in a way appropriate for the present era. The woman who asked the question was the mother of Lori Smits, a girl of seventeen, who longed for a new and spiritually true form of dance.

It was characteristic of Rudolf Steiner that he did not launch initiatives unless they were specifically asked for. In this case, he might

---

16. *Calendar of the Soul*, Ruth and Hans Pusch, trans., Anthroposophic Press, Hudson, NY, 1988; *The Year Participated: Being Rudolf Steiner's Calendar of the Soul Translated and Paraphrased for an English Ear*, Owen Barfield, trans., Rudolf Steiner Press, London, 1985. See also, Rudolf Steiner, *The Cycle of the Year as Breathing Process of the Earth*, Anthroposophic Press, Hudson, NY, 1988. See Note L in Appendix, page 273.

have been able to act several years earlier, when he had guided a conversation with the Russian painter Margareta Woloshina toward the possibility of an art of movement; Woloshina, however, was preoccupied with other questions at the time. In her autobiography, *The Green Snake*, she describes that moment as well as her deep chagrin when she later realized the opportunity Steiner had offered her, and that her lack of response had prevented him from acting.

Steiner asked Marie von Sivers to guide Lori on the path she was seeking, and their work, with periodic guidance by Steiner, led to the birth of the art known as *eurythmy*. Marie von Sivers wrote:

> In 1912, he [Steiner] gave nine lessons to a seventeen-year-old girl, who, after the death of her father, had been obliged to help support her younger brothers and sisters. She greatly wished to devote herself to an art of movement that did not originate in the materialistic impulses of the time. Her life situation created the opportunity out of which the gift of eurythmy evolved. I was asked to take part in these lessons. They included the first elements of sound formation and some exercises that, in essence, have since been incorporated into the pedagogical aspect of eurythmy—the basic principles of standing, walking, and running, some special postures and bodily gestures, many rod exercises, and techniques for keeping time and maintaining rhythm.
>
> On these foundations, several young women who had become pupils of the first eurythmist later went on to develop the educational side of eurythmy. After this, they worked on elaborating the sound aspect of poetry. This was the first phase in the development of eurythmy. Now and again, when Rudolf Steiner was shown something they were working on, he would give hints and corrections and answer questions. A second phase of development began when the young art gained a foothold at the Goetheanum in Dornach.[17]

---

17. *Life and Work of Rudolf Steiner*, pp. 179–180.

Eurythmists at Oxford in 1922

From that original question asked by Lori Smits's mother, and from those first lessons given by Rudolf Steiner, the art of eurythmy arose. Today there are twenty-three eurythmy training schools worldwide, and several thousand individual eurythmists, who perform in established stage groups and who teach, primarily in Waldorf schools.[18]

The goal of eurythmy is to express in space the creative, formative forces behind the spoken, poetic word and musical tone. Performances include literary and dramatic as well as musical selections. In addition to its evolution as a stage art, eurythmy has, from its very inception, proved of great educational value through its development of spatial awareness, coordination, rhythm, balance, and artistic sensitivity. And a therapeutic form of eurythmy known as *curative eurythmy* is a highly effective instrument for healing often prescribed by physicians familiar with its effects.

---

18. At the present time (1996), the Moscow Eurythmy School—the school most recently established—is beginning its fifth year with sixty students, having just graduated its first class.

~

If we look at these years in Steiner's biography as the gradual "incarnation process" of the living *Being of Anthroposophy* into the materialistic culture of our time, then Steiner himself can be seen as the "midwife" in its birth. The earliest glimpses of this Being of Anthroposophy was through insights into the process of knowing, or cognition, and into the nature of thought itself. These had been expressed in such works as *Die Philosophie der Freiheit* and *A Theory of Knowledge*. In *Theosophy* and *An Outline of Occult Science*, the principles of cognition were extended to include supersensible realms, made possible through a special training of inner activity. Now, in the destinies of the characters in the four mystery dramas, anthroposophy became dramatically individualized. And, in both eurythmy and speech formation, through individual practice and intensification, cognitive insights could become living artistic experience.

August, 1912, also saw the publication of a volume entitled *A Road to Self-Knowledge*.[19] In this little book Steiner presented some general, universally valid conclusions of spiritual-scientific research in the form of eight meditations, which could be pursued as exercises on the path of inner development. In the introduction, Steiner wrote:

> Here I describe what a soul can experience when it proceeds along a particular path toward the spiritual. In a certain sense, you can view the present volume as a series of inner soul experiences. However, you should note that the experiences obtained in the manner described here will take on a form consistent with the peculiarities of your own soul. I have tried to take that into account, so you should also understand that I am presenting the experiences of a particular soul. (p. 8)

One of the high points in the evolutionary process of anthroposophy was the decision, after the final separation from the Theosophical

---

19. *A Road to Self-Knowledge and The Threshold of the Spiritual World*, Rudolf Steiner Press, London, 1975.

Society, to establish the Anthroposophical Society as a community of independent seekers of the spirit. A gathering of members came to this decision in early September, 1912, after long hours of deliberation, and affirmed their determination to work independently of the Theosophical Society in all future endeavors. Although this decision was reached in September, 1912, the actual inauguration of the new Anthroposophical Society did not take place until the following February.

This remarkable year of 1912 concluded with the lecture cycle *The Bhagavad Gita and the Epistles of St. Paul*, given in Cologne.[20] Addressing, once again, the powerful polarity of East and West, of pre-Christian and Christian worldviews, Steiner guided his listeners toward seeing such polarities as part of one great evolutionary whole.

Before beginning those December lectures, Steiner asked his listeners whether or not they regarded themselves as members of the newly established Anthroposophical Society. All but three of those present said yes, and the lecture cycle therefore took place under the auspices of the Anthroposophical Society.

~

The decisive events of 1912 thus made possible the formal inauguration of the Anthroposophical Society in 1913. In addition, the momentous decision was made to construct a building to be the home for anthroposophical work. The first performances of eurythmy and the fourth mystery drama, *The Souls' Awakening*, were also given in 1913.[21] For a full picture of that year, one must realize that in addition to these various initiatives and activities Steiner also gave nearly 200 lectures, as he did almost every year. In 1913 his lecturing activity involved visits to nine countries outside Germany; there were also countless meetings, consultations, and private conversations. Steiner seemed to be moved by an immense urgency in 1913 because of the impending catastrophes he clearly foresaw.

---

20. Anthroposophic Press, New York, 1971.
21. Anthroposophic Press, Hudson, NY, 1995.

The first Goetheanum March 14, 1914

6

The
Building Rises

In the opening chapter we encountered Rudolf Steiner amid the conflicting crosscurrents of the early years of this century. We met him as a man deeply concerned for the social future at a moment of intense crisis. We met him also as a research scientist investigating the ways in which the human soul and spirit penetrate the organism to bring about thought, feeling, and will. And we met him, finally, as the designer of the building that, in 1917, stood nearly completed on a hillside in northwest Switzerland. In the preceding chapter we briefly traced the steps that led to the intention to provide a home for the work then unfolding. The artistic impulse that sparked this intention was characterized as the striving to create an outer architectural structure whose forms and colors would speak essentially the same language as the ideas that inspired them.

Several leading members of the Anthroposophical Society placed themselves in the service of this intention. With great generosity and enthusiasm they also committed the financial resources. Originally, the building was to be erected in Munich, where Steiner's mystery plays had been performed each August since 1910. By 1912 architectural plans had been drawn for a building that would stand within a city block, surrounded by residential structures. The building was to be called "Johannes Bau," after Johannes Thomasius, a central character in the mystery plays. An organization—the Johannes Bauverein—was established to pursue the project, but it was unclear whether or not the Munich authorities would approve the plans.

In September, 1912, Rudolf Steiner, Marie von Sivers, and several friends were in Basel for a lecture cycle, after which they were invited by Dr. and Mrs. Emil Grosheintz to visit their country home in the Jura foothills. Dr. Grosheintz was a well-known dentist in Basel, and both he and his wife were longtime members of the German Theosophical Society. Nelly Grosheintz-Lavall described that visit:

On what was then an untouched hillside that had been known for centuries as Blood Hill, harking back to the Battle of Dornach in 1499, we owned two hectares of land on which stood our summerhouse Brodbeck, which has since been converted and enlarged, and is now known as Rudolf Steiner Halde. After the Basel lecture cycle on the Gospel of St. Mark in the autumn of 1912, Fräulein von Sivers together with her sister Olga and Fräulein Waller spent a few days' rest there while Dr. Steiner visited Edouard Schuré in Baar (Alsace) and Christian Morgenstern in Graubünden. After this they intended to proceed to Italy.

In the *Nachrichtenblatt*, August 16, 1925, Frau Dr. Steiner (then Fräulein von Sivers[1]) reported this first stay there as follows: "The hill was green and virgin, uneven and untouched except for the northwestern slope where Haus Brodbeck stood.... In the brilliant autumn sunshine the landscape spread out before us; the cherry trees flamed red in the valley, like fire, blood burning in the play of the sunshine.... Around the Dornach hill the slopes shone in an eerie shade of yellow. For us city dwellers it was a delightful view. Thrilled, I leaned from the window to look. But the next morning Rudolf Steiner awoke as he had never been before. For no apparent reason he was bewildered, crushed, gloomy. Such a thing had never happened to him before, for despite the endless bustle and hurry he was harmonious and eventempered. It passed; yet I had the feeling, which has recurred many times since then, that in that first night he foresaw many things that he had to forbid himself to turn over in his thoughts."

---

1. Marie von Sivers and Rudolf Steiner were married December 24, 1914. Anna Steiner-Eunicke had died in October 1911.

Dr. Emil Grosheintz

To everybody's astonishment, Dr. Steiner stayed in Dornach, exploring the whole district and even climbing into the Arlesheim caves. Then he called on us in Basel, and the following conversation took place:

Dr. Steiner: What do you plan to do with this piece of land?

Dr. Grosheintz: When I bought it, I said to my wife that the future will reveal why I had to buy so much land.

Myself: I should like us to build a boarding school where children can grow up in the right way.

Then, Dr. Steiner spoke the fateful words: We have been thinking about a kind of Bayreuth.

We knew about the difficulties that were being encountered in Munich, so my husband answered: Dornach has no building restrictions....

Dr. Steiner added: And Basel has a favorable theosophical karma.

And then he told us about the steps that had been taken in Munich, which were turning out to be nothing but a waste of time. He said what he so often repeated later on: "We have no time to waste."[2]

Model for the proposed building in Munich

Indeed, the Munich plans did fall through: the city authorities finally refused permission in February, 1913, and Steiner gratefully accepted the generous offer of the Grosheintzes, joined now by several other Swiss friends who had purchased additional land, to place their combined properties at the disposal of the Johannes Bauverein. Thus the building, which was later to bear the name of Goethe, Germany's greatest poet and dramatist, did not stand on German soil but found its home in neighboring Switzerland.

The building that was to have been completely surrounded by other structures would now stand alone on a hillside, visible for miles in every direction. It had to be redesigned, and time was pressing.

~

The day of the foundation stone ceremony, September 20, was cloudy. By early evening, when the ceremony was to occur, "a great wind arose." Distant thunder rumbled, lightning repeatedly shattered the darkness, and "the landscape took on an eerie appearance."

---

2. N. Grosheintz-Lavall, *Erinnerungen*; quoted in Lindenberg, *Rudolf Steiner eine Chronik*, Verlag Freies Geistesleben, Stuttgart, 1988, p.321.

The foundation stone—made of beaten copper and formed of two interlocking dodecahedrons of unequal size—was placed into the earth as the culmination of an apparently simple ceremony which, nevertheless, carried far-reaching spiritual implications.

The first Goetheanum 1914

Steiner spoke in a way that he had never spoken before. He related his experience of the Christ Being and of that being's relationship to our time. He called on the highest spiritual powers to recognize and help the work that was to proceed within the building and to which it was then dedicated.[3]

Once the foundation stone was laid, the construction of the building itself progressed at an astonishing rate. For years afterward, neighbors in Dornach would remember the great wagon-loads of lumber that clattered through the village and up the long hill to the

---

3. See Rudolf Grosse, *The Christmas Foundation: Beginning of a New Cosmic Age* (Steiner Book Centre, Vancouver, BC, 1984), which presents a detailed study of the spiritual significance of the Christmas Foundation ceremony and the events surrounding it, as well as a discussion of the "Foundation Stone Meditation."

building site; the lumber demanded for this gigantic building project affected the timber market all over Europe.

Two huge intersecting domes of unequal size formed the basic plan of the building. They were built of wood, which was carved inside and out, and rose above a ground-level structure of concrete. This concrete base extended beyond the wooden structure and was defined by walls that followed the curving lines of the building above, creating a terrace where audiences could mingle and stroll. The larger dome faced west, the smaller east, and both were sheathed in Norwegian slate, whose gray-green surfaces reflected the light and shadow of the sky.

The first Goetheanum from the south by Katharina Eisleben

If you entered from the west, you found yourself in an entryway from which two stairways of molded concrete swung upward, to the left and to the right. Each was supported by a column of poured concrete, which carried the upward thrust in a dynamic form reminiscent of a tree trunk or sculpted bone. Climbing either of the stairs, you would be greeted by a newel post—a freely sculpted form in which the three dimensions of space came together in dynamic balance, as they do in the inner ear for equilibrium. The stairway led into an upper foyer from which two carved doors opened into the auditorium. The space of the foyer, constructed of red beechwood, was bathed in crimson light that flooded in—especially in the afternoon and toward sunset—through a grand triptych-like window of solid red glass. Forms and images had been inscribed into the glass—the more deeply the engraver's tool cut, the lighter the color, and where the glass was untouched, it glowed in deep crimson.

The first Goetheanum from the northeast

If you entered the auditorium, you would find yourself in the midst of a space flooded with color, surrounded by seven great pairs of wooden columns that curved down toward the opening of the stage. Above them, a carved wooden architrave supported the dome, whose interior was painted in flowing colors that seemed to climax in warm reds, orange, and yellow toward the stage. In addition to the color that met you from the painted ceiling, more color flooded the interior on sunny days from the four great stained-glass window triptychs in the north and south walls—windows of light green, crystalline blue, violet, and a peach-blossom rose. As in the red western window, images and forms were carved into the colored Belgian glass using an engraving technique developed by Rudolf Steiner for his designs.

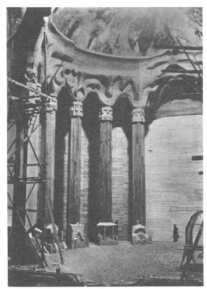 

The smaller cupola under construction and completed

Wandelhalle April 9, 1915

As you began to distinguish forms within the sea of color, you would notice that each pair of columns was crowned by carved capitals, whose forms metamorphosed from column to column as you moved toward the stage. Each pair was carved in a different wood: beech, ash, cherry, oak, elm, maple, and birch. Your eyes could follow the forms as they moved toward the arch that framed the stage, beyond which the interior of the smaller dome—supported on a circle of twelve columns—opened out to form the stage area. At the rear of the stage, beneath the smaller dome, a great wooden sculpture would have greeted those who entered the auditorium from the west.

In this sculpture, which can still be seen today, a central, free-standing figure strides quietly toward us. Above his head, a winged being plunges earthward. Below the feet of the central figure, within a rocky cave, a cramped and twisted figure reaches upward, as if to seize and hold the walking figure above his head. The central figure is not locked in combat with his cosmic brothers. His gaze is not triumphant but deeply seeing, and his mouth expresses compassion and restraint.

We have come to know the central figure as the *Representative of Humanity*—and also as the *Christ*—and the two contending beings as *Lucifer* and *Ahriman*. Steiner wanted to show his contemporaries the two faces of evil and the power who alone can help to create an inner space where we can meet the adversaries freely and without fear. Ahriman and Lucifer, each in his own rightful sphere, are necessary cosmic powers. Yet each, if left to himself, creates a caricature of what is truly human. It is only with the help of Christ that we can create that fragile balance in which we are able to experience freedom and awaken the all-transforming power of love.

These are some of the impressions one might have had upon entering this building, which stood nearly completed when it was burned to the ground during the night of the New Year's Eve that ended 1922.

~

Rudolf Steiner at work on the statue; the model for the columns

The north side of the west stairs

The Representative of Humanity

Looking back from the end of the twentieth century, it is hard to believe that, during those few embattled, fateful years, this building ever actually stood on the hill at Dornach. There, in the northwest corner of Switzerland, its rounded, carved forms and flowing colors spoke a language different in every way from the utilitarian functionalism that would soon dominate contemporary culture. It spoke of a world of living forms, of organic transformations and metamorphoses. Yet this is a lawful world, a world of forces that can be understood and grasped by an awakened and disciplined consciousness. It is a world where the human soul and spirit can feel at home.

Details of central figure

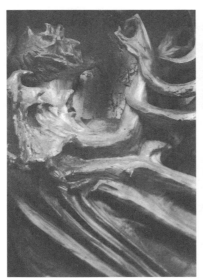

Details of the Ahriman figure and model of his head

Details of the Lucifer figure

Outwardly it was to be a festival center and a university based on a science that investigates spiritual reality, leading to research in many fields. It was intended for those asking questions that material science is largely unable to answer. For such people the school would offer study and training in the sciences and the arts, as well as in practical disciplines such as education, medicine, and the social sciences.

Enthusiasm for this vision, and the commitment to share in its realization, drew men and women from seventeen countries to work as volunteers. Alongside the Swiss workers, they carved and painted, ground and mixed plant colors, and engraved the glass.

Meanwhile, French and German guns dueled back and forth across the Rhine to the north. Many of the volunteers' home nations were at war with one another. More than one man among the workers was called away to serve in his country's army, knowing that he might meet, as an enemy in battle, a companion worker from the building in Dornach.

Although it was totally destroyed and replaced by a second, very different building, which was also designed by Rudolf Steiner, the first Goetheanum remains as an invisible inspiration and a challenge for human beings to unite in future service to a common, creative, spiritual goal.

As the building rose on the Dornach hill, it became clear that a new and very different architectural impulse was at work. Many people found that the design challenged deeply ingrained habits of thought and perception, and they reacted in outrage, anger, and derision. But for many others the building awakened the slumbering longing for a new experience of form and color. The Goetheanum, over the years, has inspired painters, sculptors, and architects to explore new possibilities of expression in their various fields. And these, in turn, have led to new opportunities for training in the visual arts, to new applications in education, healing, and social therapies, and to new approaches in interior and exterior structural and architectural design.

Steiner was asked, and was able, to design several of the structures immediately surrounding the Goetheanum. Those buildings survived the fire that destroyed the central building, and they may be seen today as examples of an organic, dynamic architectural approach adapted to structures as varied as a heating plant, a publishing house, an electrical transformer station, a building for engraving glass windows, an artist's studio, as well as various residential structures.[4]

~

While the Goetheanum was under construction, Steiner was often called away from Dornach. He spoke in many cities throughout Central Europe, and was involved in consultations concerning the developing anthroposophical work. He was also asked for countless personal conversations. Even when he was at the utmost limit of his strength, Steiner always tried to respond to individual requests, offering advice and guidance where it was sought, as well as insight and consolation arising from his research and knowledge. His help often took the form of a special meditative word or verse given to a particular person, which became a treasured source of strength and courage amid the tragedies of war.

---

4. See Note M in Appendix, page 275.

During these years Rudolf Steiner's lectures frequently dealt with the spiritual realities of death, of the life between death and rebirth, and with questions of individual destiny and karma, as well as the destinies of folk groups and nations. He often introduced his lectures by directing the thoughts and feelings of his audience to those on the battlefields, and to those increasing numbers who had fallen and had crossed the threshold. He would begin by speaking a mantric verse to help his hearers unite themselves in heart and mind with those from whom they were now physically separated. Those verses, which arose in many different ways and served many purposes, were later collected and published as *Wahrspruchworte* (*Truth-Wrought-Words*).[5] They constitute a significant part of Rudolf Steiner's creative, artistic achievement. When reading these verses in English, we need to realize that they have been "twice translated," once by Rudolf Steiner into German from direct spiritual inspiration, and then from German into English. In his autobiography Rudolf Steiner often spoke about the challenge that the esotericist experiences in trying to find earthly language to express experiences that originate in the supersensible realm.

To conclude this look at the main artistic phase of anthroposophy as it entered more and more into human cultural experience, we should realize that Rudolf Steiner was also intensively engaged in the study of great artists and great works of art when he visited cities such as Florence, Rome, Nuremberg, Prague, Leipzig, London, Vienna, and Amsterdam. He never failed to visit the museums of those cities, even with little time at his disposal. Those visits bore fruit, especially for the carvers, painters, sculptors, and engravers at work on the building in Dornach. Rudolf Steiner spoke again and again about art, and the evolution of consciousness as expressed through art. During these years, he mentioned more than seven hundred works of art, often illustrating what he had to say with lantern slides. Thus, his pioneering work in the practice of the arts, in which new forms and methods were researched and explored, was enriched and supported through a study of the art of past centuries and ages.

---

5. *Truth-Wrought-Words and Other Verses*, Anthroposophic Press, Spring Valley, NY, 1979.

7

Insight Becomes Life

The Threefold Movement for Social Reform

Anthroposophy has its roots in the perceptions—already gained—into the spiritual world. Yet these are no more than its roots. The branches, leaves, blossoms, and fruits of anthroposophy grow into all the fields of human life and action.

—Rudolf Steiner[1]

In previous chapters we accompanied Rudolf Steiner on the first two stages of his path, and observed how, through him, anthroposophy gradually unfolded into life in the twentieth century. We are at the threshold of the third and final stage, when the ideas that had been won through spiritual-scientific research, and had flowered into artistic creation, began to penetrate the world of everyday life as practical initiatives.

Steiner compared anthroposophy to a plant with its roots in the spiritual world rather than in earthly soil; it grows down, in the opposite direction from an earthly plant. Its roots draw life and nourishment from spiritual perceptions, which grow into concepts that are true to the spirit. These gradually unfold and become visible, as do a plant's green shoot and leaves. They not only sustain the plant's life but lead to the budding blossoms, and ultimately to the ripening fruits and to seeds for the future.

---

1. *The Foundation Stone / The Life, Nature, and Cultivation of Anthroposophy*, Rudolf Steiner Press, London, 1996, p. 73.

This growing down, this "incarnation," of spiritual science required it to penetrate the nature of matter itself, as well as the life processes that enable inorganic, mineral substance to be taken up, shaped, and enlivened by the living world. Spiritual science asks, for instance, how the human spirit and soul actually shape the organism in which they will live? How does the physical body support the soul in its activities of feeling and of willing? Are these activities seated in the brain as thinking is? If not, what are their physiological bases? What is consciousness, and how does it arise? What is operative in human sense perception? These were the questions with which Steiner silently wrestled and which he continuously researched while, outwardly, he worked on the new building (and on many other things not elaborated in the preceding chapter).

The simplest, most basic questions about human life carry cosmic overtones and reach cosmic dimensions. Esoteric research reveals the human physical body as the oldest, most wisdom-filled aspect of the human being and of the earthly world, in comparison with the bodies of life, sentience, and selfhood. In *An Outline of Occult Science* Steiner describes how, in the earliest stage of planetary evolution, the mightiest divine beings poured out their spiritual substance as warmth and will, which became the seeds for earthly evolution. He also describes how other hierarchies of spiritual beings brought movement, order, form, sensation, and consciousness into planetary evolution, which led to the earth and to the human being as they are today, just as the plant's development leads to blossom, fruit, and seed.

As the distant goal of this cosmic, planetary evolution, the divine world's task is to bring about a new *hierarchy*, or level of cosmic being, which will be unique among all the heavenly host, for it will develop the capacity for individual freedom. Out of freedom, humanity—destined to become the youngest hierarchy—is to bring forth love, which can be neither forced nor compelled. In order to become free, human beings gradually had to be estranged from the divine-spiritual world out of which they had been created; the strings had to be cut. This process, which took eons, is described in

An Outline of Occult Science. It has brought human beings to the point where they feel completely cut off from the supersensible realm and totally immersed in the material world. Yet, within this isolation, through the innermost activity of the human spirit, we can discover the unbroken thread of thinking that still unites us with the creative sources of existence. This discovery can awaken the potential for freedom in us.

Only when we are prepared to endure and go through the terrible isolation of being cut off—confronting the void of nothingness—can we experience true rebirth and the joy of being reconnected to the source of meaning, life, and love. In Steiner's view, it is the Christ Being who accompanies us uncompromisingly on this path and gives us the strength and courage to come through it. Other beings would like to entice us into premature spiritual experiences and short-circuit the painful process of transforming ourselves—and our world—consciously.

Steiner describes unseen beings who tempt and waylay us in two very different directions. On one side, there are the servants of Lucifer, the fallen angel of light. They are beings who have brought humanity great gifts, but who would abandon the goals of the highest hierarchies and create a blissful kingdom of spiritual light and delight for themselves. On the other side, there are immensely powerful beings who strive to blind us to the spirit, powers for whom it is self-evident that the universe is a machine and that what can be measured, weighed, and quantified is the only reality. These spirits of materialism belong to the dark power that ancient wisdom called *Ahriman*, or *Angra Mainyu*. Ahriman was the great cosmic opponent of *Ahura Mazda*, or *Ormuzd*, the divine being of light and truth, for whom Zarathustra (Zoroaster) was the prophet, as presented in the Zend-Avesta, the body of sacred text of Zoroastrianism.

Both Ahriman and Lucifer have played, and continue to play, necessary roles in human and world evolution, but only the Christ has totally united himself with the earth and with humanity. Only the Christ continually seeks to balance and transform, and to awaken in each of us our essential individuality, which alone can achieve freedom and the capacity for love.

~

During the closing months of 1916, when the possibility of a negotiated peace hung in the balance, and the world could have been spared the cruel continuation of war, Steiner wrestled with the question: How can one penetrate the physical world so that it can be truly and completely humanized? To abandon it and to seek personal, mystical bliss and gratification, while ignoring the rest of the world and its suffering, would yield to the luciferic temptation. To find no spirit in matter at all would abandon humanity to the forces of the cosmic machine and the deceptive lies of Ahriman.

It became increasingly evident to Steiner that Christ, by uniting himself with the earth and with unredeemed humanity for all time, gave us the possibility of penetrating and transforming the material world. Steiner expressed this conviction in a lecture on November 27, 1916:

> If the luciferic evolution had continued, if Christ had not entered into human evolution ... humankind would have spiritualized itself in an entirely ascetic way and would have entered into the spiritual luciferic world in this ascetic spiritualization, leaving the corporeal behind. Human souls would have found their salvation, but the earth would have remained purposeless. The bodies of human beings would never have been able to render the service to human souls that they really ought to render. To prevent this constitutes the significance of the Mystery of Golgotha.[2]

In his early years, Steiner's primary focus was the nature of knowledge itself. What is the true nature of thinking, and how can it reach beyond the senses to other dimensions of reality? Now, after thirty years of intensive research, the question had evolved: How can spiritual science illuminate the ways in which the human soul and spirit interact with and penetrate the human physical organism? How does the soul, in its thinking, feeling, and willing, actually take hold of the physical body, which is its basic instrument for earthly life?

---

2. *The Karma of Vocation*, Anthroposophic Press, Hudson, NY, 1988, p. 198.

Rudolf Steiner 1916 and 1918

It was during the storms of war that Steiner finally achieved full clarity in regard to these questions and was able to present the results of his years of research for the first time. Although those first presentations were inconspicuous, they had far-reaching consequences, for it was only on the basis of these new and radical insights that so much of the practical work, soon to follow, could find its ground in knowledge.

The research method that led Steiner to his conclusions could be considered an extension of Goethe's method of allowing the phenomena to "speak for themselves." Goethe characterized his method as a "seeing-knowing" (*anschauende Urteilskraft*), a power of knowledge consisting of both thinking and perceiving, an "intuitive discernment." Steiner developed Goethe's way of knowing into a disciplined faculty of supersensible investigation. As such, it becomes a "reading" of phenomena, in which the single factual perceptions are "letters" that form themselves into words and sentences and whole paragraphs of meaning.

Steiner recognized Goethe as an artist and thinker who spoke out of the spirit of Central Europe. He called him the "Copernicus and

Kepler of the science of the organic." Therefore, in fulfillment of the principle of a spiritual continuity in which future forms arise through a living metamorphosis of past achievements, on October 18, 1917, in a lecture in Basel, Steiner first spoke of the fact that the building then arising in Dornach would be known as the *Goetheanum*. Looking back on the process that led him to give the name of Goethe to the building, Steiner wrote:

> Anyone who has noticed the shapes from which the total formation of the Goetheanum has been composed in a living integration, can see how Goethe's ideas of metamorphosis have entered into the conception of the building.... In the same manner, moreover, anthroposophy itself has taken the course of a direct further development of the Goethean view. Anyone who has become receptive to the conception of transformation, not only of the sensibly visible forms (the point at which Goethe remained because of his particular character of soul), but also of what can be grasped by the soul and spirit—such a person has arrived at anthroposophy.... Through the concept of metamorphosis, we achieve the living. We thus impart a living quality to our own thinking. From a dead thinking, it becomes living. But, in this way it achieves the capacity to take into itself, in actual vision, the life of the spirit.... What therefore experiences itself as resting firmly upon Goethe's worldview can justly be cultivated in a building that, as a memorial to Goethe, bears the name *Goetheanum*.[3]

Through Rudolf Steiner's work, the faculty Goethe called "intuitive discernment" metamorphosed and became a faculty for perceiving supersensible realities, with which Steiner explored the complex and subtle interactions of the threefold human organism.

The same faculty of sensible-supersensible apprehension, when

---

3. Quoted in Guenther Wachsmuth, *The Life and Work of Rudolf Steiner: From the Turn of the Century to His Death*, Spiritual Science Library, Blauvelt, NY, 1989, pp. 322–323.

directed toward the shifting surface of world events, disclosed the struggle for expression of the underlying social needs of all human beings. The need for individual freedom in the cultural-spiritual sphere, for community in economic life, and for just equality in the sphere of human rights—these three necessities, all fundamental to human dignity and well-being on earth, were struggling for recognition and differentiation beneath the conflict and chaos of outer life.

As we know from our initial encounter with Rudolf Steiner in the first chapter, it was these twin insights into the threefold nature of the individual and of the social organism that enabled him to respond so immediately to Otto von Lerchenfeld's appeal for help in finding ideas that might become the basis for a real peace when the war ended. The central intention of the two memoranda circulated in Germany and Austria during the summer and autumn of 1917 was to awaken the political leadership of Central Europe to the need for decentralizing state control and allowing the economy to find natural, practical ways to associate on local, regional, and global levels. The intention was also to allow individuals to have the freedom to think and act on their own initiative, and to align themselves with whatever intellectual, religious, or ethnic groups they may choose. Steiner had no illusions; but he also knew that only the radical, yet organic, understanding of the underlying social forces could rescue Europe, and eventually also humanity, from the dead ends into which they were allowing themselves to be driven.

~

As long as the war lasted, Steiner used every available opportunity to encourage his contemporaries to look behind external events at the powerful forces of which the events were only symptoms. It was clear to him that the end of the war must bring the breakdown of the old order, and that with the breakdown would come an opportunity to reach a much wider circle than was possible under the pressures and restrictions of war. During the final months of 1918 he devoted himself especially to lecturing on social themes in a number of Swiss cities, where friends from across the border in Germany were occasionally able to take part.

Among these friends were several who recognized that Steiner's ideas carried possibilities for action. They let him know that they were ready to serve an initiative that would make these ideas known. This group included Emil Molt, owner and director of the Waldorf-Astoria Cigarette Company in Stuttgart; Carl Unger, owner of a precision tool company near Stuttgart; and Roman Boos, a Swiss political economist and lawyer.

In January, 1919, Molt and Boos along with Hans Kühn, a young German businessman who had given up a promising position to work for the threefold commonwealth ideal, met with Steiner in Dornach to discuss what might be done, especially from the economic and political side. Steiner's advice was that nothing socially effective could be accomplished unless it went to the root of the problems. Out of this discussion arose the thought of an appeal to the German people, a call to action, supported by public figures whose signatures would carry weight.

Hans Kühn described how the conversations with Steiner, which lasted several days, ranged widely over basic economic, social, and political questions.[4] These included such matters as wages, the social role of labor, how one should arrive at commodity value and price, the role of land and land ownership, and the building of unifying associations between consumers and producers, as well as the spiritual tasks of Central Europe in relation to the underlying causes and consequences of the war. Out of these broad and fundamental considerations, Rudolf Steiner said he was ready to draft a statement that would address basic social issues. His text was received in Stuttgart in February, where individuals were delegated to present the appeal to selected people, asking for their support and their signatures.

Within a short time, the signatures of 250 known and respected individuals active in public life in Germany, Austria, and Switzerland had been obtained, and the "Appeal to the German People and the Cultural World" was published in several major newspapers.

---

4. *Dreigliederungs-Zeit, Rudolf Steiners Kampf für die Gesellschaftsordnung der Zukunft* ("The threefold movement: Rudolf Steiner's battle for a social order of the future"), Philosophisch-Anthroposophischer Verlag, Dornach, 1978.

Meanwhile, during February, Steiner delivered a series of important lectures in Switzerland that dealt with current critical issues from the standpoint of the threefold social organism. These lectures were well-attended and received enthusiastic understanding, and they became the basis for a book, *Die Kernpunkte der sozialen Frage* ("The Crux of the Social Question").[5]

The effort to introduce these radically new ways of dealing with economic, spiritual, and legal life moved forward with astonishing energy and speed considering the privation and uncertainty that prevailed in both inner and outer life. The widespread chaos and conflict in Germany culminated in a general strike in early April, followed by the imposition of martial law. In many German cities this erupted into open revolution, often ending in street fighting and bloodshed. Looking back, it is hard to believe that an initiative such as the Threefold Commonwealth could actually have occurred, could have affected so many lives, and could have created prototypes that still inspire social initiatives for the future—despite the fact that this Threefold initiative survived outwardly for only a very few years.

We will mention only a few of the most important activities that arose out of the Threefold Movement at that time. Because of their potential value for current efforts toward social renewal, it is important that they are known.

Steiner traveled from Dornach to Stuttgart on April 20, 1919. When he arrived, the Association for the Threefold Social Organism (*Bund für Dreigliederung des sozialen Organismus*) was established and headquartered in a multistory business building in Stuttgart. Initially the association's activities were concentrated on disseminating Steiner's social ideas, bringing his newly published book (*Towards Social Renewal*) to public attention, and making reports of his lectures available to members of the Anthroposophical Society, students, and friends. The two memoranda written in 1917, as well as the "Appeal to the German People and the Cultural World," were widely circulated.

---

5. *Towards Social Renewal: Basic Issues of the Social Question*, Rudolf Steiner Press, Bristol, 1992.

Steiner's personal engagement in the process provided a center for these activities in the spring and early summer of 1919 in Stuttgart and southern Germany. He held more than seventy public lectures, including addresses to the workers in some of the area's largest factories, such as Daimler (now Mercedes-Benz), Bosch, and the Waldorf-Astoria Cigarette Factory. He also delivered at least twenty private lectures, as well as courses, study evenings, and consultations.

Amid this whirlwind of activity came a request from Emil Molt to inaugurate a school for the children of his factory workers. In July, the first issue of the weekly magazine, *Threefolding the Social Organism*, appeared, guided by Steiner and edited by Ernst Uehli, a Swiss colleague who later became one of the first teachers in the new Waldorf school. But these activities did not exhaust Steiner's efforts toward cultural and spiritual renewal. On May 18 and 19, Stuttgart's first public eurythmy performances were presented at the State Theater and at the Art Museum, and Steiner was actively involved in the rehearsals. The degree of interest that all these efforts aroused can be measured by the decision to quadruple the size of the first edition of *Towards Social Renewal* from ten to forty thousand volumes; eighty thousand copies were sold during the first year after publication.

The Stuttgart Waldorf school opened its doors on September 7 with 253 children and twelve teachers. Three weeks later in Dornach, Steiner met with a group of friends from Germany, Switzerland, and Sweden to discuss the expansion of the Threefold Movement to other countries—particularly to Scandinavia and Holland, and eventually to England. The possibility of establishing an international bank was also discussed, in order to finance the Threefold Movement and to counter the destructive effects of inflation in Germany, which Steiner saw coming.

Two further efforts emerged from these widening initiatives; there was an appeal to those active in cultural, scientific, and academic circles to form a central leadership for cultural life, and a working group of business enterprises was established that would coordinate activity within the economic sphere.

In June, 1919, the new Association for the Threefold Organism issued its call to the culturally active community throughout Germany under the heading, *An appeal for the establishment of a cultural parliament* (*Aufruf zur Begrundung eines Kulturrates*). It was a call to the spiritual and cultural idealism that had lived so strongly in the greatest German poets, philosophers, writers, and artists of the eighteenth and early nineteenth centuries. Only when the cultural element could rouse itself to unite as an independently active constituency within the social organism as a whole—creating a balance of forces with the economic and political spheres—would Germany find its required role as a cultural mediator between Russia to the east and the Anglo-Saxon world to the west.

To accomplish such a goal, the appeal called for an education—from elementary school through university levels—free of all state regulation and control, and free of the one-sided influence of economic pressures; and it called for the formation of associations or councils of cultural and spiritual leaders to administer all cultural activities, whether educational, scientific, artistic, or religious. The published appeal was signed by 175 writers, artists, professors, and scientists. The response from the academic and cultural communities, however, was far less than hoped for by Steiner and the Association for the Threefold Organism and did not lead to any significant practical initiative in that sphere. On the other hand, there was a very strong and active response from a group of entrepreneurs in business and manufacturing.

It was decided at the end of 1919 to form an association of economic enterprises, which became a reality early the next year. The plan called for an umbrella organization in the form of a shareholder corporation to carry the overall financial responsibility, whereas the individual enterprises would continue to be managed by their former owners. The proprietors would surrender private ownership and agree, instead, to receive equity in the general holdings and a fixed income in lieu of personal profit. The general profit, however, was to flow directly to spiritual, cultural initiatives, the most immediate being the newly established Waldorf school.

Agricultural enterprises were also included among the participating economic activities, as well as a nonprofit publishing house, a clinic, and various research laboratories.

Steiner wanted the future-directed aspect to be reflected in the name of this new organization, which came to be known as "The Coming Day: Shareholder Corporation for the Furthering of Economic and Spiritual Values" (*Der Kommende Tag, Aktiengesellschaft zur Förderung wirtschaftlicher und geistiger Werte*). On March 11, 1920, shortly before the founding of The Coming Day, Steiner spoke about the responsibility of the economic realm for the support of spiritual and cultural life:

> Now, my dear friends, we must focus our attention on economic matters, because the economic must carry the spiritual. But one cannot carry when there is nothing to carry. Our main concern will always be with carrying the spirit. We must therefore see to it that a well-grounded spiritual life can establish itself in public view. It has not been for nothing that we have recently made efforts to offer something like eurythmy from month to month, and wherever possible, to present it to the public. But this should be done in a far more comprehensive way.[6]

By the end of 1922, The Coming Day included a publishing house, a mail-order book distributor, a printing firm, a precision machine tool factory, a chemical works, a slate-oil extracting plant, a packaging plant with branches in two other towns, six farms (including a flour mill and sawmill), a clinic in Stuttgart, a pharmaceutical production plant in Schwaebisch Gmünd (now Weleda), a chemical laboratory, and a biological laboratory. The Coming Day association was also affiliated with an agricultural machine production company, a mechanical weaving plant, a limited partnership in Hamburg, and a joint stock company based in Berlin.

In June 1920, a similar, though smaller, international initiative based in Switzerland, Futurum AG, was founded, and Steiner was placed in the position of accepting the presidency, as he had for The Coming Day.

---

6. Hans Kühn, *Dreigliederungs-Zeit, Rudolf Steiners Kampf für die Gesellschaft-sordung der Zukunft*, p. 102 (H. B., trans.).

Even in 1920, Steiner clearly saw that forces, both above and below the surface of events, were creating an almost insurmountable opposition to any social renewal. Social life needed to be restructured from the ground up, and this inevitably conflicted with established interests. First of all, even the most intelligent and idealistically minded individuals were unable to free themselves from materialistic habits of thought. This was coupled with the suffering and bitterness engendered by the "peace of revenge" imposed by the Allied Powers in Versailles, which forced Germany to accept sole responsibility for causing the war—a responsibility that Steiner had done everything in his power to oppose as a one-sided misinterpretation of the facts. Those two factors united to prevent any radical rethinking or reorientation, either by a significant leadership or by the German people themselves. Nevertheless, Steiner felt that every possible opportunity must be seized until it became clear that further efforts were fruitless and that energies and resources would be more effectively channeled in other directions.

The final opportunity during this period came in 1921 when, in accordance with the new doctrine of "the self-determination of nations," the people of Upper Silesia in northeastern Germany were to decide through a referendum whether they wanted to belong to Germany or to Poland. The active members of the local section of the Association for the Threefold Organism in Breslau—the capital city of this region—saw an opportunity to offer a third alternative to an otherwise either/or situation. They appealed to Rudolf Steiner and to the Alliance in Stuttgart, and Steiner responded by calling together a number of people active in the threefold movement to prepare for a concerted action in Silesia. As a preparation, he gave them a training course in public speaking that addressed the specific circumstances that would confront them. At the time a dangerous tension was building; the emotional forces of nationalism were driving toward a violent end. It was decided to send out four teams of four members each. Each group was assigned a territory and worked out the route it would follow. Helmuth Woitinas, a member of one of the teams, writes:

We set out through the main cities of Upper Silesia in groups of four men, presenting lectures and holding discussions in an atmosphere close to the boiling point. Often, by the skin of our teeth, we escaped having the speaker arrested and a shoot-out. No immediate or direct result of our efforts was possible, since the national polarities were too powerful, but perhaps something was achieved; at least the threat of settling the disputes by armed force was avoided. The result was the division of Upper Silesia into a Polish and a German sector.[7]

Hans Kuhn adds, "Although the referendum resulted in Germany's favor by sixty percent, the valuable coal and iron industrial sections were largely given to Poland."[8] It is by no means merely coincidental that the invasion of Poland by Hitler's Germany just eighteen years later finally launched World War Two.

The actions of Steiner and these men were a courageous attempt to introduce the idea for a solution in which cultural groups would have the freedom to form their own spiritual and cultural associations—their own schools, churches, clubs, and cultural organizations. At the same time, they could integrate their economy into a regional and European economy and establish a minimal political state to secure a fair and orderly implementation of the agreements for the autonomous region. This attempt—perhaps doomed to failure from the start—serves as a point of reference for the conflicts currently raging around similar efforts to achieve the "right of national self-determination," in which the only view seems to be toward the victory of one party over the other and all-embracing control by a centralized, unified political state.

This attempt was the end of any realistic hope of achieving a breakthrough for the ideas of a threefold social order in postwar Germany. The immediate consequence for Steiner was that he was branded a traitor against his country by the Alldeutsch political

---

7. Helmut Woitinas, *Menschenschicksal*, Stuttgart, 1978.
8. Quoted in Hans Kühn, *Dreigliederungs-Zeit, Rudolf Steiners Kampf für die Gesellschaftsordnung der Zukunft.*

movement (two years later, that movement, under the leadership of General Ludendorf, backed Hitler in his attempt to seize power in Munich). A year after the Silesian action, an attempt was made on Steiner's life in Munich. An organized group tried to break up his lecture and attack him in the ensuing tumult. Their effort failed because of Steiner's extraordinarily calm presence of mind, and because of the intervention of young friends who had formed a body-guard for his protection. In November, 1923, when Steiner heard of Hitler's Beer Hall Putsch and abortive march on the Feldhalle in Munich, he commented, "If these people ever come to power, I will never be able to set foot in Germany again."

The three years that followed the First World War show us an all-too-brief moment in the history of the twentieth century when the breakdown of outer forms in Central Europe created an opportunity ripe for sowing new seeds of thought and action. As we have seen, Steiner's direct awareness of the spiritual struggles behind the scenes of external events caused him to intervene with great intensity in the day-to-day developments of the time. He tirelessly called his contemporaries to wake up to the deeper realities of the events all around them.

As a result of his initiatives, Steiner was very much in the public eye at this time, to the degree that a leading concert agency urged him to allow them to arrange a series of public lectures for him in the major cities of Germany. He agreed, and during a fifteen- day period in January 1922, Rudolf Steiner spoke to large audiences in crowded halls of twelve cities, including Munich, Frankfurt, Cologne, Berlin, Hamburg, and Dresden. In several places the lectures were accompanied by eurythmy performances in nearby large theaters, with a brief introduction to the new art given by Rudolf Steiner. In Berlin, the crowds that came to hear Rudolf Steiner at the Philharmonic Hall were so large that traffic was disrupted and many hundreds had to be turned away. Rudolf Steiner did not succumb to any sensationalism in either the content of his lectures or the manner in which he addressed these large audiences. On the contrary, he always addressed deeper, heartfelt concerns, lifting them into the clear light of consciousness. He reportedly said that in facing an audience of one or two thousand people, he spoke directly to perhaps one or two individuals. The titles of his lectures were "The Nature of Anthroposophy" and "Anthroposophy and the Riddles of the Soul."

Steiner's great interest at that time was to reach the younger generation, most of whom had grown up during the war years. And many of them, having been on the battlefields and in the trenches, had come to know death and the cruelties of war. Steiner perceived that they, having been born around the turn of the century, brought with them new experiences of the spiritual world from the pre-earthly realm, and that these experiences lived in them as questions about life's meaning, questions that were often unconscious but deeply disturbing. Steiner's awareness of this sounded through those lectures again and again, as if he were seeking to awaken the consciousness of his younger listeners to their experiences before birth, and to confirm in them the deeper intentions that had accompanied them into life on earth. He also hoped to awaken them by opening up new approaches to many fields of human activity, pointing the way for their innermost selves to strive for positive transformation in life and culture. It was as though Steiner bore within himself the ideal of a new "university," where science, art, and religion would again form the united whole they once were, on renewed spiritual foundations. The Goetheanum, standing on its hill in Dornach, was to be the home for this life of universal renewal.

Many of Steiner's lectures at that time dealt with aspects of contemporary science, always with the purpose of extending scientific methods of inquiry to include the results of spiritual-scientific research. He hoped to show his young listeners, many of whom were in the midst of university studies, that modern human beings can develop methods of knowing that lead beyond intellectual "head" knowledge to a fully conscious penetration of the realm of the living and of higher realms of supersensible cognition.

8

The First
Waldorf School

and the Independence of Education

The foundation of the first Waldorf school grew directly out of the social needs of the time. Rudolf Steiner was not alone in recognizing the need, above all, for initiatives born out of thinking that was inwardly flexible, genuinely practical, and thoroughly human. Such thinking, he knew, arises only when individuals find themselves both inwardly and outwardly free—not only to question and challenge prevailing attitudes and established forms, but also free to develop their full creative human potential. For this to happen, education must be independent of political and economic controls. And this requires a sphere of free cultural life within the social organism as a whole. This would become possible only when economic life and the sphere of political rights find healthy roles in a naturally functioning threefold society.

When the workers in Emil Molt's Waldorf-Astoria factory read an article in the local Stuttgart newspaper and saw Molt's name as a supporter, they wanted to know who this Steiner was, and they wanted to hear more from Molt about the ideas that he believed held hope for the future. His talks and the discussions that arose from them led to questions about the kind of thinking that could go to the roots of the social problems intensified by the war. His listeners were only too aware of the problems, and they realized how little their own education had equipped them to come to terms with new realities. When Molt described some of Steiner's ideas on education, the thought arose: If only our children could be educated in this way!

It was April when Steiner was finally free to come to Stuttgart to launch the Threefold Movement for Social Renewal. Two days after he arrived, on the morning of April 23, he addressed the workers in the Waldorf-Astoria factory.[1] Immediately following his talk, Steiner met with the plant managers, and Emil Molt took the opportunity to say that he hoped to establish a school for his employees' children, and he asked Steiner if he would "take on the establishment and leadership of it."

A few days later, Steiner spoke to the workers of the Daimler-Benz Automotive Works and again met with Molt and others to declare his readiness to establish such a school. He stipulated four fundamental conditions. First, the school must be open to *all* children and not just to the children of the Waldorf-Astoria employees. Second, the school should be based on a unified twelve-year curriculum that eliminated the customary segregation occurring when, at about the age of eleven, intellectually gifted students were sent to secondary schools to prepare for university entrance, whereas the great majority were left to complete their elementary education and enter a vocation or trade. Third, the new school must welcome girls as well as boys, contrary to the custom of the day. And, fourth, the teachers, who carry the daily responsibility for educating the children, should be free to teach and run the school outside the control of either government or outside economic interests.

This was to be a truly independent school, freely supported out of the economic realm, and conforming only to those conditions legally required by the state of Württemberg. The fourth condition was undoubtedly the most radical, since Germany at that time had virtually no tradition of private education, and teachers were civil servants like any other government employees. But central to Steiner's ideas was the conviction that education would truly serve the future only within the freedom of the cultural and spiritual sphere of social life.

---

1. This lecture is contained in *Education as a Force for Social Change*, Anthroposophic Press, 1997 (a new translation of *Education as a Social Problem*, with additional, related lectures).

Emil Molt gladly accepted the conditions and plunged into preparing for the school's founding. Within two months he found two
possible sites, and on May 30, 1919, Steiner visited both and
decided in favor of the site of a restaurant overlooking the city from
a hillside to the east. Molt purchased the property and underwrote
its renovation costs. Meanwhile, Steiner issued a call for teachers
willing to place themselves wholly in the service of this new initiative and sent out a young colleague to interview and recruit them.
On August 20, less than four months after Molt's initial question,
twelve teachers gathered on the Uhlandshoehe with Emil and Bertha Molt, Marie Steiner, and a few invited guests to begin two
weeks of intensive training.

Emil and Bertha Molt

Every day for fourteen days, Steiner held three courses: a fundamental study of the nature of the human being from the viewpoint
of spiritual-scientific research; an introduction to the methods of
instruction arising from those new insights; and a seminar course

dealing with specific aspects of instruction and subject material.[2]
Each session of the latter series began with speech exercises designed
to free the voice and to awaken both the dynamic and formative elements of the spoken word. On September 6, Steiner sketched the
curriculum for the various grades, and on the next day the festive
inauguration occurred. Over a thousand people gathered in the
municipal auditorium, and in the presence of local dignitaries, the
Independent Waldorf School was dedicated to its task. One week
later, with renovation sufficiently completed to allow teaching to
begin, 253 children in eight grades met their teachers, and the school
actually began.

~

What was it in Steiner's work that inspired Molt to ask him to
start a school? In a sense it was the totality of the work itself—everything that Molt had heard and read over the many years of association with Steiner. For indeed everything that Steiner had written
and spoken, from one perspective or another, shed light on what it
means to be—or perhaps better said, to *become*—a human being. But
beyond the extraordinary insights, it may well have been Molt's
experience of the man himself that became the ultimate inspiration—the teacher, the artist and thinker, and the man of selfless, creative will.

In addition to their knowledge of Steiner's work in general, Molt
and his wife Bertha—who shared completely in his hopes for the
new school—were also certainly familiar with the booklet in which
Steiner had presented his view of child development in the light of
his anthroposophical research. Based on his lectures at that same
time, the booklet was published in 1907 as "The Education of the
Child in the Light of Theosophy."[3] It characterized not only the

---

2. The three courses are, respectively, *The Foundations of Human Experience*
(formerly *Study of Man*), Anthroposophic Press, Hudson, NY, 1996; *Practical
Advice to Teachers*, Rudolf Steiner Press, London, 1988; and *Discussions with
Teachers*, Anthroposophic Press, Hudson, NY, 1997.
3. Contained in *The Education of the Child and Early Lectures on Education*,
Anthroposophic Press, Hudson, NY, 1996.

development of the child, but went on to suggest many practical ways in which this understanding might become fruitful in the classroom. His suggestions were specific enough that, when they were first published, they might well have inspired someone such as Molt, or another thoughtful reader, to establish such a school, but the time was evidently not yet ripe, and no such initiative occurred.

Whatever its source, what Molt saw was, in essence, the need for an education that could unlock the human being's full potential as thinker, as man or woman of open, loving heart and practical will. Only such human beings, he knew, could find the insights, courage, and strength to shoulder the responsibilities and take the initiatives so desperately needed in our time. Above all, such people needed to be guided by thinking that does not endlessly indulge in abstract impractical theory, but can come to grips with life's complex realities in the social, spiritual, and economic dimensions.

Emil Molt also knew that an education was needed that recognizes the fact that humanity now lives in an age when the longing for human freedom underlies all contemporary experience. No matter how the surface events of life appear to contradict this longing, Molt shared Steiner's conviction that the ultimate goal of any truly modern education must be to support the individual's striving toward this ideal. He also knew that the way to freedom requires hard work on oneself and the courage to let go of the old and move toward the new. Such self-transformation demands far more than technical skills and theoretical knowledge; it requires capacities of discernment, active, loving interest in others, and perseverance, sacrifice, and the courage to act. Only such capacities—and their many companion faculties—can equip the human being to confront and overcome the unforeseen situations in life. If this is the premise, then the goal of any true education must be to awaken, exercise, inspire, and nourish such essential human capacities. In consequence, every subject taught and every skill developed must, ideally, contribute in some degree toward the gradual acquisition of the abilities that will be necessary in the years to come.

As a student of anthroposophical spiritual science, Molt knew that the search for freedom presupposes the recognition that within every human being there lives an essentially spiritual individuality, independent of gender, race, and nation. And it is the real task of all education to prepare the instruments of body and soul so that they can best serve this individuality when the person comes of age and is ready to take the reins of self-direction. Ideally, therefore, the process of education in childhood and youth is to prepare the ground on which the individual can later walk in freedom and, if he or she wishes, pursue the most important education—self-education as an adult human being.

~

In his essay "The Education of the Child," Steiner presented the challenging observation that we as human beings are born not *once*, but *four times* on our way to adulthood. Three of the four members of the bodily organism, however, are supersensible in nature and not directly accessible to sense perception. Each member of the total human organism requires a period of about seven years to mature and to fully penetrate the physical body.

During the six or seven years following physical birth, spiritual-scientific observation recognizes a field of living formative forces at work in the organism. Such forces shape the bodily organs and stimulate their life and function according to a creative "blueprint" that governs the living architecture of each individual human body as it matures. One may think of this "field of living formative forces" as an invisible sculptor who works primarily from the head downward into the rest of the organism. It shapes and individualizes the organism, thus transforming the body originally inherited from the parents, adapting it to the needs and special characteristics of the human being for whom it is designed.

Steiner speaks of this "invisible sculptor" as the human *etheric body*. Once these etheric formative forces have penetrated the densest physical substance and have thus accomplished the major part of their sculptural-architectural task within the organism, a significant portion of this field of force is liberated from its work in the body and becomes available for the use of the child at a new and different level of activity. The physical milestone that marks the liberation, or birth, of the etheric body is the casting out of the first baby teeth and their replacement by the more individual second teeth. The formative forces that have shaped the organs go through a metamorphosis and become available to the child at the level of inner soul activity. They retain, nevertheless, their original image-forming character, and the child discovers in them a living power of *imagination*.

Just as the infant and the younger child have absorbed their surrounding world through the bodily senses—tasting, touching, seeing, and hearing their environment—and have made it their own by *imitating* it, so the older elementary age child once again "digests" the environment through the intelligence of imagination. Both imitation and imagination can be understood as truly cognitive powers of the human soul. Imitation is the least conscious, but most deeply penetrating and extraordinarily active expression of human intelligence. Through imitation the child *becomes one with* the surrounding objective world, literally transforming it into the self—into speech, gestures, and creative play. This is archetypal learning through the physical body. In imagination, the deeply unconscious, instinctive activity of imitation is transformed into a more dreamlike intelligence that is, nevertheless, also faithful to reality.

The parent and kindergarten teacher have the greatest challenge: they teach primarily through *who they are*. Their voices and gestures, their lifestyles and loving embraces are learned by the children through imitation. The elementary school teacher is then challenged to translate the world of human experience into the language of imagination. Not imagination in the sense of make-believe, but as the objective, disciplined instrument of knowledge that allows the child to penetrate *through* outer perception into the invisible reality behind and within phenomena—to "hear the story within the story," to "see the picture" that reveals the hidden being within external facts.

The ideal for the teacher of the youngest children is to strive to become worthy of their unquestioning, devoted emulation. For the teacher of the middle years of childhood it is to become, in the truest sense of the word, a beloved authority. To become an authority who "causes to grow," who helps the child to become an "author" in his or her own right, one in whom the world once again "originates."

Steiner goes on to describe the developmental phase that follows the birth of the etheric body—during the years from seven to fourteen—when a second supersensible member of the human organism is at work. If one thinks of the etheric formative forces as an invisible sculptor, then one can think of these new sentient forces as those of an inaudible musician who fine-tunes the organism, individualizing and harmonizing its rhythmic, functional life to conform with the needs of the individual for whom this particular body is to be the instrument. Steiner designates these new supersensible forces as the work of the *astral body*. Again, this developmental phase culminates in physiological events, this time in the sexual changes that accompany puberty. A significant portion of the forces within the organism is then available for the individual's use at a new level of maturity.

The birth of the astral body, liberating its wealth of emotional and sentient forces, its tidal waves of sympathies and antipathies, as well as its nascent intellectual capacity, marks the birth of what we generally think of as the human personality. However, educators proceed at their own peril if they fail to recognize the validity of Steiner's insight that another inwardly very real, though externally imperceptible, member of the human organism is still waiting to be born. This is the human *I*, or *individuality*. Language itself can give us a clue to this distinction. The word *personality*, which derives from the Latin *persona*, or "mask," used by actors, is the manifested character or "role," as in a play. *Individuality*, on the other hand, derives from the Latin *individuus*, or "indivisible"; the I is undivided and indivisible. The individual in each of us is the essential being, who, in the final analysis, we really are.

The I, in Steiner's view, may be thought of as the member of the human being through which self-transformation can occur. Its outer sheaths are the body and soul, and it opens itself to the spirit, at first through the activity of thinking. In this sense, the I in ordinary life is closely connected with the body and with the personality, but it can awaken to a higher consciousness through which it can gain even greater objectivity. Therefore, to spiritual understanding, the elimination or suppression of the I should not be striven for, but its gradual awakening and transformation.

During the adolescent years, the educator's aim is (or should be) to support and strengthen the I, to guide it toward objectivity and firmness within the surging ebb and flow of feelings and newly awakened intelligence. We may think of the I as the hidden organizer of experience, as the "knower within the knowing," who finally emerges as the self-aware, potentially self-directing adult, hopefully ready and able to continue to grow through self-education.

After coming of age, the I struggles to find itself in the drama of its own biography, and it can now become the active, transformative force in the years that follow. Steiner characterizes this later process as the I working through its outer sheaths (the astral, etheric, and physical bodies), but now from within. This activity awakens the higher aspects of the soul, which he called the *sentient soul*, the *mind soul*, and the *consciousness soul*. Their successive awakenings roughly correspond to the three seven-year periods between the ages of twenty-one and forty-two. This process, as he points out, can further evolve as the I, working within the soul, opens itself to the objective spirit, creating—at least in seed form—what Steiner calls *spirit self*, *life spirit*, and *spirit body*. In this sense, education becomes a lifetime commitment to the process of becoming a fully human being of body, soul, and spirit.

~

These few characterizations of the nature of the human being and of the child's path of development toward adulthood as revealed by spiritual-scientific research were largely foreshadowed in the booklet published in 1907. They constituted the core of the insights available to Emil Molt and the friends who gathered to establish the new school during the spring and summer of 1919. They may also serve to indicate the reservoir of living insight on which Steiner drew during the years after the school was founded. The original teachers— joined by a steadily growing number of others searching for the sources of educational renewal—turned to him for help in the daunting task of self-transformation required to become colleagues in the practice of this new pedagogical art. Beginning with a course of six lectures right before leaving Dornach for Stuttgart to establish the school there, Steiner lectured on various aspects of education for five years, until his strength gave out completely at the end of September 1924.[4]

Rudolf Steiner visited the school whenever he was able to visit Stuttgart. He would visit classes, speak to the children and their parents, and meet with the teachers for intensive pedagogical conferences that often went late into the night. During such conferences the teachers presented their questions, reported on their work and experiences, and asked for help with the problems confronting them. Steiner responded concretely, drawing on his classroom observations, and spoke about individual children, even remembering where they sat in the classes he visited. Those conferences are a gold mine of pedagogical insights and practical advice for teachers in facing their daily tasks and challenges.[5]

Starting with 253 children in eight grades, the Waldorf school soon grew to be the largest private school in Germany, with over a thousand students. By the 1923 school year it had become a full twelve-year school, and Steiner had the great joy of being asked by the school's first graduating class to meet with them and speak about their questions, hopes, and dreams.

When Hitler came to power in 1933, there were seven schools in Germany striving to implement Steiner's ideas. By 1941, after systematic harassment by the government, not one school remained. It was openly stated that the task of schooling was to educate citizens for the National-Socialist state, and there was no room for schools that attempted to teach children and young people to think for themselves. Steiner certainly recognized the fragile nature of freedom.

Although he deeply loved the Waldorf school and carried it in his thoughts when he could no longer visit there, his initial hope for the

---

4. The lectures at Dornach are *Education As a Force for Social Change*, Anthroposophic Press, Hudson, NY, 1997. There are over twenty-five volumes of Steiner's lectures on education, most of them delivered between 1919 and 1925.

5. *Conferences With Teachers*, vol. 1, Anthroposophic Press, Hudson, NY, (fall 1997).

school had been that it might provide a focus around which a widespread popular recognition would grow, and that education would become entirely free of political and state control. To this end he worked to establish a World School Association (*Weltschulverein*), whose goals would be to support the Waldorf school as a prototype of the independent school and spearhead spiritual-cultural initiatives in education, science, art, and religion, free of external control. In December 1923, however, he spoke with sadness about the fact that the Stuttgart school—despite its real success—had remained largely isolated in the cultural life of Germany; he saw no indication that Germany or any other nation had learned the essential lesson of our time.

From the vantage point of the end of the century, one can ask: How much tragedy may we avoid, and how much creative potential may we unlock, if this one basic idea becomes an *ideal* in the hearts and minds of men and women today? This question must be written large in the agenda for the twenty-first century.

9

The
Healing Arts

Just three days before his death on March 30, 1925, Rudolf Steiner was able to correct the final draft of the manuscript of a book that he and Ita Wegman had written together. That he could still find the strength to do this was a matter of deepest satisfaction for him. The volume was published the following autumn with the title *The Foundations for an Extension of the Art of Healing According to the Insights of Spiritual Science*; it was published in English as *Fundamentals of Therapy* by the end of that same year.[1] In her foreword, Ita Wegman emphasizes that it was in no way the authors' intention to deny the great achievements of contemporary medical science. Rather, they wanted to expand the science of the healing arts to include insights that open up when spiritual-scientific methods are applied to the understanding of health and illness.

We have seen how the initiative that led to the art of eurythmy in 1912, the ideas that in 1917 inspired a new initiative toward social renewal, and the inauguration of a school and a new art of education in 1919, all came about when Steiner was asked for help by an individual whose question was the expression of a real inner need. This was true also for the beginnings of the new work in medicine and its related fields.

---

1. Currently entitled *Extending Practical Medicine: Fundamental Principles Based on the Science of the Spirit*, Rudolf Steiner Press, London, 1996 (*Grundlegendes für eine Erweiterung der Heilkunst nach geistes-wissenschaftlichen Erkenntnissen*).

Ita Wegman first met Steiner in Berlin in 1902 as a young woman of twenty-six who had just completed her training in curative gymnastics and Swedish massage. Having already become familiar with the ideas of Theosophy while in Java, Dutch East Indies, where she grew up, her meeting with Steiner was decisive for Wegman's life and career. She became his pupil, and Steiner encouraged her to give up gymnastics and massage to study medicine, in which she had a long-standing interest. Wegman acted on his advice, which included, to her surprise, the suggestion that she study in Switzerland. After a general academic preparation, she matriculated at the University of Zurich, and in 1906, at the age of thirty, she entered medical training and received her degree in July 1911. She gained a practical and thorough understanding of the main aspects of medical work through a series of posts as assistant medical officer, and by 1920 she had an extensive practice, as well as a small private clinic. During those years she maintained an active connection with Steiner and consulted with him about individual cases at every opportunity.[2]

In 1901, Steiner had published an article in the Vienna *Klinisher Rundschau* entitled "Goethe and Medicine." Over the years he continued to speak occasionally about questions related to healing and medical practice. His intention was always to awaken in his listeners the realization that medicine—along with every other branch of contemporary culture—needed renewal through a new and comprehensive understanding of the nature of the human being and the relationship of humankind with the cosmos. In 1906, one of Steiner's students, Dr. Ludwig Noll, a practicing physician in Kassel, Germany, turned to Steiner for advice and help. He was facing questions to which he could find no satisfactory answers within the current schools of medicine. Soon after, during the war years, countless human beings were faced with death and illness and, in their despair, looked for meaning in the apparently blind chaos of events, as well as for help and healing.

---

2. See J. E. Zeylmans van Emmichoven, *Who Was Ita Wegman: A Documentation*, vol. 1 (1876–1925), Mercury Press, Spring Valley, NY, 1995.

Ita Wegman 1915 and 1925

Out of such experiences, a number of doctors and young medical students asked Rudolf Steiner for his help in finding new ways to understand, diagnose, and heal. His response was to offer a course at the Goetheanum in which he would attempt to bring the light of spiritual-scientific insight to bear on their problems. The course of twenty lectures took place in March and April, 1920, later published as *Spiritual Science and Medicine*.[3] This course was decisive for Ita Wegman in taking a step she had been contemplating for over a year; she dissolved her practice in Zurich and moved to Basel with the intention of establishing a private clinic in the area of Dornach and Arlesheim. She was joined the next year by a young physician, Dr. Hilma Walter, with whom she opened the clinic and began to build up the work. Hilma Walter describes this beginning as follows:

> Thus, in June 1921 the Clinical-Therapeutic Institute in Arlesheim was opened. Since then our paths [hers and Ita Wegman's] were linked by devotion to medicine and therapy,

---

3. Steinerbooks, Blauvelt, NY, 1989.

widened and enriched by spiritual science. Other doctors, too, gradually came and joined the work. Outwardly, it was a very modest beginning, but a close cooperation between Dr. Wegman and Dr. Steiner in the sphere of medicine had been initiated. Dr. Steiner visited the clinic regularly, and it gave him great joy to see the work gradually develop.[4]

During the four years he was able to continue his outward activity, Steiner found several occasions to meet with physicians and those in related therapeutic fields. Those meetings and the accompanying lectures took place in Dornach, Germany, Holland, and England. During the last nine months that his strength sustained such activity— from January through September 1924—Steiner was able to contribute to the healing arts with a new level of intensity. In January, he spoke to young physicians on ethics in the study and practice of medicine, seeking to awaken, as he put it, a "medical attitude of mind." [5]

In the months that followed, there were courses on curative education and curative eurythmy.[6] And, during July and August in Holland and England, he met with and lectured to physicians.[7] When he returned to Dornach, during the last four weeks before his strength gave out, Rudolf Steiner gave four courses daily, one of which was for physicians and priests of the newly established Christian Community and dealt with their common tasks.[8] Also, it should be remembered that during Steiner's last two years, he and Ita Wegman collaborated in writing their book *Extending Practical Medicine*, which was published shortly after his death.

Inevitably, as Steiner opened up new possibilities of treatment, it became urgently necessary to explore and produce medicines that would support these new procedures. Dr. Hilma Walter described this process:

---

4. *Memories of Ita Wegman*, Anthroposophical Publishing, London, 1943.
5. *Course for Young Doctors*, Mercury Press, Spring Valley, NY, 1994.
6. *Curative Education*, Rudolf Steiner Press, Bristol, 1993; *Curative Eurythmy*, Rudolf Steiner Press, London, 1983.
7. *What Can the Art of Healing Learn through Spiritual Science*, Mercury Press, Spring Valley, NY, 1986.
8. *Pastoral Medicine*, Anthroposophic Press, Hudson, NY, 1987.

A small chemical laboratory already in existence was available for this purpose; it had previously been used to produce the colors for painting the first Goetheanum, which was then almost completed. Within the first year, however, because of the close cooperation with Dr. Wegman and the clinic, demands grew and required more space, and a house nearby was secured. This was the beginning of what became the Weleda Company, with its various branches abroad.

The clinic in Arlesheim 1926

After a year it became necessary to extend the clinic. For the accommodation of patients who needed convalescence only, the property called "Sonnenhof" was acquired. This also provided opportunity for agricultural work on a small scale. In 1924, a country house called the "Holle," close to the Sonnenhof, was acquired as a home for a number of children who were physically or mentally in need of special care. Besides the garden, a private bakery was begun and maintained according to special principles of dietetics. Soon, however, the number of children increased to the extent that it was necessary to turn the Sonnenhof into a home for them. The clinic itself had to be enlarged by adding adjacent buildings and, in 1926, by considerably extending the main house.

Thus, over time, the clinic together with the Sonnenhof became a center where young doctors could be introduced to these particular methods of healing. It also became necessary to arrange training courses for those who wished to take up nursing and curative educational work; for, as the years passed, an increasing number of doctors—largely from other countries, especially Germany—desired to join in this broader medical activity. Foundations with the same goal also sprang up in other countries, particularly in relation to curative education. This expansion of the work subsequently necessitated journeys [by Wegman], for example, to Germany, England, France, and even Iceland. Other journeys were undertaken for the purpose of study, especially for the study of "geographic" medicine, in which Dr. Wegman was deeply interested.[9]

The Sonnenhof in Arlesheim

9. See Rudolf Steiner's 1917 lecture on geographic medicine in *Geographic Medicine: The Secret of the Double*, Mercury Press, Spring Valley, NY,

In July, 1926, the journal *Natura* was started to help promote
a wider understanding of the methods and possibilities of healing that were opened up by anthroposophical spiritual science.
A supplement issued to doctors and medical students published
articles and notes on the practical experiences already obtained.
In connection with the clinical work, a research laboratory was
established that, following Steiner's suggestions, worked out
new methods for preparing medicines. There was also valuable
research into early diagnosis and treatment of cancer. (*Memories
of Ita Wegman*)

What were the new capacities that Steiner wished to awaken in
the physician, teacher, scientist, artist, and therapist? What was the
necessary inner step that would prevent the stagnation of human civilization, which is incredibly informed but essentially helpless to deal
with the real complexities of life? Anthroposophy is Steiner's answer,
and he expressed repeatedly its essence: We must learn to "read" the
book of nature, the universal cosmos, the planet earth, ourselves, and
human society.

~

Today's medical science has penetrated the realm of the physical
body to the most minute detail. The physician and master surgeon
have access to nearly unbelievable amounts of information about
how the body functions; such information constitutes the "letters,"
sometimes even the "syllables" or "words." But, are we able to read
their meaning? Are we learning to read the living, healing wisdom of
the world and the human organism as a whole? Steiner's call to the
physician of his day was: Learn to read how the etheric, formative
forces shape and transform the physical organism; learn how the
astral forces penetrate the living, vegetative functions with the
death-bearing, nerve-forming force of consciousness; and, above all,
learn how the forces of the human I, or ego, individualize and structure the entire organism. Learn through supersensible research how
substances are changed within the living organism, and how this
process differs in the animal from that in the human being. Study the
living interplay of sulfur, phosphorus, silica, and carbon in their

etheric, elemental as well as in their chemical, substantial roles. Discover how the I works in the nervous system's activity, on the one hand, and in the blood's circulatory system, on the other. Is the heart really just a mechanical pump? Is the human organism seen differently when the heart is perceived as an inner sensor of soul and spirit life within the body? Ask yourself, what, in terms of human destiny, is the true meaning of illness, and how you can understand it and help your patients find a relationship to illness that genuinely supports their human growth.

Steiner spoke to physicians and medical students at the Goetheanum in the hope of awakening a deep and joyful interest in such explorations. He also discussed individual cases with Ita Wegman and the other doctors at the clinics in Arlesheim and Stuttgart. He had such fundamental questions in mind when, with the coworkers in the medical laboratory, he explored the ways of producing and enhancing effective new medications.

Steiner was particularly satisfied when he could bring colleagues together from various fields to work on a common educational or therapeutic task. For instance, they explored ways that doctors and teachers could work together on the problems of chronic fatigue, hyperactivity, weakness of memory, or excessive nervousness in certain children. They asked what teachers could do in the classroom to support a doctor's treatment of a child with a tendency toward asthma, rheumatic fever, epilepsy, or diabetes. How could eurythmy movement enhance the healthy activity of a particular organ, or strengthen the I so that it could penetrate the digestive processes? How could the unbridled influence of astral forces be tempered—forces that overwhelm, perhaps unnecessarily, a child's vital functions?

Such questions led to the development of curative eurythmy, a collaborative effort between artist and physician. And despite his failing strength, as already mentioned, Steiner gave a course in September, 1924, for physicians as well as priests of the recently established Christian Community, on ways that religion and the healing arts could fructify one another in the form of pastoral medicine.

Although ignored, ridiculed, and attacked initially, the insights of spiritual science have been taken up by an ever-increasing number of physicians as an important extension of their medical training. There are hospitals in Germany, Switzerland, Holland, and Sweden where the diagnostic and therapeutic treatments arising from these insights are practiced and available to the general public. Their contribution is beginning to be recognized and included in the training offered in some medical schools.

Steiner's indications for new remedies were being practiced during his lifetime, and since his death this research has been vigorously extended. Several pharmaceutical companies now provide medications internationally. Of these, the largest, Weleda, has research, production, and distribution facilities in several countries, including the United States and Canada.

This new approach is working as a powerful leaven, not only in medical practice and in nursing, but in the whole range of health services. These include therapeutic techniques that involve nutrition, music, painting, sculpture, eurythmy, speech, massage, and movement, which supplement and support the primary medical work.

Therapeutic, or curative, eurythmy is well established within the practice of anthroposophically extended medicine and is beginning to be recognized as a supporting therapy by nonanthroposophical physicians. Training in curative eurythmy is overseen by the Medical Section at the Goetheanum and may be pursued after completing the required four to five years of basic eurythmy training.

Medical therapy, as developed under Rudolf Steiner's guidance and through the efforts of Ita Wegman and many others, also came to include a broad range of curative educational endeavors. It became evident that spiritual-scientific insight could lead to significant new ways of understanding developmental problems, and create new and practical means for addressing such difficulties.

In this context, Steiner considered it fortunate that he was led in Vienna during his twenties to care for the developmentally handicapped son of the Specht family. Through that experience he gained firsthand knowledge of how the human soul and spirit may be forced to struggle against the limitations and imbalances of the physical body. He began with that experience and widened his investigation to every level of developmental handicaps, including the physical, mental, emotional, and spiritual. Beyond this, in the broadest sense, he researched the destinies of repeated earth lives and the laws governing karma in human life, which cast new light on questions of illness and developmental problems of all kinds. A growing number of individuals, especially young people in the years immediately following the war, were drawn to one therapeutic vocation or another. They recognized Steiner's work as a source of extraordinary insights and asked for guidance, and again he responded by offering a course.

The course on curative education, given in Dornach during June and July, 1924, was intended for those engaged in new initiatives in this field and for those who intended to enter into such work. Steiner was in touch with the work developing at the Sonnenhof in Arlesheim, and, while returning in June from the agricultural conference in Silesia, he visited the Lauenstein near Jena to visit the home for children in need of special care. He spoke of this visit during the course for curative education in Dornach:

And then I was able to go on Tuesday to Jena-Lauenstein, where a number of our younger friends, together with Fräulein Dr. Ilse Knauer, have established a curative and educational institution, not for poorly endowed children, but truly ill, constitutionally ill children, who were to be educated and brought as far as possible within their illness. This institute is actually in the process of being established. I was able, in a way, to inaugurate this and see the first children admitted. Thus, we have been able, in a sense, to place this thing in Lauenstein, near Jena, on its feet.[10]

From such beginnings, a worldwide curative educational movement has developed. In 1995, according to the Conference for Curative Education and Social Therapy in Dornach, there were a total of 374 homes, schools, workshops, and village communities—both

---

10. Quoted in Guenther Wachsmuth, *The Life and Work of Rudolf Steiner*, Spiritual Science Library, Blauvelt, NY, 1989, p. 552.

residential and day programs—in twenty-eight countries. Also, seventeen Waldorf schools had specialized groups and classes for children unable to benefit from regular schooling. Sixty-five of the curative institutions belong to the Camphill Community that began in Camphill, Scotland under the leadership of Dr. Karl König immediately after World War Two. As in the other curative initiatives, Camphill has residential and some day-care facilities for adults as well as for children and adolescents.[11]

Dr. Karl König

More than seventy years have passed since this therapeutic impulse was born from the insight and efforts of anthroposophy, and as a result many hundreds of handicapped individuals have been able to experience human dignity and, within the limits of their capacities, a productive life. When one visualizes how, in contrast to this endeavor, a materialistic Darwinism—survival of the fittest as a basic law of life—has also been applied in this century,

11. See *A Candle on the Hill: Images of Camphill Life*, Cornelius Pietzner, ed., Floris Books, Edinburgh, 1990.

one is again confronted with the reality that the twentieth century has indeed been a "battleground for human individuality," a battle won or lost in each individual human soul. No matter what outer forms this battle may take, at its core is the question: Who *is* the human being? Is the individual identical with the bodily instrument? Or, could it be that, when the instrument is damaged, the musician is still intact?

10

Religious
Renewal

In 1921 Rudolf Steiner was making a final attempt to enkindle awareness that social healing requires spiritual and economic life to be freed from centralized political control. As we have seen, he was also responding to initiatives and requests for help in the fields of education, medicine, and social therapy.

Meanwhile—still in the aftermath of World War One—a group of young theologians and theology students asked his advice toward a renewal of religious experience and religious life. They were concerned about the intellectualism of Protestantism, which during the eighteenth and nineteenth centuries had eroded the foundations of a heartfelt, more instinctive religious life, bringing genuine religious seekers to crisis and despair. Through spiritual science this group of theologians had discovered that the human soul today could regain access, in freedom, to knowledge and inner experience of supersensible realities and the divine ground of existence. Steiner responded to their appeal with genuine warmth, though he made it clear that his own task was to extend and deepen spiritual science as a source of knowledge rather than to foster the renewal of religious life as such. Nevertheless, it was self-evident that the light of spiritual-scientific research penetrates to the wellsprings of religious striving and can provide a modern path to the Christ. Steiner expressed this on a number of occasions. In Basel, Switzerland, he said:

One cannot make anthroposophy directly into a religion. But, from a true understanding of anthroposophy, a genuine, honest, unhypocritical need for religion will arise. The human soul requires a variety of paths to ascend along the way toward its goal. The human soul needs not only the path of cognition, but also needs to be warmed through, to be inwardly set aglow by the approach to the spiritual world as found in religious confessions, in genuine religious feeling.[1]

And in Berlin:

One should not present things in such a way that spiritual-scientific endeavors appear as if they were a substitute for religious life and practice. Spiritual science can be a support in the highest sense, and very particularly in relation to the Christ mystery, as well as a foundation for religious life and for religious practice; but it should not be made a religion. One should be clear, however, that religion as a living experience, as a genuine practice within a human community, kindles spiritual awareness of the soul. In order for this spirit awareness to come to life in a human being, that person cannot stay with an abstract idea of God or Christ, but must enter, renewed, into religious practice, into religious activity, which can assume the most varied forms in many different human beings. If this religious sentiment is deep enough and finds a way of stimulating the soul, it will soon find a longing—a real longing—for the very ideas that can be developed in spiritual science.[2]

In 1921 this circle of young religious seekers was joined by a man who had a considerable following within the Protestant community.

---

1. October 19, 1917, *"Anthroposophie stört niemandes religiöses Bekenntnis"* ("Anthroposophy disturbs no one's religious beliefs,"), in *Freiheit, Unsterblichkeit, Soziales Leben*, Rudolf Steiner Verlag, Dornach, 1990 (GA 72).
2. February 20, 1917, in *Cosmic and Human Metamorphoses*, Spiritual Research Editions, Blauvelt, NY, 1989, p. 27.

Friedrich Rittelmeyer (1872–1938) was at the time a leading representative of true spiritual and heartfelt religious efforts. When he preached, the church was sure to be filled, and his writings on religion were widely read. He was deeply respected and influential within the Lutheran church. In 1916, he was called from his pastorate in Nuremberg to the Neue Kirche in Berlin, one of the leading Protestant churches there.

Dr. Friedrich Rittelmeyer

Late in 1910, while searching for a broader and more encompassing view of the religious life, Rittelmeyer met the work of Steiner. This meeting was decisive for Rittelmeyer, who sensed that Steiner was a thinker who could lead him farther in his search for a contemporary Christianity. Yet he took nothing on faith; each of Steiner's statements was challenged, questioned, and thought through. This process is wonderfully described by Rittelmeyer in his book, *Rudolf Steiner Enters My Life*, from which one gains not only a warm and vibrant impression of Rudolf Steiner, but also of Rittelmeyer himself.[3] After years of strenuous testing, Friedrich Rittelmeyer joined the Anthroposophical Society in 1916.

The theologians who formed The Christian Community in 1922

In 1921 Rittelmeyer was instrumental, along with others, in arranging for two courses to be given by Steiner to a circle of theologians. Although his health prevented him from participating, Rittelmeyer studied the content of these courses and the text for the communion service, "The Act of Consecration of Man," which became the central sacrament in a body of seven sacraments. His study, and especially his study of the sacrament, convinced Rittelmeyer that he was called to join the initiative working toward the founding of The Christian Community. He realized that this would probably mean giving up his Lutheran pastorate in Berlin and anticipated being misunderstood and severely criticized. In September 1922, Rittelmeyer was in Dornach as one of the founders of The Christian Community, when he was asked, and agreed, to accept the leadership of the new endeavor.

Since its establishment, The Christian Community has become an active participant in contemporary religious life. Today there are

3. *Rudolf Steiner Enters My Life*, Floris Books, Edinburgh, 1982.

close to three hundred congregations in twenty-five countries on four continents. Although the majority of its priests, as individuals, are members of the Anthroposophical Society, The Christian Community as such is entirely independent from the society. As Steiner clearly stated, "Anthroposophy does not interfere in any way with an individual's religious convictions," although it does open the doors of insight that may lead to the central experience of religious life.

Steiner's participation in establishing The Christian Community led to misunderstandings, both within the Anthroposophical Society and without. To some anthroposophists it seemed that The Christian Community was now "their church," and to others it seemed that anthroposophy had fulfilled its task and was now irrelevant. However, for the man who personally sacrificed and resigned his position as a leading figure of the Protestant church in Germany to accept the leadership of The Christian Community, there was great inner clarity about the relationship between the two movements. At the end of his book describing his own meeting with Steiner and anthroposophy, Rittelmeyer characterized the relationship between the two movements:

> When Dr. Steiner was asked, "What is the difference between the anthroposophical movement and The Christian Community?" he answered, "The anthroposophical movement addresses the human need to know and brings knowledge. The Christian Community addresses the human need for resurrection and brings Christ." One who lives within The Christian Community may experience being in the presence of Christ during the ritual. One has nourishment for the soul and help for life—help as strong and powerful as one could possibly want. One need not be troubled about the details of anthroposophical knowledge, but shares in the highest goal to which anthroposophical knowledge can aspire. When the demand for knowledge is there, we who lead The Christian Community and have received such wealth from anthroposophy, can give to the individual, out of anthroposophy, whatever help is needed. For our aim is to keep pace with the view of the world that is coming into being, and

not to remain with the one that is passing away. But, in all these things, the individual is left the fullest freedom—priest and member of the community alike. No anthroposophical teaching is a dogma of The Christian Community. What welds The Christian Community are the great basic truths of Christianity, viewed, of course, in the light of a new spiritual teaching (and the history of modern times shows that they would be lost without this), but given in such a form that they express what leads to the actual salvation of humanity. The Anthroposophical Society is a movement in civilization that embraces all domains of culture. The Christian Community is a church of salvation that can embrace all people.

If all these things are clearly perceived and openly stated, and if ignoble human feelings do not crop up here and there, then all can know for themselves where they belong. What helps a person most to become a helper of humanity and a coworker with Christ—this is the right thing for a person.

This was the sense in which Rudolf Steiner became an "advisor and helper" in establishing The Christian Community. (*Rudolf Steiner Enters My Life*, pp. 141–142)

Steiner had the deep conviction that knowledge itself—achieved by thinking transformed through inner effort—can also lead one to experience the Resurrection. It was his conviction that, at this time in human historical development, it is most important for individuals to find their way in inner freedom to this experience. This was, for him, the path of anthroposophy.

It was an act of destiny that, on the last three evenings of 1922, Steiner interrupted the cycle of lectures on the history of science to speak about communion through knowledge.

11

Out of Fire

It was December 31, 1922—New Year's Eve. The Goetheanum crowned the hill at Dornach. It spoke a language of inner beauty and outer harmony with its surrounding landscape. It had for some time been in use and provided a home at last for the university now coming into being. Rudolf Steiner had spoken often in the domed hall; the color, movement, and speech of drama and eurythmy had resounded from the stage beneath the smaller dome. Curiously, however, the building had not yet been dedicated. Steiner seemed to be waiting for the decisive moment, for something yet to come.

Extraordinary moments had been experienced and were turning points in many fields; among them were the courses on national economy and drama, meetings with the clergy and theologians in search of religious renewal, and significant work with physicians, teachers, and artists. And always, there was a widening and deepening of insight into the realities beyond the threshold of sense perception. Now, at the end of December, a series of lectures was almost concluded on the origins and evolution of science since the fifteenth century. In the midst of these, Steiner gave three lectures on the spiritual communion of humanity.[1]

---

1. *The Origins of Natural Science*, Anthroposophic Press, Hudson, NY, 1985; *The Spiritual Communion of Mankind*, contained in *Man and the World of Stars*, Anthroposophic Press, New York, 1963.

The large cupola and auditorium

These three lectures were a kind of culmination and explored a new path to the spirit; thinking itself can become a communion, or union of the human soul with the innermost—and outermost—divine. Guenther Wachsmuth, a scientist and a personal secretary for Rudolf Steiner, assembled a year-by-year record of Steiner's immense activity from the point where his autobiography ends; Wachsmuth describes those lectures, the mood awakened by them, and the tragedy that followed:

> The first five lectures of the science course were delivered by Dr. Steiner until the end of December in the domed auditorium of the Goetheanum building. On December 29, 30, and 31, he wove three lectures into these considerations that drew on the entire spiritual-scientific research and activity of the preceding ten years, and he gave the foundation for a "cosmic ritual," which raises knowledge to the level of consecration and raises the recognition of the forces active in cosmic rhythms to festivals of the great moments occurring over the course of the year. The lecture

on December 29 outlined the progression of the day and the year as the basis for this cosmic ritual. The lecture on December 30 raised the tasks of the Anthroposophical Society into consciousness, along with those of the Movement for Religious Renewal.... On the afternoon of December 31, in the domed hall, we experienced once again the luminous beauty, the color miracle, the mirroring of spiritual-cosmic laws, and the harmonious interweaving of the performers who represented word and tone forms in movement through the eurythmy presentation of the "Prologue in Heaven" from [Goethe's] *Faust*. There was a unique harmony between the art being presented and the living colors and forms of the encompassing building.

That evening, New Year's Eve, 1922, Rudolf Steiner, as his final gift within the building, offered the language and power for the spiritual communion of humanity. Having made us aware in the previous lectures that the continuous changes in beings, forces, and substances over the course of the year are mirrored in the human being, he now showed the response that human beings can give to the cosmos through spiritual knowledge and activity: "Spiritual knowledge is true communion, the beginning of a ritual that is appropriate for human beings of the present time." He caused the forces of life and death to stand before our inner vision in powerful images.

The human being is not only a receiver in this world but also a giver: "Human beings transform the world through their own spiritual nature when communicating with the world out of their spiritual nature, as their thoughts are enlivened toward Imagination, Inspiration, and Intuition, as they fulfill the spiritual communion of humanity. First, however, one must be conscious of this.... What would otherwise be mere abstract knowledge becomes a felt and willed relationship with the world. The world becomes the dwelling place of God. Through active knowing, human beings elevate themselves in feeling and willing and become beings who offer sacrifice. The fundamental relation of the human being to the world moves upward from knowing to a universal ritual, or cosmic festival rite."

In the domed hall, the assembled people listened to his words. Around them, in the highest artistic expression, the great columns and the forms of their capitals, the paintings in the arched dome in this most living of all human buildings, spoke to them of spiritual initiative and the meaning of sacrifice, of a decade of creative working and molding—led by a human being who was pointing toward the spiritual communion of humanity. Deeply moved by what was being bestowed upon them in this earthly place, never dreaming that it would be their last glimpse of so much beauty, they went out into the stillness of New Year's Eve.

What then occurred can be reconstructed from the report of an eyewitness: "By about ten o'clock, the last member of the lecture audience had left the building. Shortly thereafter, the watchman on duty noticed smoke. He, together with a Goetheanum employee, alerted the Goetheanum firemen, who were soon assembled. 'Smoke in the White Hall!' was the report, and all of the rooms in the south wing of the building were immediately opened and searched. But no fire was found in any of those rooms. Then smoke was seen seeping from the external west wall of the south wing into one of the outer corner rooms. This wall was immediately broken through, and it was discovered that the structural work inside this outer wall was in flames."

When the alarm and the terrible news reached the homes in the neighborhood, we all rushed out and up the hill. Within a few minutes, many lines of hose were laid, the terrace of the building ascended, and the center of the fire flooded with water. We still believed that the blaze could be brought under control and eventually put out. The firemen, aided by hundreds of helpers, bravely risked their lives. But the smoke, with its sinister implications, rose more and more thickly from the south wing of the building. We plunged inside, holding handkerchiefs soaked in vinegar over our faces so that we could breathe to some extent in the smoke-filled stairway hall. When we arrived in the domed hall, we were met by the roar of flames devouring their way between the two walls. What could still be carried away was saved, but very soon the smoke was so thick that breathing was almost impossible. A voice shouted to us that Rudolf Steiner had ordered everyone out of the building. The power of fire had won a victory over human will. All our energies now had to be directed toward saving the neighboring houses, the workshop, and the studio that sheltered the statue. We broke through the wall of the studio and carried the wooden sculpture, *The Representative of Humanity*, into the open air; it was thus saved for the future.

When this had been made safe, we stood for the remainder of the night and watched the flames. Around midnight the domes collapsed, and even as late as seven o'clock the following morning, the mighty columns were still ablaze in the destructive fire.

During the night, Rudolf Steiner walked around the building in silence. Only once was he heard to say, "Much work and many years." Until morning came, he stood before the ruin of the building, quiet, concerned only that no one should be endangered. His greatness, dignity, and goodness gave all of us the strength to endure during this night. As the dawn of New Year's Day broke, he said, "We will continue to fulfill our inner obligations at the place we still have left to us." He gave instructions to get the spare rooms in the workshop in order, so that the conference could continue, and said, "We shall continue with the lectures that have been announced." He asked us whether we felt strong enough to perform the Three Kings Play, which had been scheduled for the afternoon, and received our "yes" with thanks and appreciation.

That afternoon at precisely five o'clock, the play began; the three kings, Joseph and Mary, Herod, the angel and devil, the star singers—all played their parts. The mood that united the actors and audience on this first day of January cannot be put into words. In the evening, Rudolf Steiner stepped up to the podium and gave the sixth lecture in his cycle on the origin of natural science in the course of world history. The work for 1923 had begun.

The foundation stone of the building was still there, and upon this the Goetheanum would be built anew.[2]

---

2. Guenther Wachsmuth, *The Life and Work of Rudolf Steiner*, Spiritual Science Library, Blauvelt, NY, 1989, pp. 473–476.

Rudolf Steiner 1923

And so 1923 began. It was a year of powerful, tragic premonitions and tests, both inner and outer. On January 11 the French occupied the Ruhr, the industrial heartland of Germany, to force payment of reparations. In doing so, however, they removed the only means left to generate the income to pay them. When autumn arrived, the currency presses were printing millions, then billions, then trillions of marks, and the German economy was in total collapse. On November 9, Hitler made his first bid for power. Steiner knew that the battle lines were drawn and that another world war had already begun behind the scenes. The German government gave Hitler a year of relatively comfortable incarceration and the leisure to write *Mein Kampf.*

For Steiner this was the year when everything would either be won or lost. The opposition had become unmistakably visible through the burning of the Goetheanum; those who were perceptive had come to view anthroposophy as a challenge to the very foundations of their vested interests—economic, political, and spiritual.

Steiner was forced to realize that, even within the anthroposophical movement, there was opposition to what he was trying to bring.

Old ways of thinking found it very hard to let go. The intellect could analyze and categorize the fruits of spiritual-scientific research, just as it could those of materialistic science. Anthroposophical dogma and sectarianism were as tempting as any other kind—but more irritating and offensive because their proponents claimed to be spiritually correct. Steiner suffered not so much for himself as for the being of *Anthroposophia*, as she struggled to gain a foothold in life, despite the obstacles that even her most devoted pupils placed in her path.

Of particular concern was the estrangement that arose between younger and older members. In the early days of the movement, the insights of spiritual science were the cherished treasure of very few, cultivated in small groups of like-minded friends without interference or disturbance. The older members rightly considered themselves to be Steiner's personal pupils, and this relationship was the deepest, most sacred element in their lives. The generation now storming the gates and demanding entry, however, wanted to put these insights to work. They wanted to establish public institutions that challenged those around them. The protective sheath of reverent silence in which these seeds of wisdom had been cultivated was experienced by them as secrecy, as a denial of fundamental openness and honesty, which for them was a basic fact of life. In these and many other ways, the new generation felt misunderstood, suffocated, and estranged.

The situation within the German Anthroposophical Society became so serious that Rudolf Steiner was forced to do something that contradicted the very nature of anthroposophy; he created a separate society within the existing society, one in which the young people might feel at home. In the Free Anthroposophical Society, younger members and their friends could meet and work together in ways that they felt the older generation could neither understand nor tolerate. They were grateful to Steiner for making space for them. Nevertheless, in Steiner's mind, the Anthroposophical Society—of all human societies—should be a community where young and old, conservatives and radicals, sophisticated and simple, could all find themselves as pupils on the common path of "becoming human."

~

The destruction of the Goetheanum became a tremendous rite of passage, literally a trial by fire, a test of the will to live. It was also a powerful call for reflection, questioning, and renewal. If the Goetheanum was to be rebuilt, if the movement was to have a home once again, the sacrifice and strength needed for such an immense effort could come only from the courage to confront the past and the willingness to work toward the future.

Steiner devoted the first two months of the new year to a "forward-facing retrospect." He hoped that this would enable his colleagues, who were also his pupils, to find a common inner ground where their individual initiatives could come together with a genuine understanding of what was essential and necessary. Steiner did this in many lectures, especially in Dornach and Stuttgart. Again and again in these lectures, from various perspectives, Rudolf Steiner led his audience to an essential thought: The insights that flow in a thoroughly human way from spiritual science can bring about the genuine renewal culture so urgently needs in the world today. When such insights become one-sided and specialized, no matter how brilliant and valid, they lack the power of real renewal. And when the energies of the co-workers in the movement become exclusively absorbed in developing and teaching in a school, in the practical work for social renewal, or in The Christian Community, causing the "mother"—the Anthroposophical Society as the carrier of the movement—to be neglected, such narrowness undermines the effectiveness of anthroposophy to work as an essential leaven in today's world culture:

> For we must not turn into a circle of teachers, a circle for religious renewal, a circle of scientists, or a circle of young people, old people, or middle-aged people. We must be an anthroposophical community, aware of the sources that created it and nourish its offspring. We must be strongly conscious of this!
>
> Please take very seriously all that I have had to say, with a grieving heart, to you today. May it invoke the strength to work, the will to work, and especially the will to hold together in the

anthroposophical movement as a whole. No one should feel singled out as an outstanding contributor to the work of *Der Kommende Tag* ["The Coming Day"], the Waldorf school, the movement for religious renewal, and so on. But all of these, along with those who have not entered into any special field, and those who are old or young or middle-aged—may all become conscious of their mother—the Anthroposophical Society itself—which has brought them all forth, and in which all the various specialists must work together. Specialization has grown too great among us, without our being properly aware of it. In some cases specialization has become so great that the mother has been too much forgotten. [3]

Two related themes resounded through the lectures given early in 1923, two themes that, at first glance, may appear contradictory. The first was a powerful call to overcome every vestige of sectarianism, and the second was a call to recognize the need for a "home" in which spiritual science could be cultivated for its own sake, not for a specific vocational, social, economic, or age group, but for its intrinsic human and spiritual value.

Speaking in Stuttgart on January 23, 1923, Steiner stressed the first aspect, using the Waldorf school as an example:

The proof lies in the fact that the Waldorf school is not set up to teach anthroposophy but to solve the problem of how to teach, so that the best possible development of the whole wide range of human capacities is achieved.... It cannot be too strongly emphasized that it is a universally human characteristic that is worked toward in the Waldorf school. Similarly, a person who acknowledges the true spirit of anthroposophy is not in the least concerned with the name *anthroposophy*; such a person is concerned only with what it is about, and it is about universal, human concerns. (ibid., p 10)

3. *Awakening to Community*, Anthroposophic Press, Spring Valley, NY, 1974, pp. 19-20.

Nevertheless, in the same lecture, Steiner pointed out the urgent need for a strong Anthroposophical Society if there was to be any hope of rebuilding the Goetheanum. After expressing the overwhelming sense of loss caused by the destruction of the original building, he said:

> Let us hope that the terrible misfortune that struck us will at least serve to cure our good members of their illusions and convince them of the need to concentrate all the forces of our hearts and minds on advancing the anthroposophical movement. Now that the wish is emerging to build something like another Goetheanum, above all else, we must recognize that, without a strong, energetic Anthroposophical Society in the background, it makes no sense to rebuild. Rebuilding makes sense only when a strong, self-aware Anthroposophical Society, thoroughly conscious of its responsibilities, stands behind it. (ibid., pp 7–8)

Steiner's immense exertions during 1923 seem to have been directed one way or another toward working and struggling with these two themes. On the one hand, he worked toward the ideal of a community that was open in every aspect of its being, in which one worked to transform every lurking vestige of sectarianism, and at the same time he worked to build the foundations for a society in which a purely human anthroposophy may live without reservation, compromise, and cover-up, but with openness and inner integrity.

Could there be a human community in which it is possible to unite these two apparently irreconcilable opposites? Would their union "merely place the issues side by side," mutually "canceling each other out," or would it be a true meeting with all its inherent risks, but with the possibility of transcendence? Steiner struggled, suffered, and waited.

His struggle often took the form of a question, a challenge: What is a true festival? How can it come about? Can it make a real difference in reconciling our needs, both for nonsectarian community and for celebrating the fruits of anthroposophy? As he searched and probed and struggled it became clear that a truly human festival must be rooted in a vital experience of nature and also reach spiritual sources of being. If this was possible, the outcome would not be the mere addition of something, but something entirely new—a spiritual, chemical change, an act of true "combustion." Each element would die and yield its individual identity, and a third element, absent to begin with, would arise. It would indeed be a resurrection, a new birth.

Much of Steiner's effort during 1923 went toward exploring, characterizing, and enkindling an understanding for what such festivals might be. He described festivals of the past, in which—at a very different stage of consciousness than our own—human beings were embedded in a world experience that was connected with both nature and spirit, both earthly and divine. He spoke of how this paradisiacal state of being was destined, over the millennia, to change and die away. The intelligence, or cosmic wisdom, that built the world in its inconceivable living complexity, balance, and beauty, gradually surrendered its original divine sovereignty and fell into the heads and hearts of men and women. These human souls, into which the cosmic wisdom-intelligence descended, were free to recognize, understand, and treasure it, or to exploit and abuse it.

From this descent, or interment, Steiner pointed to the possibilities of rebirth, and particularly to the possibility of a festival that did not yet exist in any traditional form—a festival of initiative and courage, whose time was the autumn of the year when the earth, which "breathes out" in spring and summer, "breathes in" and turns toward winter. Outer life dies and inner life awakens and becomes active. Steiner characterized such a future festival as inwardly related to the angelic being woven together with the very essence of cosmic intelligence, who once reigned creatively, but has now given over sovereignty and waits to see what humanity does with it. This being is the Archangel Michael, who is spiritually and intensely active in our historical age and who allows human freedom.

Through finding the right way to celebrate Michaelmas (traditionally September 29), we may awaken new human forces needed to create completely open community, grounded in spiritual reality.

It was clear to Steiner that much depends on our awakening to such new festivals.

At Easter, 1923, he gave five lectures calling for a renewal of the year's festivals.[4] In these lectures, Steiner describes how the ancient festivals were bound to space and were possible only at certain places and under certain configurations of earth and cosmos. He then shows how, through the transforming power of the death and Resurrection of the Christ Being, festivals became experiences within the rhythms of time. We can learn once again to live with these rhythms. If, in our soul life, we can learn to accompany the outbreath of the earth in spring and summer, allowing the cosmic Christ to unite with us at midsummer, then with Michael's help in autumn we can accompany the elemental world's withdrawal into itself during winter's death and darkness. The evil, estranging ahrimanic powers that seek to possess the earth while it is breathed out and united with the cosmos at midsummer, must now be transformed and illumined from within at Christmas. Steiner points out that Michael clears the inner and outer paths that lead from midsummer to Christmas, and that he enables the Christ to reunite with the earth each year. The human soul, now independent in its isolation and aloneness, can learn to accompany this great earthly-cosmic breathing process in which the polarities of light and dark, life and death, cosmos and earth are transmuted into the experience of a living rhythm. The duality of apparent opposites becomes the trinity of rhythmical transformation.

In these remarkable Easter lectures, Steiner shows how this new understanding of the yearly festivals prepares us for our current historical transition. The supersensible experience of the *risen* Christ has faded from human experience (it is, at best, a miracle in which we want to believe), and in its place we are left with the *crucified* One upon the cross. During the Middle Ages, the Easter experience gave way to Good Friday, with which the suffering and devoutly longing

---

4. *The Cycle of the Year*, Anthroposophic Press, Hudson, NY, 1988; see also five lectures given in the autumn of the same year, *The Four Seasons and the Archangels*, Rudolf Steiner Press, London, 1996.

souls of men and women united themselves with fervor. Their profound religious experience of death and isolation from the divine ground of the world gave rise to the impulse that directed Western humanity's intense preoccupation with death and materialism in all its forms. Steiner was convinced that we are inspired to rediscover the reality lost from view only through a profound and powerful experience, such as that of the crucified Christ during the Middle Ages. He expressed his conviction on this point:

My dear friends, whatever people are hoping for from a renewal of the social life will not come about from all the discussions and all the institutions based on what is sensed externally. It can come about only when a powerful inspiration-thought goes through humanity, when an inspiration-thought takes hold of humanity through which the moral and spiritual element will once again be felt and perceived along with the sensed, natural element. (*The Cycle of the Year*, p. 39)

In the concluding lecture, after summarizing the religious festival experiences of the more recent past, which were deeply rooted in humanity's relationship with the changing seasons and the course of the year, Steiner went on to say:

What men and women formerly received from the life of the year's course has now been taken over within individual human beings themselves. It will come into consideration precisely in relation to the Michaelmas festival, however, that there will have to be a festival to honor human courage, to honor the human manifestation of Michael's courage. For, what is it that holds humanity back today from spiritual knowledge? Lack of soul courage—not to mention soul cowardice. Human beings want to receive everything passively, to sit down in front of the world as though it were a movie, and to let the microscope and the telescope tell them everything. They do not want to temper the instrument of their own spirit, or soul, through activity. They do not care to be followers of Michael, which requires courage. Such inner courage must have its festival in Michael-mas. Then, what gives the other festivals of the year the right content will radiate from the *Festival of Courage* and from the inwardly courageous human soul. (pp. 86–87)

This theme of the festivals, which sounded so powerfully at Easter, continued to resound throughout the year, ending with a great festival event at Christmas, the subject of the next chapter.

~

In August 1923, Steiner went to England to be the principal speaker at a summer conference in Penmaenmawr on the coast of Wales. This site afforded an opportunity to visit and study some of the many Celtic stone circles and dolmens in the area. Rudolf Steiner requested that Guenther Wachsmuth accompany him on a visit to one of these high, isolated, nature-mystery centers. Wachmuth's report sheds an intimate light on Steiner's response to the ancient ritual site. At the time of the visit, Steiner was intensely engaged in reawakening, in modern terms, a sense for the festivals as "window moments" through which human beings today could rediscover their connection with the cosmos.

After the morning lectures, various sized groups and individuals visited the dolmens of the ancient Druid centers high on the surrounding crags. Their origins and decay, their significance and function, had been brought much closer to us through these lectures. One of these trips remains with me as an unforgettable memory. Rudolf Steiner asked me to climb alone with him one day to the high plateau that rests on the cliffs above Penmaen-mawr, in order to visit one of the Druid circles. Despite his sixty-two years, he climbed the slope rapidly and energetically. In keeping with the spiritual atmosphere of the place, our conversation centered on the mysteries of the Druids and their polar opposite in Europe, the cult of Mithras, in the Southern mysteries. While walking I was able to tell him about an experience I'd had some years before when an ancient Mithras center had

been discovered on the Danube. Climbing steadily and tirelessly, Dr. Steiner spoke about the great antithesis between the
Druid rituals and those of the Mithras religion, about the
Northern and Southern mysteries of Europe, the effects of the
spiritual streams from Ireland and northern Europe, moving
from north to south, and those from Italy and the Danube area,
moving from south to north, and how both then met their fate
in the rise of Christianity.

When we reached the crag high above Penmaenmawr, a
lonely plateau surrounded by rocky peaks lay before us. In the
middle stood the mighty stone relics of the Druid circle. This
was one of those vivid, unforgettable moments in life. Here was
a unique and remarkable picture: In the solitude of this lofty plateau, Rudolf Steiner stepped into the middle of the Druid circle.
He suggested that I look beyond the jutting stones of the circle
to the mountain peaks that surrounded the plateau and
described—with an intensity that made it seem as though these
things were happening at that very moment—how the Druid
priests, by surveying the signs of the zodiac as they passed along
the horizon in the course of the year, experienced the spiritual
cosmos, the beings working within it, and their mandates to
humanity. He described how they formed the festival celebra-
tions and rituals of the year according to these cosmic rhythms,
and gave their priestly directives to the members of their communities; how the seasonal events of the year had to be spiritually reflected in the rituals, and even physically in managing the
agricultural work. He spoke of the sunlight and shadow experience within the stone chamber of the ancient sacred site, and of
the visions and impulses flowing out, received there into the
wide expanses of the earthly sphere.

Rudolf Steiner later let the words and images that were
evoked here in solitude shine forth in many lectures, and also
supplemented them through further research. When we left
the Druid circle and the silent plateau to return to Penmaenmawr at the foot of the mountains, I was inwardly certain that,
within the sphere of this place, something real and timeless

had happened, because a seer such as Rudolf Steiner had once lingered here, had read the spiritual events of the past in such a place, and could now communicate what he had seen to human beings—to those in our time who desire to take a path of schooling for the future. (*The Life and Work of Rudolf Steiner*, pp 508–509)

~

The events and activities of 1923 were borne on a particular tide, beginning in the spring and gathering momentum as it flowed toward Christmas. Five new national societies were founded in preparation for the reestablishment of an international Anthroposophical Society. In July there were meetings of delegates from many countries, which led to a decision to rebuild the Goetheanum. On May 17, the Norwegian Anthroposophical Society was instituted in Christiania (now Oslo), and Steiner participated in the festivities. On September 2, following the educational lecture cycle in Ilkley and the anthroposophical conference in Penmaenmawr, Steiner inaugurated the society in Great Britain. On that occasion in London he said, "No spiritual movement can really flourish in our day if it represents only a special group within humanity. This is simply an esoteric law, that every truly enduring and fruitful spiritual movement must be universally human; they must be (what is called in trivial ordinary life) 'international,' universally human."

In October and November, societies in Austria and Holland were similarly constituted. These national (or "country") societies, as well as those established in later years, are autonomous as long as they do not conflict with the basic constitution of the general organization. The society in each country, for example, chooses its own General Secretary to represent it in the General Society. The leading council of the General Society in Dornach has no authority to appoint a General Secretary for any national society, but it has the freedom to say whether or not it can work with a particular individual. It has the right to veto such an appointment, because the council may not be forced to work with someone if this is genuinely impossible. Such autonomy is a key factor in creating a free, nonbureaucratic society.

~

Negotiations with the Goetheanum's insurance companies and with government authorities were vigorously pursued throughout the early months of 1923. By June they had concluded, opening the way to rebuilding the Goetheanum, provided the will and the means were present. A meeting of the Swiss members on June 10, and a general meeting of the Goetheanum Association one week later, unanimously voted in favor of moving forward with this work. Once again Steiner emphasized the importance of continuing the central spiritual-scientific work without any decrease or interruption. He expressed this at the General Meeting of the Goetheanum Association on June 17, 1923:

> It became self-evident for us, as we stood there and directly experienced the burning of the Goetheanum, that we must by no means give up the continuity of the work of our spiritual life; this must always live in our souls. What is especially important is that we really know how to conduct ourselves in the sense of what I said yesterday: Let us work from the center of what is spiritual and, despite the most painful or the most exalted experiences from the outer world, not allow ourselves to be confused or go astray in this truly inner work and mood coming from the center. The true perspective for the anthroposophical movement depends on exactly this. It does not depend on the number or type of blows with which destiny strikes us from the outside. They must be met from the perspective that is a natural result of the anthroposophical view of life.
>
> Yet, in spite of all the blows of destiny, and also in spite of all the positive events of destiny, this inner energy in working out of the center of spiritual life must not be crippled; it determines what should be achieved by the anthroposophical movement and also what can be achieved.... I would like to comment here that, in a spiritual movement such as that of anthroposophy, we have to be very serious if we are to find the right path. Basically, success and failure do not mean much: the

only thing that matters is to proceed from the inner strength and the inner impulses of the cause itself. (ibid., pp. 502–503)

Steiner and those who shared responsibility with him saw that only the united will of the entire membership could rebuild the Goetheanum. For this reason, it was announced that a meeting of delegates from the groups and branches in every country would take place the following month in Dornach, July 20-23. Guenther Wachsmuth reported that their decision was unanimously ratified, and the process ensured a united spirit and the unwavering energy that would be required to complete the rebuilding project. Steiner was asked to design and direct the new building's construction. At the close of the meeting he stated:

This gathering will undoubtedly prove to be memorable if it results in a new Goetheanum being built. It would be good if, in its forms, this new Goetheanum could also radiate to us what needs to be said to humanity through the word, out of the ground of anthroposophy. In this way you will have done very much for anthroposophy. (ibid., p. 505)

Thus, out of the ruins of the old building, and out of the profoundly difficult inner and outer circumstances with which it was confronted—as was all of Central Europe—the Anthroposophical Society took the initiative to work with all possible energy and determination toward creating something genuinely new. Rudolf Steiner modeled the outer form of the building in plasticine during the following months, and in this outer form it was to be totally different from the one that stood so briefly on the Dornach hill. It was to be built of poured concrete and reinforced with steel. Instead of the two harmoniously intersecting wooden domes that had graced the old building, it was deeply sculpted. It looked westward with a powerful, awakening gaze—at times skull-like, at other times sphinx-like, but always arresting, always challenging, through boldness, grace, and beauty. The first building had been achieved through gifts that flowed toward it out of love and sacrifice; the second was made possible initially by insurance money that flowed because it had to. This fact and others, its designer said, needed to be reflected in its outer form.

The Society that was to be rebuilt would also prove to be a radical transformation, a metamorphosis, of what had emerged from the Theosophical Society some ten years before.

Rudolf Steiner 1923

12

Renewal from Within

The Christmas Foundation

In the autumn of 1923, Rudolf Steiner spoke with increasing urgency and anticipation about reconstituting the Anthroposophical Society, which was to take place in Dornach at Christmas. In mid-December, the final invitation and daily schedule were published in the weekly *Das Goetheanum*. Members were invited to Dornach for the founding of the *International Anthroposophical Society*.

~

Seven or eight hundred members, including delegates from all the major branches, responded to the call. Snow was on the ground, the charred ruins of the Goetheanum were still visible; but the work of clearing the wreckage, enlarging the site, and preparing for the new structure had already begun. Arvia MacKaye, a young American artist traveling in Europe, had met Steiner a few months before and came to Dornach for the Christmas conference; she describes her impressions:

The Dornach hill in deep snow. Brilliant, starry nights. Cold, sparkling, clear days. The ruins of the old Goetheanum—the gray, charred concrete lower structure, partially swept by drifts, was a gaunt, mute reminder of the tragic night one year ago.

Behind the ruins, and just above them on the hill, stood the low wooden barracks of the *Schreinerei*, the carpentry shop. Here, during the days prior to the Christmas Conference, intense activity had been going on. The walls of the small audi-torium, situated in part of this building, were being ripped out on two sides to open the hall toward the adjoining outer work-shops. In this way it was hoped that the many people—some coming from distant parts of the world—who had sent word that they were coming for the Conference would be able to see and, in any case, to hear. No one had anticipated such a large number. There was an atmosphere of intense expectation and preparation.

Then, overnight, people began to arrive. On the twenty-fourth, long processions came climbing up the hill through the snow, past the ruins, along the winding paths that mount steeply from the valley below. All converged upon the small weather-beaten door of the carpentry shop. Inside, the auditorium and adjoining work-shops gradually became packed to overflowing as the people streamed in. Tightly placed chairs filled every available bit of floor space and the stage as well. People sat upon piles of planks in the background, on workbenches, and on anything they could find. It was impossible to heat the whole enlarged space adequately in the bitter cold, and especially in the outlying areas, people sat wrapped in heavy overcoats and blankets. Young people were asked to give up their seats to the arriving visitors, so many of us stood along the walls at the rear, or perched upon window ledges. Finding myself near a big machine for sawing lumber, I climbed up onto it and found myself a somewhat precarious seat on a small metal slab. From it, I was able to look out over the heads of the assembled people to the small speaker's stand that stood at the far end of the auditorium, from which Rudolf Steiner was to speak. This perch, being suitable only for a young climber, I was fortu-nately able to keep throughout the Conference.

A sense of deep earnestness, of almost breathless expectation, and of high festivity pervaded the gathering. There seemed to be so much going on in the way of last-minute preparations. Then at 10:00 A.M. Rudolf Steiner stepped to the podium.

The calm, moving dignity of his frail form clad in black, against the blue curtains, the power and erect carriage of his head, the profound kindness and gravity of his features, the unforgettable depths of his gaze—these rise again in memory. For a long moment he stood silent, as was his custom before he spoke, an enormous quiet surrounding him. Then his deep voice sounded, and with a few simple, impressive words, he pronounced the opening of the Christmas Conference, welcoming all who were present.[1]

With words of warmest appreciation, Steiner introduced Albert Steffen, who spoke on the history and destiny of the Goetheanum. Following Steffen's address, at 11:15 A.M. Steiner then opened the proceedings:

> My dear friends! We begin our Christmas Conference for the founding of the Anthroposophical Society in a new form with a view of a stark contrast. We have had to invite you, dear friends, to pay a visit to a heap of ruins. As you climbed the Goetheanum hill here in Dornach, your eyes fell on our place of work, but what you saw were ruins of the Goetheanum that perished a year ago. In the truest sense of the word, this sight is a symbol that speaks profoundly to our hearts, a symbol not only of the external manifestation of our work and endeavor, on anthroposophical ground both here and in the world, but also of many symptoms manifesting in the world as a whole....
>
> Let us begin with the immediate situation here. We have had to invite you to take your places in this wooden shed.... Our initial introduction to these circumstances showed us yesterday that our friends felt the cold dreadfully in this shed, which is the best we can offer. But dear friends, let us count this frost, too, among the many other things that may be regarded as maya and illusion in what has come to meet you here. The more we can find our way into a mood that feels the external circumstances surrounding us to be maya and illusion, the more we shall develop the

---

1. Arvia MacKaye Ege, *The Experience of the Christmas Foundation Meeting*, Adonis Press, 1981, Ghent, NY, pp. 4–5.

mood of active doing, which we shall need here over the next few days, a mood that may not be negative in any way, a mood that must be positive in every detail.

Now, a year after the moment when the flames of fire blazed skyward from the dome of our Goetheanum, everything that has been built up in the spiritual realm during the twenty years of the Anthroposophical Movement may appear before our hearts and before the eyes of our soul not as devouring flames but as creative flames. For everywhere, out of the spiritual content of the Anthroposophical Movement, warmth comes to give us courage, warmth capable of bringing countless seeds to life for the spiritual life of the future—seeds that lie hidden here in the very ground of Dornach and all that belongs to it. Countless seeds for the future can, in their ripeness, begin to unfold through the warmth that may surround us here. Thus, one day they may stand before the world as fully matured fruits as a result of what we want to do for them. Now more than ever before we may recall that a spiritual movement—such as the one encompassed by the name *anthroposophy*, with which we have endowed it—is not born out of any earthly or arbitrary consideration....

Our starting point today will be something that we would have gladly seen as our starting point years ago in 1913. This is where we take up the thread, my dear friends, and inscribe into our souls the foremost principle of the Anthroposophical Movement, which will find its home in the Anthroposophical Society—that is, everything in it is willed by the spirit; this Movement desires to fulfill what the signs of the times speak in a shining script to human hearts.

The Anthroposophical Society will only endure if we make the Anthroposophical Movement the profoundest concern of our hearts. If we fail, the Society will not endure. The most important deed to be accomplished during the coming days must be accomplished within all your hearts, my dear friends. Whatever we say and hear will only become a starting point for the cause of anthroposophy in the right way if our heart's blood is capable of beating for it. My friends, this is why we have brought you all together here: to evoke a harmony of hearts in a truly anthroposophical sense. And we allow ourselves to hope that this is an appeal that can be properly understood.[2]

With powerful strokes Steiner reminded his hearers of the beginnings of the Movement, of how it had been possible for the spiritual world to speak through a few individuals of the momentous changes occurring behind the scenes of world events. Steiner spoke of the years immediately preceding the war, and how his mystery dramas showed that individual destinies are linked with the great events of our time.

I do believe that during those four or five years when the mystery dramas were performed in Munich—a time much loved and dear to our hearts—much of what is involved in this link between the individual human soul and the divine working of the cosmos in the realms of soul and spirit did indeed make its way through the souls of our friends. (ibid., p. 47)

Then the four terrible years of the war followed. Every effort was directed toward keeping the movement relatively intact. Nevertheless, there were serious misunderstandings. The forces that splintered humanity inevitably penetrated the Society as well. Steiner went on to say:

As yet there exists no proper judgment about the enormity that lives among us all as a consequence of the World War. Thus, it may be said that the Anthroposophical Society—not the Movement—has emerged riven from the war. (ibid., p. 48)

---

2. *The Christmas Conference for the Foundation of the General Anthroposophical Society 1923/1924*, Anthroposophic Press, Hudson, NY, 1989, pp. 43–47.

The friends assembled in that hastily improvised auditorium were once again called on by Steiner to look through outer appearances, to see it as *maya*, or illusion; for this is what it is, once the eyes of one's heart have opened to the hidden reality.

> I want to tell you that if this gathering runs its course in the right way—if this gathering really reaches an awareness of how something spiritual and esoteric must be the foundation for all our work and existence—then the spiritual seeds present everywhere will be able to germinate through the warmth of your mood and your enthusiasm.... Prepare your souls, dear friends, so that they may receive these seeds; for your souls are the true ground and soil in which these seeds of the spirit may germinate, unfold, and develop. (ibid., p. 48)

Steiner knew very well what was at stake. To unite an esoteric movement with an open, public society was a daring endeavor. How could one hope to reconcile the freedom of the individual member, on one hand, with the necessity for disciplined research and the authority of spiritual insight on the other? But this was, in fact, exactly what was intended if the Anthroposophical Movement was to become one with the Anthroposophical Society. Steiner alone had been responsible for the Movement that flowed through him into the culture of his time. He had not even been a member of the Anthroposophical Society as it emerged from the Theosophical Society in 1912 and 1913. He was its adviser, counselor, and guide but had remained free as an individual to establish communication with the beings who spoke and acted through him. Their collaboration constituted the insights and initiatives that inspired the Movement. Now this wellspring of spiritual life and wisdom was to find its earthly home within a very human society; a society into which any individual was free to enter.

This was the dilemma with which Steiner wrestled throughout the fateful year of 1923 following the destruction of the Goetheanum. Despite powerful inner resistance, he reached a momentous decision that gave him the ability to lead the Movement within the Society.

In this regard he stated:

> In recent weeks I have pondered a question deep within my soul:
> What should be the starting point for this Christmas Confer-
> ence, and what lessons have we learned from the experiences of
> the past ten years since the founding of the Anthroposophical
> Society?
>
> Out of all this, my dear friends, two alternate questions
> arose. In 1912 and 1913 I said for good reasons that the
> Anthroposophical Society would now have to run itself, that it
> would have to manage its own affairs, and that I would have to
> withdraw and become an adviser who would not participate
> directly in any actions. Since then things have changed. After
> grave efforts in the past weeks to overcome my inner resistance
> I have realized that it would be impossible for me to continue
> to lead the Anthroposophical Movement within the Anthro-
> posophical Society if this Christmas Conference were not to
> agree that I should once more assume in every way the leader-
> ship—that is, the presidency—of the Anthroposophical Soci-
> ety to be established here in Dornach at the Goetheanum.
> (ibid., p. 49)

Rudolf Steiner knew the risk. To unite his destiny, his individual
karma, with that of the Society's membership might very well cloud
his relationship with the spiritual beings who guided and nourished
the Movement. It might no longer be possible for him to have the
kind of transparent communications on which the truth and integrity of the Movement depended. Yet, as he assessed the situation
within the membership, he became convinced that he could continue to carry responsibility for the Movement within the Society
only if he was fully free to act on its behalf.

What observations had contributed to Steiner's realization that—
despite his inner resistance—this was a step that he must be willing
to take? He spoke frankly about one of the most important symptoms that had awakened this realization, In so doing, he also
revealed the character of the society he hoped would come about.

As you know, during a conference in Stuttgart it became necessary for me to make the difficult decision to advise the society in
Germany to split into two societies, one of which would be a
continuation of the old Society and one in which the young
members would chiefly be represented, the Free Anthroposophical Society.[3]

Let me tell you, my dear friends, that the decision to give this
advice was difficult indeed. It was so serious because, fundamentally, such advice contradicted the very foundations of the
Anthroposophical Society. For if this was not a Society where
today's youth could feel fully at home, then what other human
association in the earthly world of today was there that could give
them such a feeling! Such advice was an anomaly. (ibid., p. 49)

Behind Steiner's concern that, of all human societies, the
Anthroposophical Society should be one in which the youth might
feel at home, was his awareness of the mighty spiritual transformation that occurred during the final years of the last century. About
this he said:

You see, at the turn of the century something took place very
deeply within spiritual events, and the effects of this are evident
in external events among human beings here on earth.

One of the greatest possible changes occurred in the spiritual
realm. Preparation for it began at the end of the 1870s, and it
culminated right at the turn of the century. Ancient Indian wisdom pointed to it, calling it the end of Kali Yuga. Much—very
much, my dear friends—is meant by this. When I have recently
been able to meet in various ways with young people in all the
countries of the world accessible to me, I have repeatedly said to
myself: Everything that beats in these young hearts, everything
that glows toward spiritual activity in such a beautiful and often
indeterminate way, this is the external expression of what was

---

3. See *Awakening to Community*, Anthroposophic Press, Spring Valley, NY,
1974, lectures 6 and 7.

completed in the depths of spiritual world-weaving during the last third of the nineteenth century until the twentieth century.

My dear friends, what I now want to say is not something negative but positive, so far as I am concerned. I have frequently found, when I have gone to meet young people, that their efforts to join one or another organization encountered difficulties because again and again the association's form did not fit what they themselves wanted. There was always some condition or other concerning the sort of person you had to be or what you had to do to join any of these organizations.... The human soul today feels that anything dogmatic is foreign to it; to carry on in any kind of sectarian way is fundamentally foreign to it. And it cannot be denied that within the Anthroposophical Society it is proving difficult to cast off this way of doing things. But cast it off we must. Not a shred must be allowed to remain within the new Anthroposophical Society that will be established.

Young people must feel that here they have found something that emerges to meet their youth. When the Free Anthroposophical Society was established, I dearly longed to reply to young people's inquiries about the conditions for joining by giving them the only answer I now want to give: The only condition is to be truly young, in the sense that we are young when our youthful soul is filled with all the impulses of the present time.

Dear friends, how does one become old in the proper sense in the Anthroposophical Society? You are old in the proper sense if you have a heart for what is welling up into human beings today, both young and old, out of the spiritual depths through a universal youthfulness that renews every aspect of our lives.

By suggesting moods of soul I am indicating what it was that moved me to take on the task as President of the Anthroposophical Society. (ibid., pp. 50-51)

It was at this point that Steiner also asked that the name of the new society be the "General Anthroposophical Society" rather than the "International Society" as stated in the invitation. General, in this context, might be characterized as the "generally human" or what is "commonly human," which is better conveyed by the German words *Die Algemeine Anthroposophische Gesellschaft*. Every implication of nationalism—even in the negative sense of disavowal—was to be avoided.

> Dear friends, it is to be neither an "international" nor a "national" society. I beg you heartily never to use the term *international society*, but always to speak simply of a "General Anthroposophical Society" that wants to be centered here at the Goetheanum in Dornach. (ibid., p. 51)

With this, Steiner turned toward formulating the statutes he wished to present to the meeting. As they were presented and discussed in detail each morning during the following days, it became overwhelmingly clear that the members accepted with deep gratitude and confidence Steiner's request to be the Society's president. In preparation for presenting the statutes he characterized the intentions underlying them in the following way:

> You will see that the Statutes are formulated in a way that excludes anything administrative, anything that could ever turn into bureaucracy of its own accord. These statutes are tuned to what is purely human.... These statutes say: Here in Dornach is the Goetheanum. This Goetheanum is run in a particular way. In this Goetheanum work of this and that kind is undertaken. In this Goetheanum endeavors are made to promote human evolution in this way or in that way. Whether these things are "right" or "not right" is something that must not be stated in statutes that are intended to be truly modern. All that is stated is the fact that a Goetheanum exists, that human beings are connected with this Goetheanum, and that these human beings do certain things in this Goetheanum in the belief that, through doing so, they are working for human evolution.
>
> Those who wish to join this Society are not expected to adhere to any principle. No religious confession, no scientific conviction, no artistic intention is set up in any dogmatic way.

The only thing required is that those who join should feel at home in being linked to what is going on at the Goetheanum. (ibid., pp. 51-52)

In order that this new association not harbor the seeds of bureaucracy, it would have to develop the confidence and courage to recognize and support the autonomy of its organs. Just as in a healthy living body in which heart, liver, and lung enjoy autonomous lives and functions within the organism as a whole, so in a healthy human social organism centralized direction and control must give way to confidence in the autonomous function of its various organs within the association as a whole. For this to happen, the various national, or country societies (*Landesgesellschaften*)—in whose establishment Steiner had participated so actively and enthusiastically during the preceding year—would become autonomous organs within the body of the General Anthroposophical Society. The only restriction that they would have to freely accept would be to refrain from actions that would contradict the intentions of the General Society. He underlined this aspect:

Then the Anthroposophical Society will become what I have often pointed to when, to my deep satisfaction, I have been allowed to be at the founding of individual national, or country, societies. The Anthroposophical Society will then be able to arise independently on the foundations of all that has come into being in those national societies. If this can happen, then these national societies will be truly autonomous as well. Then every group that comes into existence within the Anthroposophical Society will be truly autonomous. (ibid., p. 52)

Steiner nevertheless felt it necessary to point out two difficulties that would need to be overcome if the Anthroposophical Society was to become the purely human association that he hoped for and that was so urgently needed.

The first difficulty was the very understandable tendency that had characterized the early years of the movement—the wish to protect the fledgling work in secrecy, to cultivate it very privately, away from public view, where it would not be exposed to conflict and controversy. Here again, times had changed and the new Society could no longer afford this luxury.

> A Society built on firm foundations must, above all else, not offend this demand of our time. It is not at all difficult to prefer secrecy, even in the external form, in one case or another. But whenever a society like ours, built on a foundation of truth, seriously desires secrecy, it will surely find itself conflicting with contemporary consciousness, and the most dire obstacles for its continuing existence will ensue. Therefore, dear friends, for the General Anthroposophical Society that is to be established we can lay claim only to absolute openness. (ibid., p. 53)

To illustrate this point, Steiner spoke of the Society's dilemma regarding the publication of his lectures, which had, in theory, been available only to members of the Society; in fact, however, they almost immediately came into the hands of those who were interested only in attacking what they had to say and their source. "The history of these lecture cycles," Steiner observed, "represents a tragic chapter within the development of our Anthroposophical Society." (ibid., p. 53)

> To continue in our old ways regarding the lecture cycles would be to hide our head in the sand, believing that because everything is dark for us, everything must be dark in the outside world too.
>
> This is why for years I have been asking myself what can be done about these cycles. We now have no alternative but to put up a moral barrier in place of the physical one we tried to erect earlier, which meanwhile has been breached at every point.
>
> In the draft of the Statutes I have endeavored to do just this. In the future all the cycles, without exception, are to be sold publicly, just like any other book.... We sell the cycles to all who wish to have them, but declare from the start who can be considered

competent to form a valid judgment on them, a judgment to which we can give some credence. Everyone else is an amateur as far as the cycles are concerned. We also declare that in the future we shall no longer consider any judgments passed on the cycles by those who are such dilettantes. This is the only moral protection available to us. If only we do this properly, we shall bring about a situation in which the matters with which we are concerned are treated no differently than books about the integration of partial differential equations. People will gradually come to agree that it is just as absurd for someone, however learned in other spheres, to pass a judgment on a lecture cycle as it is for someone who knows nothing of logarithms to say: This book on partial differential equations is nonsense! We must bring about a situation in which the distinction between an amateur and an expert can be drawn in the right way. (ibid., pp. 54-55)

The second difficulty that, in Steiner's view, needed to be overcome before the new association could truly become the outer bearer of the movement was the illusion that one can win people over by denying the Anthroposophical Movement—"by seeing it as something parallel to the very things it is supposed to replace in human evolution." He went on to say: "Whatever the realm, we must stand in the world under the sign of full truth, as representatives of the essence of Anthroposophy" (ibid., p. 55).

Steiner illustrated what he meant by citing work in the fields of eurythmy, speech, and medicine. He concluded by saying:

We must carry anthroposophy courageously into every realm, including medicine. Only then will we make progress in what eurythmy ought to be, in what recitation and declamation ought to be, in what medicine ought to be, not to mention many other fields living within our Anthroposophical Society, just as we must make progress with anthroposophy itself in the strict sense of the term.

Here I have at least hinted at the fundamental conditions that must be placed before our hearts at the beginning of our

Conference to establish the General Anthroposophical Society. In the manner indicated it must become a society of attitudes and not a society of statutes. The Statutes are intended to express externally what lives within every soul. (ibid., pp. 56-57)

The "Statutes of the General Anthroposophical Society" as presented by Steiner and approved by the membership are public documents and readily available to anyone interested in them.[4] They state that membership in the Society is based not on adherence to theoretical principles but on the recognition of what exists and strives to manifest. They characterize a society that is open to every individual who sincerely wishes to join it, yet one that also distinguishes clearly between the member's individual freedom and the tasks of those who represent anthroposophy and who are responsible for the conduct of the School of Spiritual Science that carries the obligations for research. In this regard a few key paragraphs are essential.

> 1. The Anthroposophical Society is to be an association of people willing to nurture the life of the soul, both in the individual and in human society, on the basis of real knowledge of the spiritual world.
>
> 3. The people gathered in Dornach as the nucleus of the Society recognize and endorse the view of the leadership at the Goetheanum: "Anthroposophy, as fostered at the Goetheanum, leads to results that can serve every human being as a stimulus to spiritual life, regardless of nationality, social standing, or religion. These results can lead to a social life genuinely built on mutual loving interest. No special degree of academic learning is required to claim them and to base one's life on them; only open-minded human nature is necessary."

---

4. *The Christmas Conference for the Foundation of the General Anthroposophical Society 1923/1924*, pp. 57–63; see also *The Foundation Stone / The Life, Nature and Cultivation of Anthroposophy*, Rudolf Steiner Press, London, 1996, "Letter to the Members, 13 January 1924," which contains the statutes along with Steiner's commentary on them.

Research into these results, however, as well as competent evaluation of them, depends on spiritual-scientific training, which is acquired step by step. The results are, in their way, as precise as the results of any true natural science. When they attain the same general recognition as these, they will bring about comparable progress in every sphere of life, not only in the spiritual life but also in the every-day realm.

4. The Anthroposophical Society is in no way a secret society but entirely public. Anyone can become a member without regard to nationality, social standing or religious, scientific, or artistic conviction, and who considers the existence of an institution such as the Goetheanum in Dornach justified as a School of Spiritual Science.

The Anthroposophical Society rejects any kind of sectarian activity. Party politics are not considered to be within the scope of its task. (ibid., pp. 57–59)

~

This preparatory meeting on the morning of Christmas Eve day would have been incomplete and inconclusive if Steiner had not proceeded to name the individuals with whom he was prepared to carry responsibility for the Society. They had demonstrated, over many years, a readiness and capacity to commit themselves wholly to the anthroposophical path of knowledge and had demonstrated their ability and their willingness to work with Steiner and share responsibility both for anthroposophy in general and for their special field of work. They were to live in Dornach, since in order to do fruitful work they had to be able to meet personally and to communicate easily and directly. Each of them had carried a particular initiative in developing a special field out of anthroposophical research. The five individuals Steiner named and submitted to the gathering were already well known within the membership for their achievements. (Brief biographical notes on each are included in the appendix.)

Albert Steffen, the creative author and the editor of the weekly *Das Goetheanum*, was proposed as Steiner's "representative" (*Stellvertreter*) and vice-president. Marie Steiner had been an active leader in the stage arts of eurythmy and speech, and was, in Steiner's words, "united with the Anthroposophical Society from the very beginning ... and active anthroposophically in one of the most important fields." Ita Wegman was the person with whom Steiner had "the opportunity to test anthroposophical enthusiasm to its limits in the right way, by working with her to elaborate the anthroposophical system of medicine." Lili Vreede was "tried and tested down to the very last detail as a most faithful colleague," and was actively engaged in mathematical and astronomical research. And, as secretary and treasurer, Guenther Wachsmuth would "take many cares off our shoulders, cares that cannot all be borne by us because, of course, the initiatives must be kept separate. This is someone who will have to think on everyone's behalf.... What is needed is someone who does not knock heads together, so to speak, but holds them together.... The Executive Council (*Vorstand*) must be kept small, and so my list is now exhausted" (ibid., pp. 64–66). Steiner made it clear that he would reserve for himself the responsibility for establishing the School of Spiritual Science, which was to be at the heart of the new Society.

With the nomination of the Executive Council, the preparatory meeting closed. The ground had been wonderfully prepared for the festive laying of the Foundation Stone. The act of founding the society took place on the morning of Christmas Day. A "Foundation Stone," in the form of a light-filled structure of mantric verse, was laid in the only ground appropriate for a truly human social community—in the hearts of those participating, whether physically present or spiritually linked through their own activity at whatever time or place. Arvia MacKaye Ege describes this moment:

> Never had I seen Rudolf Steiner as he appeared then. There was a light from his eyes, a power and majesty about him, which gave the impression that he had grown to a great size. There was an intensity and activity, united with a cosmic calm, that was breathtaking, and indicative of what was to come.

He opened this event by giving three strong, incisive, measured raps with a gavel upon the speaker's stand, such as those given in the temple in the Mystery Plays. It was as though the room became thronged with unseen spectators. —Then as he spoke, giving for the first time the words of the Christmas Foundation Mantra ["Human Soul ..."], it was as though, in this little carpentry shop, he spoke not only to the whole earth but to the assembled heavens; as though he became like a sun, light-outpouring, his voice like gold, a Michaelic fire infusing his words. Something poured forth of such a magnitude, and in a realm of such awakened consciousness, on this Christmas morning that it can only be likened to a spiritual birth.

From my perch in the background my heart cried out, and I thought it would burst, because something so far beyond my grasp was taking place. Then something gave way within me, and I drank in, like a great tide, all that followed, knowing that only in later incarnations would I approach any adequate realization of what was actually taking place.

His words resound to us again today. "Out of these three—the Spirit of the Heights, the Christ-power encircling us, the creative Father-activity streaming out of the depths—we will in this moment form in our souls the twelve-sided Foundation Stone that we now sink deeply into the ground of our souls."

That morning the dodecahedric Foundation Stone was laid into the hearts of all those present and of all those who truly wish to unite themselves with the Being of Anthroposophy. From what transpired it was apparent that a mystery deed had been enacted through Rudolf Steiner. We sense that this deed, while taking place here on the earth, was enacted on the highest spiritual plane and as such was a deed that cannot pass away. It is there awaiting us always. And because it was enacted on that plane, it can multiply itself infinitely and become a reality in the hearts of each one of us. Thus we are able today to begin to approach it as an archetypal seed sown within humanity—the seed of a free spiritual community of human beings. (*The Experience of the Christmas Foundation Meeting*, pp. 8–9)

The Foundation Stone verse, spoken for the first time on Christmas morning, sounded again each day in a particular rhythmic configuration, as Steiner guided his listeners into the experience of its three aspects, each presented as a kind of dialogue between the activity of the individual human soul and the cosmic reality that underlies and makes it possible. Three times the human soul is called on to become active—to practice *spirit recalling*, to practice *spirit communing*,[5] to practice *spirit beholding*. This means becoming active in each of the three realms of our own humanity: in the limbs, bearers of the human will; in the pulse of heart and lung, bearer of the human power of feeling; and in the stillness of the head, bearer of human thought activity. Three times the response rings out from the cosmos:

> For the Father Spirit of the heights holds sway;
> For the Christ-Will reigns in the spheres encircling us;
> For the Spirit's World-All Thoughts reign.

Elemental beings already hear this—will we human beings hear it? This is the question, the plea, with which each double stanza ends. All three seem to be placed on the altar of the fourth stanza, in the service of the God-given Light, the Sun of Christ, which entered the stream of earthly evolution, warming the humble shepherds' hearts and enlightening the wise heads of the kings. We too may warm, we too may enlighten, our hearts and heads, so that a community of hearts, and wills, and minds may work for the good, for all humankind.

The entire mantric, poetic Foundation Stone verse is included in this volume. It is Steiner's gift to everyone who takes it up and works with it, thus joining his or her own self with those who have committed themselves to working for a human spiritual community of free, striving, souls.

---

5. Here Rudolf Steiner uses the verb *besinnen*—"*Übe Geist-Besinnen.*" This has both the quality of "sensing" and, from an older form of German, the quality of "walking"; one might, therefore, speak of "going a contemplative, sensing path." *Communing* has something of this quality.

~

The nine days of the conference surrounding the events of Christmas morning were permeated by the light and warmth that radiated from that festive moment. They were days of activity so intense that even a simple recounting of the program may serve to convey something of the scope and magnitude of what occurred.

Each morning at ten o'clock the members gathered in the improvised auditorium. On five of the seven mornings that followed the laying of the Foundation Stone, Steiner called on a colleague to speak from experience about anthroposophy in that person's special field of work.

After each of the opening lectures, and, in the case of the two scientific reports, immediately preceding them, Steiner read passages from the Foundation Stone meditation, each time in a different grouping. Then he wrote certain of these lines on the blackboard as a kind of meditative crystallization, which, in the course of the seven days, built up a rhythmic pattern that led his hearers more and more deeply into the experience of the Foundation Stone verse as a whole. This meditative interlude helped to set the mood out of which the discussion—paragraph by paragraph—of the new statutes and other matters could then proceed.

Among those who Steiner asked to speak from their own research were two scientists: Dr. Lili Kolisko of the Biochemical Laboratory in Stuttgart and Dr. Rudolf Maier of the Scientific Research Institute of The Coming Day, Inc. in Stuttgart. Kolisko's report was entitled "Physical Proof of the Effectiveness of Microorganisms," and Maier's was "The Connection, Discovered through Anthroposophy, between Magnetism and Light."

In connection with Kolisko's report, Steiner spoke urgently of the need for the anthroposophical movement to engage itself with scientific research. It is significant that he did so as an essential element in reconstituting the society as the bearer of the movement. In his introduction to Kolisko's report, Steiner said:

> If it should become possible for anthroposophy to give impulses
> … to the different branches of science that can lead to certain

research results, then, one of the main obstacles to spiritual research existing in the world will have been removed. This is why it is so important that the right kind of work be undertaken in the proper anthroposophical sense.

Today there is an abyss between art and science; but within science, too, there is an abyss between, for instance, physiology and physics. All these abysses will be bridged when scientific work is done in the right way in our circles. Therefore, from a general anthroposophical viewpoint, we must interest ourselves in these different things as much as our knowledge and capacities will allow. A scientific impulse will have to emanate from the Anthroposophical Society. This must be made evident the moment we want to take the Anthroposophical Society into entirely new channels. (ibid., pp. 207–208)

Dr. Lili Kolisko with daughter

Following Dr. Kolisko's report, Steiner concluded:

Now, my dear friends, you have seen that quiet work is going on among us on scientific questions, and that it is indeed possible to provide, out of anthroposophy, a stimulus for science in a way that is truly needed today. In the present situation of the anthroposophical movement, however, such things are really possible only because there are people like Frau Dr. Kolisko who take on the work in such a devoted and selfless way....

These experiments are, from an anthroposophical viewpoint, details that lead to a wholeness needed by science today—more urgently than can be said. Yet, if we continue to work as we have been in our research institute, then perhaps in fifty, or maybe seventy-five years, we shall come to the result that we need, which is that innumerable details go to make up a whole. This whole will then have a bearing not only on the life of knowledge, but also on practical life as a whole.

People have no idea today how deeply all these things can affect practical daily life in such realms as the production of what human beings need to live or for the development of healing methods, and so on.

Now, you might say that human progress has always gone forward at a slow pace, and that there is not likely to be any difference in this field. However, with civilization in its present brittle and fragile state, it could very well happen that, in fifty or seventy-five years' time, we will have missed the chance to achieve what so urgently needs to be achieved. We are confronted with having to work very quickly, since we can work only when there are devoted colleagues such as Frau Dr. Kolisko; and the speed of our work might lead to results in fifty or perhaps seventy-five years. In the face of such speed, let me express, therefore, not a wish or even a possibility, but perhaps merely an illusion—that it would be possible to achieve the necessary results in five or ten years. And I am convinced that if we could create the necessary equipment and the necessary institutes and have the necessary colleagues—as many as possible to work out of this spirit—then we could achieve in five or ten years what will now take us fifty or seventy-five years. All we would need for this work would be fifty to seventy-five million francs. Then we would probably be able to do the work in a tenth of the time. As I said, I am not expressing this as a wish or even as a possibility, but merely as an illusion, though a very realistic illusion. If we had seventy-five million francs, we could achieve what has to be achieved. This is something that we should at least think about. (ibid., pp. 208–209)

~

Even a brief sketch of these nine days would be incomplete without mentioning that, in addition to artistic performances every afternoon, Steiner met in the early mornings and afternoons with leading members from the various national societies. And he crowned each of those nine days with a lecture that wove a historical tapestry out of the light of mystery wisdom.[6]

~

On the two last mornings of the conference, Rudolf Steiner spoke about his ideas for the new Goetheanum. As we know, the decision had been made during the preceding June and July to rebuild, and the insurance company had agreed to settle. Steiner had been given complete freedom to design the new building, working with the appropriate architect and engineers, and at his suggestion, it had been agreed that the new structure would be built with reinforced concrete. He introduced this topic:

As you may imagine, I have recently given much thought to the idea of the building in Dornach, and the situation will most certainly necessitate the earliest possible execution of this idea. (ibid., p. 210)

He went on to comment on many aspects of the new building that needed to be taken into consideration: that the cost should be kept

---

6. *World History in the Light of Anthroposophy*, Rudolf Steiner Press, 1977.

within definite limits (three to three and a half million Swiss francs); that it should be a multi-purpose building, whereas the first Goetheanum was essentially a single-purpose structure; that a practice stage of the same dimensions as the main stage was needed to avoid continuous conflicts for the use of the hall; and that many smaller spaces were required to house the section offices, the society's administrative offices, meeting rooms, studios, and so on. Exhibition spaces, storage facilities, and a library would also be needed. He said that the decision to build in concrete required very different treatment of structural forms; the building would no longer be circular but "more rectangular, a building with angles."

It will be unnecessary to make the new Goetheanum very much taller than the old Goetheanum, since I am not considering a new cupola. I am endeavoring to create a design for the roof which will consist of a series of planes arranged in relation to one another in a way which will, I believe, be no less aesthetically attractive than a cupola.... There will also be entrances at the sides. By making the stage space smaller on plan than the storage area, and by extending the walls forward, we shall gain space for the different rooms. At the top it will be possible to light the whole space with daylight, so that we can alternate between daylight, when it is there, and artificial light when we need it.

In this way it will be possible to have a really practical building in which every cubic foot of space can be used to the full. Many things will be able to occur in this building simultaneously, whereas in the old building only one thing could occur at any given time.

You must consider, my dear friends, that this is not simply intended to be an improvement—which perhaps some might consider a "dis-improvement"—but it is designed to take into consideration all the developments that have come about. Among ourselves, I have often stressed that if you want to live in reality and not in ideas, then the realities of time must be given particular recognition. The age in which one lives is a reality. But, it is difficult to generate an understanding for this time as something real. There are still those today who speak of the threefold social organism with the very sentences I used in regard to the conditions prevailing in 1919. History is indeed advancing so rapidly just now that, when someone describes things just as they were described in 1919, it seems hundreds of years out of date. Thus, since things have after all been happening in the Anthroposophical Movement, you cannot build in 1924 as you did in 1913 and 1914. In 1913 and 1914 the idea of the Goetheanum arose simply from the realization that an artistic space would have to be created for the Mystery Dramas. At that time we really only thought of the Mystery Dramas and the lectures.

Steiner then went on to speak of the artistic challenge presented by the new building material, concrete.

Much will have to be done, on the one hand, to force the intractable material of concrete into forms that the eye of the human soul can follow artistically and, on the other hand, mold seemingly decorative features (which really are a result of the concrete itself) in an artistic and sculptural way, so that the substance of concrete can be revealed for once in an artistic way. I ask you now to regard this idea as the seed out of which the Goetheanum shall actually emerge.

In the remarks that followed, it became clear that Steiner had been approached by well-meaning friends with suggestions that he look for inspiration to this building or that which had been constructed in concrete, at that time still a relatively new medium.

I have stated that I alone am allowed to work on the artistic creation of the Goetheanum, and it will not be possible, to any great extent, to accept any of the offers or suggestions that have already been made—of course, with the best intentions. There is no point in telling me about concrete buildings that have been erected here or there, or about factories here or there that are working efficiently. If the Goetheanum building is to come about in concrete, it will have to emerge from an original idea, and nothing that has so far been achieved in concrete can serve as a basis for what is to come into being here.

On the following morning, New Year's Day, Steiner carried his discussion of the building further, concentrating on its exterior. He emphasized that, unlike the first building, which was circular, the new building was to be partially circular and partially rectangular, and that it would be necessary to find a modern style appropriate to concrete as a building material. As there was no time to go into details, he said that he wished to concentrate on "one essential feature, the underlying theme of the portals and windows, so that you can see how I want to let the inner formative force that was latent in the old forms (of the first building) assert itself once more also in the new forms of the intractable material, concrete."

> I want the walls coming down from the roof, which is shaped in flat surfaces, to give the eye a definite impression of load. I want to bring it about that this downward pressure is caught and held, also for the eye, by the portal as well as the window surrounds. I also want to bring it about that inwardly the spiritual impression is of a portal that draws you in, or a window that takes in the light in order to usher it into the space within. But at the same time I want to bring it about that in a certain way this form reveals how the Goetheanum is to be a kind of shelter for the one who seeks the spirit within it. (ibid., pp.249–250)

With the help of a color sketch he had drawn on a blackboard, Steiner described in a wonderfully tactile and visual way that the forms of the portal interacted to create a "protective form that appears above the head of the one who enters ... but at the same time carries the roof section with an appropriate form that grows out of it" (ibid., p. 551)[7] Steiner then concluded his discussion about the building:

---

7. This black-and-white reproduction of Steiner's original sketch (color plate XX in *The Christmas Conference*) may help the reader to imagine how the elements, which Steiner described in greater detail, worked together to create the desired impression.

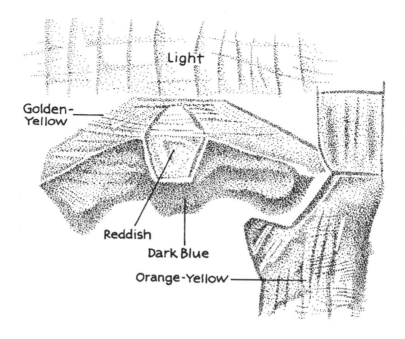

Light

Golden-Yellow

Reddish

Dark Blue

Orange-Yellow

The essential thing about an angular building is the harmony between the forces of support and load. If we are to carry this out in an organic building, every part must reveal the indwelling character of the whole. The pillars in the old building reached from bottom to top. Now they will be metamorphosed so that on the lower level, the ground floor, they will develop like roots—architecturally conceived, of course. Out of these the actual pillars will grow on the upper level, becoming bearers of the whole. They will then bring the forms of the roof to completion from within outward. The roof will not terminate horizontally, but rather in the way the cupola was terminated. The pillars and columns will be metamorphosed into supporting elements while at the same time expressing what in the old Goetheanum was intended to express the roundness of the building.

We shall have to endeavor to calculate how basic the forms will have to be, merely hinted at perhaps, in order to keep the whole building, given this shape, within three to three and a half million francs. Once we have made this decision—and I do not believe any other is possible—then I hope we shall (if our friends' willingness to make sacrifices does not let us down) soon be in a position to begin construction, and the building will then appear as a new Goetheanum where the old one stood and in a much more basic and simple form. (ibid., pp. 251–252)

~

The evening lectures culminated with two addresses on New Year's Eve and New Year's Day. In them Steiner spoke directly to the heart of our time. The first was delivered exactly one year after he spoke for the last time in the first Goetheanum, which must have been already on fire at the time. This time he spoke with powerful words concerning the fire that destroyed the temple of Ephesus on the night Alexander the Great was born. Into those flames, Steiner said, was written the "Jealousy of the Gods." Now, he said, in the dawning age of human freedom was written "Human Jealousy." But this, he said, should be for us a call to action.

> The Goetheanum could be taken from us. The Spirit of the Goetheanum, if our will is truly upright and honest, cannot be taken from us. And least of all will it be taken from us if at this solemn and festive hour—separated by such a short time from the moment a year ago when the flames leapt from our beloved Goetheanum—we not only feel the pain anew, but also vow out of this pain to keep faith with the spirit for whom, over ten long years, we were permitted to build this home. If this resolve wells up today in all sincerity from the depths of our hearts, if we can transform the pain and grief into an impulse to action, then we shall also transform the sorrowful event into blessing. Through this, the pain cannot be made less, but it rests with us to find in the pain the urge to action—to action in the spirit. (ibid., pp. 242)

On the evening of New Year's Day, the members gathered once again in the carpentry shop amid the piles of lumber and the wood-working machines to hear Steiner's final lecture. His message was *responsibility*. This message sounded already in his opening words:

My dear friends! We are gathered together for the last time in this Conference, from which much that is strong and important is to go forth for the Anthroposophical Movement. So let me now shape this final lecture in a way that connects it inwardly, in its impulse, with the various prospects thrown open to us by this series of lectures as a whole, but also in a way that will allow us to gain a sense for the future, especially the future of anthroposophical endeavor.

When we look out into the world today we see something that has already been there for many years—that is, a tremendous amount of destructiveness. Forces are at work that give us an inkling of the abysses into which Western civilization has yet to plunge. Looking at those who, outwardly, are the cultural leaders in the various fields of life, we notice how they are enmeshed in a terrible cosmic sleep. (ibid., p. 260)

Steiner underlined the urgent reality in which we find ourselves by describing the experiences available to those who can observe the situation of human souls within the spiritual world.

In recent decades it has been possible for someone with a sense for the spiritual world to wander, in spiritual observation, past many personalities, gaining bitter sensations with regard to the future destiny of humanity on earth. It has been possible to wander past one's fellow human beings in the manner available to spiritual insight, observing how they lay aside their physical and etheric bodies in sleep and live in the spiritual world with their I and astral body. Wandering among the destinies of those I-beings and astral bodies while human beings sleep has, in recent decades, given rise to experiences that can indicate the heavy responsibility incumbent on anyone who can know such things. These souls, having left behind their physical and etheric bodies between going to sleep and waking up, were often seen approaching the Guardian of the Threshold. (ibid., p. 262)

Steiner then described how those sleeping souls demand entrance into the spiritual world, which the Guardian is forced to deny them.

One can hear the voice of the grave Guardian saying, "For your own good, you may not cross the threshold; you may not gain entrance to the spiritual world. Go back!" How are we to understand such an enigmatic observation? At a time in human history when, for humanity, so much depends on gaining insight into the world beyond the senses, how can one understand that the Guardian of the Threshold—whose duty is to accompany and protect human beings on their spiritual journey—refuses the soul's entrance into the world beyond the threshold? The answer, in Steiner's view, lies in a peculiarity of contemporary consciousness, instilled in each of us by our education and contemporary civilization. This peculiarity consists in our ability to enter the spiritual world in our current materialistic soul condition, but a paralysis of soul results. The consequence is that we return to earthly human consciousness, paralyzed in our ability to grasp and experience the living reality of thoughts and ideas.

> If the Guardian of the Threshold did not gravely reject these souls, if he did not reject very many of today's human souls, but instead let them step over into the spiritual world, then, waking up on their return, waking up at the decisive moment on their return, they would have the feeling: I cannot think; my thoughts do not grasp my brain; I have to live in the world without thoughts. (ibid., p. 264)

Steiner carries this observation one significant step farther. If the present condition of civilization were to continue indefinitely into the future, and if souls were to carry their inner content of civilization into the world after death—not just into the world we enter in sleep—then human beings would reenter life "incapable of bringing any strength of ideas with them into their new life on earth. For, although you can enter the spiritual world with today's thoughts, you cannot leave with them. You can only leave in a state of soul paralysis."

> You see, present-day civilization can be based on the kind of cultural life that has long been nurtured. But life cannot be based on it.... [If this condition were to endure] a sick human

race, living only in instincts, would have to populate the earth. Terrible feelings and emotions alone, without orientation through the force of ideas, would come to dominate human evolution. (ibid., p. 264)

If, as an open-minded individual today, I am prepared to think these thoughts through as Steiner presented them in 1924, and if I then observe the almost total absence of any significant, deeply grounded, and morally vibrant ideas in public life today, I will find myself forced to wonder: Shouldn't I take Steiner's observations seriously, even though I may be far from able to duplicate them through my own spiritual-scientific research?

Before ending the final lecture of the Conference, Steiner approached the same theme once more, this time from a very different perspective. He describes a situation in which someone gifted with supersensible perception is on a journey of soul observation accompanied by a human being from an Eastern civilization; such a human being of the East would be heard speaking spirit words of terrible reproach toward the whole of Western civilization:

> You see, if this continues, the earth will have fallen into barbarism by the time those who are alive today return for a new incarnation; people will live by their instincts alone, without ideas; this is what you have brought about by falling away from ancient Eastern spirituality. (ibid., p. 265)

As always, for Rudolf Steiner the confrontation with realities, however dire, is never cause for pessimism or despair; rather, it motivates action and renewed courage. Here, out of a deepened sense of responsibility, he urges us to find the courage to stand unequivocally, straightforwardly, and simply for the fact that life in its totality must always include the invisible realities of the supersensible.

> Therefore, we shall not present a tirade of arguments on the inadequacy of current scientific theory.... [Things, such as the descriptions of souls when asleep and after death] have to be

said, not because it is necessary to brood upon them, but so that heart and mind and soul may be filled to the brim with them.... With thoughts that are not easy but serious, we must depart from this Conference that has led to the founding of the General Anthroposophical Society.

My dear friends, yesterday was the anniversary of the day on which we saw the tongues of flame devouring our old Goetheanum. Today we may hope—since a year ago we did not allow even the flames to distract us from continuing with our work—that when the physical Goetheanum stands here once more, we shall have worked in such a way that the physical Goetheanum is only the external symbol for our spiritual Goetheanum that we want to take with us as an idea into the world.

Here we have laid the Foundation Stone. On this Foundation Stone shall be erected the building whose individual stones will be the work achieved in all our groups by the individuals outside in the wide world. Let us now look in spirit at this work and become conscious of the responsibility toward the human being who stands before the Guardian of the Threshold and has to be refused entry into the spiritual world.

Certainly, it should never occur to us to feel anything but the deepest pain and the deepest sorrow about what happened to us a year ago. But let us not forget that everything in the world with any stature has been born out of pain. Therefore, let us transform our pain so that from it may arise a strong and shining Anthroposophical Society through the power, my dear friends, of your work.

For this purpose we have immersed ourselves in the words with which I began, in those words with which I wish to close this Christmas Conference, which is to be for us a festival of consecration—not merely to begin a new year but to begin a new turning point of time. To this we want to devote ourselves by enthusiastically cultivating the life of spirit. (ibid., pp. 265–270)

The Foundation Stone Mantra

Human soul!
You live within the limbs,
Which bear you through the world of space
Into the ocean of spirit being:
Practice *spirit-recalling*
In depths of soul,
Where in empowering
World-Creator-Being
Your inmost I
In God's own I
Takes being;
And you shall truly *live*
In human world-all being.

For the Father-Spirit of the heights holds sway
In the depths of the world, begetting being;
You Spirits of Strength,
Let out of the heights ring forth
What in the depths finds there its echo,
Speaking thus:
Out of the Godhead is created humankind.

This is heard by the Spirits in East, West, North, South;
May human beings hear it!

Human Soul!
You live within the pulse of heart and lung,
Which leads you through the rhythms of time
Into the feeling of your own soul being:
Practice *spirit-communing*
In the soul's fine balance,
Where the on-surging,
World-Evolving-Deeds
Your inmost I
With the world's own I
Unite,
And you shall truly *feel*
In human soul inner-working.

For the Christ-Will reigns in the spheres encircling us
In the rhythms of the world, shedding grace upon souls;
You Spirits of Light
Let from the East be enkindled
What through the West takes on form;
Speaking thus:
In Christ death becomes life.

This is heard by the Spirits in East, West, North, South;
May human beings hear it!

Human Soul!
You live within the quiet of the head,
Which from out eternal foundations
Lays open unto you the world-all thoughts:
Practice *spirit-beholding*
In thought, stilled through,
Where the eternal aims of the gods
Cosmic-Beings'-Light
On your inmost I
For your free willing
Are shedding
And you shall truly *think*
In human spirit foundations.

For the Spirit's World-All Thoughts reign
In the being of the world, light-beseeching;
You Spirits of Soul,
Let out of the deeps be entreated
What in the heights may be heard;
Speaking thus:
In the Spirit's World-All Thoughts the soul awakens.

This is heard by the Spirits in East, West, North, South;
May human beings hear it!

At the turn of time
Cosmic-Spirit-Light descended
Into earthly stream of being;
Darkling night
Had run its course;
Day-clear light
Streamed into human souls;
Light
That enwarms
The humble shepherds' hearts;
Light
That enlightens
The wise heads of kings.

God-given light,
Christus-Sun
Enwarm
For us our hearts,
Enlighten
For us our heads,
That good may be
What we
From our hearts do found,
What we
From our heads
Would from our heads
Direct with single will.

~

And so my dear friends, bear out with you into the world your warm hearts in whose soil you have laid the Foundation Stone for the Anthroposophical Society; bear out with you your warm hearts in order to do work in the world that is strong in healing. Help will come to you because your heads will be enlightened by what you all now want to be able to direct in conscious willing. Let us today make this resolve with all our strength. And we shall see that if we show ourselves worthy, then a good star will shine over what is willed from here. My dear friends, follow this good star. We shall see whither the gods will lead us through the light of this star.

> God-given light,
> Christ-Sun
> Enwarm
> For us our hearts,
> Enlighten
> For us our heads![8]

---

8. Ibid., p. 272–273.

13

Months of Grace

On the evening of New Year's Day, January 1, 1924, Rudolf Steiner closed the Conference by speaking once again the Foundation Stone verse that had sounded for the first time on Christmas morning. Three times the words rang out:

> *Spirit beings hear it in East, West, North, South,*
> *May human beings hear it.*

For its author this was no mere poetic turn of phrase but a cry from the depths of world evolution. For him, the time was at hand—but would human beings hear it?

~

That the spiritual world heard and blessed it became evident in the outpouring of creative activity on Steiner's part during the weeks and months that followed. Never in all his years had there ever been anything to equal it; but this time he was not alone, and the responsibility was shared. Help was needed, however. Word of what had happened in Dornach must reach every member. The weekly *Das Goetheanum* would now have a supplement, a newsletter for members that would report the Society's activity. The magazine itself was a public organ and would continue as such. Steiner's autobiography was appearing in it each week. Now, he also wrote a weekly "Letter to the Members" for the supplement, *What is happening in the*

Anthroposophical Society, for which he also designed a graphic mast-head, as he had for the public weekly.[1]

The first newsletter appeared January 13, 1924 and contained an introductory article by Steiner about the Christmas Conference, the Statutes, and the members of the new Executive Council (*Vorstand*). In the opening paragraph of the second issue, Steiner expressed, in the first of his "letters," the challenging thought that the Christmas Conference could be only a beginning—not something finished and complete:

> The foundation of the General Anthroposophical Society at the Christmas gathering cannot be fulfilled by what was done or witnessed by the members present at the Goetheanum while it lasted. Its true meaning will be fulfilled only when, in the future and in all the world, those devoted to anthroposophy can feel the coming of fresh anthroposophical life as they give effect to its intentions. Otherwise the meeting would not have done what it set out to do. Such was undoubtedly the unspoken language in the hearts of those who took part in it....
>
> Might it not be necessary to acknowledge that the Anthroposophical Society must work to embody *even more of Anthroposophy* than it has thus far? And how can this be done?[2]

Along with this first "Letter to the Members" was Steiner's opening article on the character and tasks of the School of Spiritual Science, which he was to inaugurate the following month. Here was an important part of his answer to the question: How can even more anthroposophy be brought to life within the Society?

Thus, right from the beginning these weekly letters carried the double impulse of the Christmas Conference out to the membership, which then numbered around twelve thousand. On one hand, Steiner urged the members to strive in every way to rid themselves of the last

---

1. See Appendix on this aspect of Rudolf Steiner's artistic work.
2. *The Foundation Stone / The Life, Nature and Cultivation of Anthroposophy*, Rudolf Steiner Press, London, 1996, pp. 81, 84.

vestiges of secrecy, sectarianism, and dogmatism in every form, so that the Society could become a truly open, fundamentally human community of free individuals. On the other hand, they had to admit that they were only beginning and needed, in every way, to strengthen the spiritual-scientific foundations of their work. It was intended that this should be the responsibility of the School for Spiritual Science through esoteric classes and research work within the special sections. The Society, on the other hand, through the work of its groups and branches, would foster the life of soul that can arise where individuals meet freely to deepen their knowledge of the spiritual world.

The Society, which was reestablished at Christmas, had to provide a membership card that expressed both the *fact* and the *spirit* of this new foundation. Action followed thought and Steiner designed the new card. Well-meaning friends urged him to have a rubber stamp made of his signature to spare him the time and strength necessary to sign twelve thousand cards! But Steiner took seriously the fact that bureaucracy should not find a home in the new Society in any form. To him it was very important that his eyes could rest, even for a moment, on each individual member's name. This is a reality. Each signature creates a contact, no matter how tenuous. For the next several weeks a batch of unsigned cards was always awaiting Rudolf Steiner's attention and his personal signature.

In February the Letters were enhanced and greatly concentrated in the *Anthroposophical Leading Thoughts*, in which Steiner condensed—in terse, lapidary form—the gist of the lectures he had given to the members. Presented in numbered paragraphs (eventually there were 185), these *Leading Thoughts* offered a living "thought extract," a jewel-like seed, that Steiner hoped would come to life in the hearts and minds of active members everywhere. Received in this way, they could help to build "a unity of consciousness" through which the society might grow "from a chaos of separate groups, into a society with real spiritual content."[3]

---

3. *Anthroposophical Leading Thoughts*, Rudolf Steiner Press, London, 1975, p. 11.

Rudolf Steiner in 1924

At the same time that Steiner was intent on allowing the impulse and the reality of the Christmas Foundation Conference to radiate out to the furthest periphery of the membership of the General Anthroposophical Society, he was also immensely engaged in his work in Dornach. He continued in early January with six lectures on Rosicrucian spirituality in the Middle Ages and its transformation and rebirth in our time.[4]

On January 18, he spoke to the members about the School of Spiritual Science, soon to be constituted. The following day he gave the first of nine lectures addressing the essence of the anthroposophical path of inner esoteric schooling.[5] These lectures challenged

4. *Rosicrucianism and Modern Initiation*, Rudolf Steiner Press, London, 1982.
5. *Anthroposophy and the Inner Life: An Esoteric Introduction*, Rudolf Steiner Press, Bristol, 1994.

his audience—most of whom had been students of Anthroposophy for many years—to make a completely new beginning. They felt called upon to reexperience everything they already knew, and to bring it to life through their individual meditative activity as willed knowledge, tempered and reborn in the fire of each individual I. During the Christmas Foundation Meeting Steiner had emphasized that anthroposophy should no longer be merely contemplated but must be *done*. He now showed that this doing should occur at every level, that each person must awaken to a new level of intensity in thinking.

On February 15, Steiner held the first of the nineteen basic lessons comprising the First Class of the esoteric School for Spiritual Science. The next day he gave the first of the many lectures on karma that were to follow during the coming months.[6] A few days later he began the course *Eurythmy as Visible Music* on musical tone eurythmy.[7] Meanwhile, hardly a day passed that Steiner did not continue to work on the statue and wrestle with questions about the new building awaiting its final design. Guenther Wachsmuth was the one who took the day's correspondence in to Rudolf Steiner each morning and received his replies and daily instructions. He describes these morning visits:

> By the time I took his letters and other mail into his studio in the mornings, he had usually already received several visitors, or was in the midst of writing an article, or was carving on the wooden statue that had been set up in his workroom, or was modeling, or painting, or writing. In the midst of whatever task he was engaged in, he was immediately ready to turn to the correspondence to be dealt with. He entered fully into this activity without hesitation and quickly and clearly gave his answers or specific indications (*The Life and Work of Rudolf Steiner*, p. 537)

---

6. *Karmic Relationships: Esoteric Studies*, vols. 1–8, Rudolf Steiner Press, London, 1973–1989.
7. Rudolf Steiner Press, London, 1977.

Rudolf Steiner's model for the second Goetheanum

During the early weeks of 1924 Steiner continued to struggle inwardly with the structural, architectural, and sculptural problems of the new building. Gradually, the imagination of the building as a whole began to take shape. Finally, in March, the moment came when he was able to sculpt its outer form in three-dimensional reality. Ita Wegman described how Steiner plunged into modeling the forms in plasticine, working for three days, almost without interruption, until the model stood there, ready for him to hand it over to the architects and engineers to be translated into building plans. The practical work was ready to begin by Easter, and during the ensuing months the scaffolding arose and the sheathed forms were built, into which the concrete would be poured. Again the sounds of hammers, saws, and many workers' voices could be heard on the Dornach hill. These were the sounds Steiner loved to hear as he lay in bed in his studio just above the construction site in the final months of his life.

These few weeks constituted a new beginning, especially in the way the ideas shared asked to be received, understood, transformed, and acted on. Although anthroposophy was now intended to be *done*, it would no longer be carried, as it had been, by a single, gifted individual. Now the doing would be fulfilled by the community inwardly and outwardly united with Rudolf Steiner. Those who had been pupils now became responsible colleagues who shared the necessity to make anthroposophy—the methods of research and action—their own to a much higher degree. Only through understanding this can we also understand the intentions underlying the incredible outpouring of initiative that occurred during the first nine months of 1924. This initiative flowed primarily through three channels: the lectures given in Dornach; the letters and articles that appeared week by week in *Das Goetheanum* and its supplement; and Steiner's visits to Prague, Stuttgart, Bern, and Paris, and to Poland, Holland, and England.

The second Goetheanum

Amid this crescendo of activity one event in particular stands out. It opened an entirely new field for spiritual-scientific initiative. The event was the Agricultural Course, which took place from June 7 to 16 in Koberwitz, on the Keyserlingk estate, south of Breslau (now Wroclaw, Poland) in Silesia.[8] Among the diverse members of the Anthroposophical Society were farmers. They were concerned about declining soil fertility, about the weakening vitality of plants and animals and their increasing vulnerability to pests and disease. They had repeatedly requested Steiner's help, and he promised to work with them but had to postpone his trip to Koberwitz several times. A date was finally set for Whitsun 1924. Plans included eight lectures for the farmers and landowners and a few guests at Koberwitz, in addition to lectures and performances in Breslau, the main city in Silesia.

More than a hundred guests arrived at the estate, and the Keyserlingks received everyone with great hospitality. In his opening address Steiner christened them the "Iron Count and Countess," not only because of the concentration of iron in the local soil and water but also because of their determined persistence in persuading him to come. These ten days constituted a historic landmark, the birth of a radically new approach in modern agriculture.

In these lectures Steiner presented astonishing perspectives concerning soils and plant and animal fertility. He gave directions for enhancing and strengthening the effectiveness of composts and manures by using preparations that could be made by farmers themselves. He spoke of the influence of planetary rhythms and cosmic forces in daily agriculture and suggested organic methods for controlling pests and disease. If these methods had been widely adopted then, the massive dependence on chemicals already beginning at that time, poisoning and threatening the biosphere, could have been avoided.

A group of farmers began to work with these insights and suggestions, and the newly established Section for Natural Science at the Goetheanum shared responsibility for carrying out agricultural research. In this way, the worldwide biodynamic agricultural

---

8. *Agriculture*, Bio-Dynamic Farming and Gardening Association, Kimberton, PA, 1993. See Note O in the Appendix.

movement gradually developed; it continues to make significant contributions to organic and sustainable agriculture today.

~

In addition to the Agricultural Course and the lectures mentioned, 1924 also brought an astonishing variety of other activities. These included important pedagogical lecture series as well as more courses for physicians, a series of fifteen lectures on speech eurythmy, and twelve on curative, or special, education. Throughout those months, Rudolf Steiner continued to speak to the workers building the Goetheanum, hold conferences with the teachers of the Waldorf school in Stuttgart, and introduce eurythmy performances. As always, there were countless requests for personal appointments.

Rudolf Steiner also significantly extended and deepened the foundations of anthroposophical insight in three essential directions: esoteric reflections on karma and reincarnation; the role of the supersensible Michael Being, whom Steiner described as guiding the decisive twentieth century toward the future; and the illumination of human experience at the threshold of consciousness through basic esoteric training. On this last theme, Steiner gave the series of lessons that constitute the First Class of the School of Spiritual Science, as well as important lectures relating to the Easter festival and to the future festival of Michael. Almost always initiated in Dornach, these themes radiated outward through the written word and were sounded again and again on his travels.[9] After his return from England in September, during the last four weeks in which his strength still held out, he gave nineteen lessons on speech formation and dramatic art, eighteen lectures specifically for priests of The Christian Community, and the Pastoral Medical Course for priests and doctors.[10]

---

9. See *True and False Paths in Spiritual Investigation*, Rudolf Steiner Press, London, 1985; and *Karmic Relationships: Esoteric Studies* (*The Karmic Relationships of the Anthroposophical Movement*), vol. 3.

10. On education, see *The Roots of Education* and *The Essentials of Education* (fall 1997), and *The Kingdom of Childhood*, Anthroposophic Press, Hudson, NY, 1995; *Speech and Drama*, Anthroposophic Press, 1986; *Curative Education*, Rudolf Steiner Press, 1993; *Pastoral Medicine*, Anthroposophic Press, 1987.

~

The first of these new directions—Western, and deeply Christian knowledge of reincarnation and karma—had been a central theme for Rudolf Steiner throughout his life. Even as a child, Steiner could follow those who had died as they journeyed in the spiritual world. At a young age he became convinced that the human individuality, or entelechy, passes rhythmically through lives on earth and through spiritual existences between death and rebirth. By 1904, Steiner had included a general knowledge of reincarnation and destiny in his book *Theosophy* and had expanded it in *An Outline of Occult Science* and in other writings and lectures. These early works focused primarily on the soul's experiences. Readers and lecture audiences could follow, with everyday consciousness, the soul's experiences after death, from one life to another. He later supplemented this earlier approach with far more detailed descriptions of the soul's progress in relation to the planetary and stellar cosmic environment.[11]

After the Christmas Foundation Meeting, Steiner drew on the general principles of karma and reincarnation to illumine the biographies of specific individuals. He also clearly wished to awaken in his hearers, and to help them develop, a new sense of "karmic self-knowledge." Only through learning to know ourselves in terms of our own karmic backgrounds, and through becoming aware of our connections with others in karmic streams and groupings, may we gradually approach a true and objective picture of ourselves. Through such deepened self-knowledge, we begin to grow toward freedom and toward an experience of love.

~

The second stream of knowledge that came to light from Steiner's spiritual-scientific research during this year had to do with the Michael impulse, or as he referred to it, the "Michael thought." As described in chapter 11, "Out of Fire," during the months leading up to the Christmas Foundation, Steiner characterized the role of the Michael Being in relation to a new experience of the year's cycle of

---

11. See Appendix, Note N, page 277.

seasons and festivals. Now, in the months following that conference, it was especially Michael's relationship with cosmic intelligence and the evolution of human consciousness that was emphasized.

In lectures during this time, Steiner described the stages through which cosmic consciousness became individualized and isolated from the world of its origins. In very early times, human beings felt embedded in the weaving life of spiritual, divine beings. They were united with them, without separate consciousness or independent will. This was a life of *instinctive intuition*, in which being experienced being— similar, in a sense, to a small child's experience through imitation of the beings who surround him or her. The cosmos was permeated by wisdom-filled intelligence, and individual human beings experienced themselves as extensions of that cosmic being.

Over immense periods of time, a separation gradually took place. Creative, cosmic being withdrew and stood behind what it had created, still shining through its manifestation but no longer one with it. Human consciousness experienced creative cosmic being "breathing through," "shining through," and "sounding through." Human consciousness was *instinctively inspired* by cosmic wisdom and intelligence.

Transformation continued; the creator beings withdrew further, leaving behind in their wisdom-filled creation only the divine signature of their creative activity. Human consciousness then awakened to the experience of the world as picture, as *imagination*, in which it recognized the handiwork of divine artistic creation and recognized itself to be filled with this creative life. It no longer experienced divine being, however, nor even the direct power of divine inspiration.

The separation went still further; the world became fully accomplished and finished, became *wrought work*. Human consciousness awoke to a sense of independent selfhood and lost all awareness of the original creative powers. Human intelligence awakened to itself, alone in a finished world of sense-perceptible reality with no ruling power to challenge its right to explore, investigate, and know. What had once been divine, creative, cosmic intelligence had now completely fallen into individual human minds. The rational intellect reigned supreme.

As cosmic intelligence fell away from the hands of the wisdom-filled beings who had harbored and used it to shape the world, it became more and more accessible to other powers who sought to master it for their own ends. All the great mythologies of the past portray this drama—the battle for intelligence, the light of the human mind. The ancient Persians spoke of Ahura Mazda, the spiritual power of the Sun, opposed by Angra Mainyu, or Ahriman, the father of lies and deception; Osiris was entrapped and destroyed by his brother Set, or Typhon; Baldur was tricked by Loki and fell at the hand of his blind brother Hödur, and his death led directly to the Twilight of the Gods. But in all these myths there is also the distant hope, and promise, of a resurrection. In the Norse stories, the golden world of Gimle appears as a gleaming image on the far shores of the vast ocean of destruction; the Persians said that Ahriman's days were numbered; and in Egypt, Isis gave birth to Horus, Osiris's spiritual son.

Today, spiritual science recognizes the death and resurrection of the Christ as the fulfillment of these ancient mysteries. What had been portrayed, foretold, and prophetically enacted in ritual and symbol became reality in the Mystery of Golgotha. Christ united with humanity and with the earth and became the seed-force of resurrection within every human being. Through Him, the cosmic intelligence—which had to go through a form of death and dismemberment in order that human beings might awake to the possibility of individual knowledge and freedom—could be brought to new life.

Steiner used the name that the Bible and Hebrew esoteric tradition give to the divine regent of cosmic intelligence—the Archangel *Micha-el*. In the past this being had been the "countenance of Jehovah" and later became the "countenance of Christ." Steiner described Michael as "the fiery cosmic prince of thought." Michael remains faithful to his task of watching over, guarding, and guiding cosmic intelligence. He saw it descend to earth and die into the minds of individual human beings, and he had to let it go, and wait for them to freely rediscover what it was.

Over the years Steiner spoke about the spiritual power of Michael and of the Michaelic impulse. At a certain point, however, there seemed to be a new urgency in his remarks about this cosmic-human intelligence, an urgency that came to a climax in the final months of his life. Starting in August with issue 79, the *Letters to the Members*, and especially the *Leading Thoughts*, were devoted to the theme of Michael and the cosmic drama of intelligence. They are therefore known also as *The Michael Letters*, or *The Michael Mystery*.[12]

Step by step in the earlier letters, Steiner built up a spiritual-scientific understanding of the human being and of each person's relationship with the worlds of nature, soul, and spirit. He proceeded to questions of karma and destiny, and of connections with the beings of the hierarchies. Only then did he turn to the Michael theme with the essay "At the Dawn of the Age of Michael." It concluded:

> The Michael age is dawning. Hearts begin to have thoughts. Enthusiasm no longer springs from mere mystical darkness but from thought-upborne clearness of soul. To understand this is to take Michael into the heart. Thoughts that today strive to grasp the spirit must spring from hearts that beat for Michael as the fiery Thought Prince of the universe. (trans., Arvia M. Ege)

~

Every individual today is, to some degree, part of the battle for human intelligence. As a contemporary in the age of the consciousness soul, each person must ask: Am I able and willing to work with the experience of my own thinking until my heart's blood beats in every thought? Can I stand behind my thoughts with all of my humanity? Or does my thinking instead unfold as an automatic, impersonal, perhaps brilliant, but essentially amoral, mechanical sequence of logical conclusions? Can I distinguish between the two? Is my thinking faithful to the reality it seeks to know, or am I actually in love with myself when I think?

These questions—naive as they may at first appear to be—may lead the self-observant thinker toward the experience of two realms of

---

12. Published as *Anthroposophical Leading Thoughts: Anthroposophy as a Path of Knowledge: The Michael Mystery*, Rudolf Steiner Press, London, 1985.

being: on the one hand, a realm where beings seek to know the world for the world's own sake, and on the other hand, a realm where beings seek to experience themselves and are actually indifferent to the world about which they think. In one of the Michael letters, Steiner contrasts Michael's and Ahriman's relationship to intelligence:

> Ahriman appropriated intellectuality in an age when he could not make it an inner reality within himself. It remained in his being as a force completely detached from anything of heart or soul. Intellectuality flows forth from Ahriman as a cold and frosty, soulless cosmic impulse. And those human beings who are taken hold of by this impulse unfold a logic that seems to speak for itself alone, without compassion and without love; a logic with no evidence of a rightful, heartfelt, inner relationship of soul between the human being and what is thought, spoken, and acted on. In reality, it is Ahriman who speaks in this kind of logic.
>
> Michael, however, has never appropriated intellectuality to himself. He fosters it as a divine-spiritual force while feeling united with the divine, spiritual powers. When he penetrates intellectual intelligence it becomes manifest that the intellect can just as well be an expression of the heart and soul as an expression of the head and mind. Michael has within himself all the original forces of gods as well as those of humanity. Therefore, he does not transmit to the intellect anything that is cold, frosty, and soulless, but he stands by it in a way that is full of soul and inner warmth. (ibid., p. 97–98)

In the same letter, this characterization is condensed into two contrasting imaginations:

> One of the imaginations of Michael is the following: He rules through the course of time, bearing the light from the cosmos in the reality of his own being, giving form to the warmth from the cosmos as the revelation of his own being; he keeps steady on his course like a world, affirming himself only through affirming the world, as if guiding forces from all corners of the universe down to earth.

Contrast this with an imagination of Ahriman: he wishes, in moving through the world, to capture space out of the realm of time; he has darkness around him into which he sends the rays of his own light; the frost around him grows stronger as he accomplishes his aims; he moves like a world that contracts into a single being—his own—which he affirms only by denying the world; he moves as though he carried with him the sinister forces of dark caverns in the earth.

When human beings seek freedom with no trace of egoism, when freedom becomes pure love for the action itself, it is possible for human beings to approach Michael. If, on the other hand, they seek to act in freedom by unfolding egoism, if freedom becomes for them the proud feeling of manifesting the self in their action, then there is danger of falling into Ahriman's sphere. (ibid., p. 99)

Whether or not one is willing to entertain the possibility that there are spiritual beings who influence human lives and actions, one knows from experience that there are ways of thinking that speak directly to the heart and to one's whole being, and that there are other ways of thinking that leave one totally untouched, though their content may be fascinating, informational, and clever.

If one engages, in an open-minded and serious way, with the nature of thinking and the different qualities of intelligence as Steiner characterizes them in the Michael letters, one is confronted with questions that can be neither easily answered nor ignored. These are the kinds of questions that stood before Rudolf Steiner with such urgency as he prepared for the Christmas Foundation meeting in December, 1923. They were also the questions that moved him powerfully as he inaugurated an esoteric school that would exist in full public view and would, nevertheless, lead its pupils to a genuine renewal of the mysteries in a way appropriate to our time.

~

The inauguration of the School of Spiritual Science was the third stream that flowed within the flood of spiritual-scientific insights that poured forth during the first nine months of 1924. The inaugural lesson for the First Class of the School was given by Rudolf Steiner on February 15. Those lessons continued weekly until the essential sequence of nineteen lessons was completed on August 2. Steiner had hoped to carry this work farther when he returned from England in September, but the number of new members awaiting him when he returned required him to recapitulate the early lessons until he no longer had the strength, and the lessons had to be discontinued.

Rudolf Steiner spoke of the School as the *School of Michael.* He linked it with the supersensible school that Michael had guided behind the scenes of historical events between the fifteenth and seventeenth centuries, and with the ritual enacted as a cosmic imagination at the end of the eighteenth and beginning of the nineteenth centuries. The mystery wisdom that lived in the supersensible School as *Inspiration* condensed and became *Imagination* in the cosmic ritual. It was transformed once again and brought to expression as *living concept*, or *idea*, in anthroposophy. The School of Spiritual Science was born in order to offer an esoteric training ground, a path of schooling, for those who freely choose this way.

Due to physical exhaustion, as already mentioned, Steiner was able to lay only the groundwork for this esoteric school, in which he introduces the pupil to the being who stands at the threshold between the sense-perceptible world and the world of spirit. In concentrated mantric verse, he describes modern human beings' experience as they follow the path toward an existence free of the body. He presents a path across the threshold that can be taken in full, clear consciousness, from which we can return with confidence to the tasks and responsibilities of the physical world. What distinguishes these lessons from the wealth of spiritual-scientific insight in Steiner's other work is not so much their content as the concentration of their form. Intellectually, one finds the material presented in other contexts in Steiner's work, but it is never the intellectual content that distinguishes what is esoteric from what is exoteric knowledge; it is the quality of inner activity that one brings to the material.

As described in the preceding chapter, the School of Spiritual Science includes departments, or *Sections*, as Steiner refers to them, devoted to research in special fields of knowledge and practical, cultural activities such as medicine, agriculture, and the arts. In its organizational form, therefore, the School is structured like the traditional university. As a student, one enters the central Section, originally intended to comprise three esoteric classes in which one's capacities would be trained for spiritual-scientific research. And then, on the basis of these newly awakened and developed capacities, one could enter a Section and join those already at work there.

On September 28, 1924, the evening before Michaelmas Day, Rudolf Steiner left his studio in the Schreinerei for the last time. He walked the few steps across the hall and ascended the stage to speak to the members who were assembled there. Because his strength gave out, he could only give part of his intended talk.

In this final address, Steiner spoke of a significant individual. Twice in recent times this individual died young, first as the sublime painter Raphael, and then as the poet Novalis, whose magical idealism endowed the facts of nature with their original divinity. Steiner's spiritual researches had, many years before, established that this being had also lived in the prophet Elijah and in John the Baptist. Now, in his last address, Steiner suggested a correspondence between this individuality and Lazarus, who became John, the beloved disciple, the author of the fourth Gospel. Following the address, Steiner's physician asked for clarification concerning this matter; Steiner told him:

> At the awakening of Lazarus, the spiritual being John the Baptist, who since his death had been the overshadowing spirit of the disciples, penetrated from above into Lazarus as far as the consciousness soul; the being of Lazarus himself, from below, intermingled with the spiritual being of John the Baptist from above. After the awakening of Lazarus, this being is Lazarus-John, the disciple whom the Lord loved.[13]

---

13. Quoted in the preface to *The Last Address Given by Rudolf Steiner*, Rudolf Steiner Press, London, 1967, p. 10.

To those gathered in the carpenters' shop on that Michaelmas evening, Steiner spoke of this individuality, in whom the Christ experience lived in the deepest possible way. He said that this being would be one of those who will help to guide humanity through its great crisis at the end of the twentieth century. He characterized the power and help that will lead humankind through the coming crisis as the power and the will of the Archangel Michael, which are "none other than the Christ Will and the Christ Power, going before to implant the power of the Christ in the right way into the earth" (ibid., p. 18).

Even during the early years of this century, Steiner had experienced the Christ Being as already present. He experienced the resurrected Christ within the etheric sphere of earth. As he predicted, a growing number of human beings have experienced Him during the intervening years. Yet, if the Christ's presence is to become effective as a redemptive force in response to the tragedies surrounding the close of the pivotal twentieth century, Michael's light-filled thought needs to be taken in, understood, and put into action.

~

After Michaelmas, Rudolf Steiner never again left his studio. Guenther Wachsmuth, whose task was to keep Steiner in touch with the Anthroposophical Society members and with the world at large, writes about this period:

> His bed was at the foot of the Christ sculpture in the studio where he had worked for decades, giving counsel and helping thousands of people. The room now had to be kept quieter. He could speak intimately with only a few people. His voice grew weaker and listening taxed his physical strength. His features became pinched. Suffering brought the form of his noble head into clear relief. His eyes spoke of pain, but they were kinder and brighter than ever. His noble spiritual power created, in that stillness and concentration, the gifts that from now on could flow out to people only in the form of the written word.

When you came into the studio during these weeks and months, you would usually find Rudolf Steiner half sitting up in bed, reading or writing. He never stopped working. Almost every day during this time, he asked me to bring in his correspondence at our accustomed hour of eleven o'clock, had me read the letters to him, and dictated the replies or gave guidelines and suggestions for these letters, which would go out to all the corners of the world. The stream of questions and requests for advice from around the world never ended. If you tried to protect him by revealing as little as possible, his questions drew whatever had been left out into the discussion; even at this time of apparent separation, he shared most intensively in the life of the Anthroposophical Society, of his friends, and of his students. (*The Life and Work of Rudolf Steiner*, p. 571)

Steiner's interest, however, was by no means limited to the members and the affairs of the Society. Through omnivorous reading, he reached out into almost every current of contemporary life. Wachsmuth continues:

In addition to the creative work that Rudolf Steiner accomplished day by day during these months from his sickbed, he also did a tremendous amount of reading, continuously keeping up with newly published books in the sciences, arts, history, and in every other conceivable field. Since he could no longer visit book stores and explore for himself the treasures of secondhand dealers, he delegated to me the difficult task of selecting and acquiring books that might be of interest to him. This was a challenging assignment, full of interesting experiences, for it was really hard to guess what he was already familiar with, what might or might not interest him, what he would consider important or not so important. Every few days I visited the bookstores in Basel, and sometimes those of other cities, in my search for books that might be what he would like to read. Every time I came to his bedside with a great pile of books for him to examine, there was always a moment of suspense while he thoughtfully picked up one book after the other, considered the title and the author, turned a few pages, and made his choice. The books that he wanted to keep and read he stacked on the right side of his bed, and those that were not so interesting he put on the left side. I was naturally proud whenever most of the books ended up on the right side, but if the pile on the left was bigger than the one on the right, I had to go out again very quickly to look for more books.

It was extremely instructive to see which books he considered interesting or important in the flood of new publications from around the world. He often summed up their authors and themes in a few words and placed them succinctly into a bigger contextual picture. How he found time to study the tremendous pile of books lying on the right side of his bed in addition to all his other work, and in spite of his illness, is a puzzle, but from the occasional comments he made when the next batch of books was delivered, it seemed that in the meantime he had thoroughly examined their contents. (ibid., pp. 572–573)

Through his written communications, Steiner maintained a vital connection with the spiritual life of the Goetheanum. Each week he wrote another chapter of his autobiography, as well as a *Letter to the Members*. The Letters, which since August had dealt with some aspect of the Michaelic theme, were published in the newly established newsletter.

These Letters are significant, and their spiritual gesture gives them an important place within the entire body of Steiner's lifework. Their scope and character are indicated by titles such as "At the Dawn of the Age of Michael," "Michael's Task in the Sphere of Ahriman," and "Michael's Mission in the Age of Human Freedom."

There is probably nothing in contemporary literature that compares with these Letters. Each is a masterpiece of living thinking, and each accompanying "Leading Thought" a crystalline essence of it. The Letters comprise—right down to their sentence structure—a meditative intensity of experience that requires a similar inner activity on the part of the reader to penetrate and comprehend the power of thought embodied in them. Because of this, they offer an inner path of schooling.

Their purity and intensity remind us of the efforts of the great Scholastics of the thirteenth and fourteenth centuries, who battled spiritually for the integrity of human intelligence. It was as though their power now streamed into the present time with a new sovereignty, to enact the triumph of human thought over its desolate, mechanistic ghost existence, which wants to penetrate every corner of contemporary consciousness. Here is the sunrise of a kind of thinking that is itself alive and can enter into qualitative processes and gradually change or completely transform itself at will. We see the dawn of a consciousness that can penetrate and know life.

Because it is alive, such conscious thinking recognizes the chasm between living nature and mechanistic subnature and thus reveals the ultimate battleground for our time.

It seems prophetic that the very last Letter, written a day or two before his death, contrasts nature and subnature. The Michael Letters as a whole, and this final Letter in particular, challenge us to recognize that mechanical technology has created a realm into which the human life of will is already deeply submerged and in danger of being lost. Our current task is to discover and to ascend to a realm of knowledge and experience that is as far above nature as are the depths of subnature below it, into which technology threatens to draw us down. We cannot wish Ahriman out of existence but must learn to know him as he is and find a relationship with him in which we remain inwardly free and completely human. Steiner says in his final Letter that this is possible only when we can rise in consciousness to a sphere of experience inaccessible to Ahriman. Steiner observes that science has not yet discovered the path to such knowledge:

> Thus far in the age of technical science, the possibility of finding a true relationship to ahrimanic civilization has escaped humankind. Human beings must find the strength and inner force of knowledge necessary to avoid being overcome by Ahriman in this technical civilization. Humankind must understand

subnature for what it truly is. People can do this only by rising—in spiritual knowing—into a non-earthly, cosmic realm above nature, at least as far as they have descended through technical sciences into subnature. In order to come to terms in our inner life with something dangerous, real, and living that has sunk beneath nature, our age needs a kind of knowing that goes *over* nature. Needless to say, it is not a matter of advocating a return to earlier states of civilization. The point is that humankind shall find the way to bring the conditions of modern civilization into their true relationship to humanity and to the cosmos. (*Anthroposophical Leading Thoughts*, p. 218)

This last communication—published two weeks after Steiner's death—is a real farewell. In it, he points the way to a science that can lead us toward achievements in the realm of life as far-reaching as those achieved by materialistic science through a technology of the lifeless world. This is, indeed, the path of anthroposophy and Steiner's life.

~

Rudolf Steiner's final months were filled with suffering, which often seemed intense. Yet on March 5, a few weeks before his death, he wrote to Marie Steiner, who was touring with a eurythmy group in Germany (he had specifically asked that she not interrupt this work because of his illness):

My condition is improving only very slowly. I must be able to work soon—after all that has happened, it is impossible to calculate what might result if work on the building were delayed because of my illness." (*The Life and Work of Rudolf Steiner*, 583)

It was not only, as Wachsmuth writes, that Steiner "loved the lively sounds of hammering and activity coming from the building site of the Goetheanum into the quiet of his sickroom," but that he, more than anyone else, knew the difficulties that this great endeavor faced and the importance of its unhindered progress.

It was just at this time that Friedrich Rittelmeyer, in Berlin, was to become the leader, or *Erzoberlenker*, of the newly established Christian Community. In February, Emil Bock, a close associate of Rittelmeyer, went to Dornach to ask for Steiner's advice on some important matters. Steiner could no longer see visitors, but through Guenther Wachsmuth he asked Reverend Bock to remain in Dornach, since there was something he wanted to give him. Wachsmuth writes:

> Two days later I was able to hand him the ritual for [Rittelmeyer's] ordination as the ruling bishop, as composed by Dr. Steiner.... The intensity and depth of the experience remain in my memory to this day, when Rudolf Steiner, from his sickbed at the foot of the Christ statue, prepared to hand me this document, full of destiny, and asked me first to listen to its contents and to absorb it. In a voice that had become faint and weak from illness, but nevertheless allowed the words to sound out in a vastly spirit-filled and intimate way, he read the sublime words of this liturgy of investiture. Only in such rare and exceptional moments did I ever see Rudolf Steiner so inwardly moved, while at the same time so filled with the joy of accomplishment. When he had finished speaking the words of the ritual, he said as he handed the text to me, "This came directly from the spiritual world." (ibid., p. 582–583)

On March 15, Steiner wrote for the last time to the teachers of the Waldorf school in Stuttgart:

> My dear teachers in the Waldorf School,
>
> That I am unable to be with you all is a great deprivation to me. And so I must hand over the important task of decision making—which I have shared with you ever since the school opened—into your care. This is a trial given by destiny. I am with you in thought. I cannot do more just now without risking the indefinite prolonging of this period of physical incapacity.

May the active power of thought unite us,
Since we must be parted in space.
May the achievements thus far
Work strongly among the teachers of this school.
May it live within their counseling,
Since the counselor—who would so gladly come—
No longer has wings that are free to fly.

So let us work all the more strenuously for spiritual communion now that this is the only way left open to us. The Waldorf school is truly a child that needs special care, but above all, it is a visible sign of the fruitfulness of anthroposophy within the spiritual life of humankind.

If all the teachers faithfully carry the awareness of this fruitfulness within their hearts, then the good spirits who watch over this school will be able to work actively; divine spirit-power will prevail in everything the teachers do.

With this in mind, I send you my affectionate thoughts and greetings. I enclose a short letter to the pupils, which I ask you to read out to each class.

With heartfelt greetings,
Rudolf Steiner[14]

Three days before his death, Steiner corrected proofs of the book *Fundamentals of Therapy*, which he and Ita Wegman had worked on together, and he continued to the very end with his *Letters to the Members, Anthroposophical Leading Thoughts*, and his autobiography, *The Course of My Life*.

~

On March 30, 1925, Rudolf Steiner crossed quietly, in clear wakeful consciousness, into the world from which he had drawn his spiritual-scientific insights. Guenther Wachsmuth described his experience at that time:

---

14. "Last Letters to Teachers," March 15, 1925, *Towards the Deepening of Waldorf Education*, Pedagogical Section of the School of Spiritual Science, Dornach, 1991.

*Rudolf Steiner's
death mask*

The last moments of his earthly life were free of any struggle with his physical organism, free of any of the uncertainty that characterizes the deaths of so many human beings—his countenance spoke of peace, grace, inner surety, and spiritual vision. He folded his hands over his breast; his eyes were alight and strongly directed into the worlds that he was united with in vision. As he drew his last breath, he himself closed his eyes; this filled the room not with the experience of something at an end, but rather with the sense of the highest spiritual activity. An exalted, transfigured wakefulness spoke from the features of his countenance, and from the prayerful power of his hands. Just as the artists of the Middle Ages gave the figures of knights, resting upon their stone coffins, an expression as though their closed eyes still see—as though their resting forms could still step forth—so did the figure resting here speak of a wakefulness beyond the earthly, of stepping forward into the spheres of spirit. (*The Life and Work of Rudolf Steiner*, p. 584)

Thus the life of one who fought with all his strength for the spiritual freedom of human individuality in the great crosscurrents of this age came to its close.

To the Goetheanum

Calm, silent thunder of the soul of things!
Vast immanence of passionate thought, made free
In archetypal purpose! Solemnly
As dawn your sculptured spirit floats, and flings
The curved escarpments of your massive wings
To nestle the offspring of Immensity
In the human mind. Prescience of life to be:
Reverence of man for God's imaginings.
His brow from whom you sprang through Phoenix fire
Here broods alike on April cherry-bloom
And autumn storm from your deep sunken eyes.
Himself your silent thunder and your choir
Of sacred dawn. Above his quickening tomb
You lift the stature of his sacrifice.

— Percy MacKaye (1875–1956)[15]

---

15. Arvia MacKaye Ege, *The Power of the Impossible: The Life Story of Percy & Marion MacKaye*, The Kennebec River Press, Falmouth, Maine, 1992, p. 440.

Afterword

Thank God our time is now
When wrong comes up to face us everywhere,
Never to leave us till we take
The longest stride of soul men ever took....

Christopher Fry wrote these words out of the heart's cry of the twentieth century—the bitter fruit of that most terrible war, World War Two. Fry knew, and we know, that wars are always fought because another battle, on some very different battlefield, has not been fought.

What other battle, rightly fought and won, might have made the two World Wars, Vietnam, Korea, El Salvador, Cambodia, Iraq, Palestine, Bosnia—and every other conflict that has filled this century—unnecessary, if not impossible? At the dawn of the twenty-first century, is that not the question? Does not everything else depend on the answer?

In any battle, who is responsible? Is it one government or another? Perhaps the United Nations? Power-hungry, self-styled and would-be rulers in faraway lands? Or, in the end, does responsibility come home to roost with me—helpless though I may feel myself to be?

If the responsibility is mine, who am I? What do I need to know about this I? What do people need to know about themselves? Should I equate myself with my physical body, the remarkable, efficient organism of physical, chemical, and biological energies that serves me and identifies me to others? Or is my self more than that: what of my intentions, my hopes, my fears, my moral actions—in short, my conscious life?

When I die, everything that I borrowed goes back to the mineral and chemical world. What of my life and consciousness? The parts of me that are most real to me; where do they go when I die? Where did they come from to begin with? Are my innermost human experiences mere by-products of organic, physical life, or do they have their own independent existence? Above all, can I really know such things to the degree that I can build my whole existence, my whole confidence in life, on such knowledge?

~

How have I learned what I already know? By thinking; yes, I have thought, and I can think. I can go a step farther and shut out every other impression, placing my own thinking, my own process of thought, at the center of my consciousness. My entire attention is focused on what I alone can produce. I am observing my own thought activity. In this moment of experience, I realize that my power of knowing—which, until now, I have used to explore and understand the world—has now been taken hold of by itself, by me as knower, and I, in my inmost activity, have become the object of my own knowing.

My knowledge of self takes a mighty leap: subject and object become one; concept and percept unite in the act of cognition. The gulf—which has thus far separated me as knower from the world outside—has been bridged. I discover I can participate in the only activity that can reunite the two halves of experience and make the world whole. I also learn to identify with the activity as part of my own being.

If I have experienced this breakthrough and have learned that it can be practiced, I can observe that my thinking slowly gains new muscle, begins to touch and grasp what it thinks. Thought associations that popped up and disappeared, unsolicited and never followed through, give way to self-directed probing, which I can observe inwardly. I experience that my thinking is less dependent on the physical body, on the brain, than it was; I experience myself, as *knower*, as "I," and as more substantial and real.

This process can continue—if I will it. My thinking becomes more and more free of the body and gains a quality of picturing, of imaginative perception, which becomes very alive. I am growing into a new way of knowing, a power of cognitive *Imagination*, through which the phenomena of the living world begin to reveal themselves in me. This is a new and vivid consciousness—colorful, mobile, and metamorphic.

Such imaginative consciousness is not the ultimate goal, however; the process may be continued. Having worked so hard toward this accomplishment, can I now summon up an even stronger force of will and bring this refreshing pictorial life to a standstill? Can I find the strength to erase what has become so alive? If I succeed, the pictures yield to stillness, to an inner quiet, deeper than any silence I have known so far. Into this silence a new world begins to sound, to speak. Spirit beings begin to be heard. I "breathe in," spiritually, and a new quality of knowing awakens, which Rudolf Steiner called *Inspiration*. Feeling grows alive and becomes an organ of perception.

I am also potentially capable of yet another significant step on the ladder of knowledge. Can I allow even this new spiritual language to go, allow the beings themselves to be in me and I in them? Spiritual science calls this the deepest and most intensive cognitive capacity accessible to human beings as we are now constituted. This is pure cognition, touching the essence of love, a sheer activity of knowing, which Steiner called *Intuition*.

~

If I set foot on this path, what have I done? I will have grasped the powers within my own being that, if left to themselves, become powers of destruction, violence, and overt evil. These, too, are spiritual powers, but, because they have not been taken hold of by the human I, lifted into consciousness and transformed, they become nourishment for beings who feed on human soul substance, seeking to destroy what divine powers have built up over the ages.

We need those destructive powers, since only through meeting and transforming them can we can become truly human. The food we eat would poison and kill us if we did not totally destroy it through the processes of digestion and then rebuild it as human substance. Our humanity would be destroyed if we did not take the evil present in all of us as potential and digest and transform it into human good.

This is the battlefield on which each human individual must find the courage to confront, recognize, and transform the self through the awakened spiritual power of one's innermost being—the *I am*, or I-being. Anthroposophy, as a path of knowledge, illumines the battlefield and guides individuals to the sources of their own spiritual being and to the insight that, within the darkness, the Being we know as the Christ stands by, ready to accompany every human being across the abyss.

~

There is scarcely an area of practical life today that has not been fructified in some way by the insights of Rudolf Steiner's spiritual science. Thousands of people have experienced an education that draws its life from a new knowledge of human development. Many have been helped to maintain health and balance in life, overcoming illnesses in a way that not only cures the symptoms but rebuilds the foundations of bodily and soul health. The science and practice of agriculture has been opened to a new understanding of earth as a living organism, embedded in a network of spiritual, universal forces. Artistic experience has been immeasurably enriched, and religious life has been deepened. There are new ways of thinking about the social future. Each new insight and achievement is in some way the fruit of Steiner's courageous, ground-breaking research.

Yet, Steiner's central contribution to this century, and to our time, does not lie in any one of these achievements. In his own life, and in the path of anthroposophy that grew from it, he showed the way, step by step, along which anyone who wishes to can take life and destiny into his or her own hands and grow in freedom toward the goal of fulfilling one's greatest potential as a human being. This is the ultimate reason why Rudolf Steiner needs and deserves to be discovered, understood, and known.

In January, 1925, less than three months before his death, Rudolf Steiner wrote the following verse. As we enter the new century and the new millennium, may it en-*courage* us to transmute the outer fires of destruction into the innermost spirit fire of human creativity. In the sense of Rudolf Steiner, this is the *alchemy of our time*.

I would enkindle all human beings
From out of the Spirit of the cosmos
To become a flame
And unfold in fire
Their being's very nature

The others, they would take,
Out of the cosmos, water
To quench with it the flames;
And dampening all being,
Lame it from within.

Oh joy, when the human flame
Is aglow, even there where it rests;
Oh bitterness, when the human thing
Is bound there, where it longs to be active.[1]

---

1. *Truth-Wrought-Words*, Anthroposophic Press, Hudson, NY, 1979, p. 77
(revised).

The first Goetheanum and surrounding area

Appendix

NOTE A: In reference to the origin of Rudolf Steiner's verse "To the Berlin Friends," Anna Samweber (*Aus Meinem Leben*, Verlag die Pforte, Basel, 1981, pp. 43–47) writes of her experience at that time. Samweber was a colleague and close coworker of Rudolf Steiner and Marie von Sivers in Berlin. In November 1923 she was on vacation in Dornach and volunteered to take her turn in the watch that was maintained day and night at the site of the burned-out ruins of the Goetheanum and neighboring buildings. On the night of November 9, Samweber experienced a waking vision of Berlin in flames. Deeply distressed and disturbed, she spoke of this with Rudolf Steiner. After describing her experience, she said:

> Anthroposophy is like a vessel from which we can drink again and again. When the hard times overtake us, and we no longer have you with us, Herr Doctor, could you give us words that can then help us come through?

Steiner agreed and appointed a time for her to come and get what he would write. This was the poetic verse "To the Berlin Friends." Steiner asked Samweber to share it with the friends in Berlin and to convey his instructions that the lease of their apartment in the Motzstrasse should be canceled. Anna Samweber was greatly distressed, but Rudolf Steiner said: "Yes, Sam, if these people (the National Socialists) ever come to power, I can never set foot on German soil again".

At this same time, Steiner also remarked to Guenther Wachsmuth, "If these fellows have their way, it will mean terrible destruction for Central Europe" (Lindenberg, *Chronik*, Verlag Freies
Geistesleben, 1988, p. 541).[1]

NOTE B: Count Otto von Lerchenfeld,(1868–1938) was a member of the Anthroposophical Society; member of the Imperial Council in the Kingdom of Bavaria and nephew of the Bavarian
ambassador to the Imperial Court in Berlin, Count Hugo von
Lerchenfeld. Excerpts from his diaries describe his reasons for turning to Rudolf Steiner, their first meeting, and subsequent weeks of
daily work together (which resulted in *Memorandum* A & B, exten-
sively quoted in Boos, *Rudolf Steiner Während des Weltkrieges*). This
volume (not in English) is an invaluable source for understanding
the origins of the Threefold Movement and for a knowledge of
Steiner's activity in relation with World War One.

NOTE C: Herman Grimm (1826–1901) was the son of Wilhelm
Grimm, younger of the two Grimm brothers. He was married to
Gisela von Arnim, daughter of Bettina von Arnim, known for her
correspondence with Goethe as a child. Grimm's correspondence
with Ralph Waldo Emerson was published by Houghton, Miffflin
in 1903. Grimm introduced Emerson to the German public. Their
correspondence spanned the years between 1856 and 1871. Grimm's
essay on Emerson, written in 1861, is included in his *Fifteen Essays*,
first series. In this essay he tells how he first encountered Emerson's
work and the impression it made upon him:

> I took Webster's Dictionary and began to read. The build of the
> sentences seemed to me very unusual; soon I discovered the
> secret: There were real thoughts; there was a real language—a
> true man whom I had before me—not a.... I need not enlarge
> upon the opposite—I bought the book. Since then I have never

---

1. The Hitler-Ludendorff Putsch in which the Nazis attempted to seize the
Feldherrnhalle in Munich occurred on November 9, 1923.

ceased to read in Emerson's Works, and every time that I take
them down anew, it seems to me that I am reading them for the
first time.... I read the essay entitled *Nature*, and as I continued,
sentence after sentence, I seemed to feel that I had met the simplest and the truest man, and that I was listening to him as he
was speaking to me. (pp. 7–8 in *Correspondence*, quoted from
Grimm's essay on Emerson, by Holls in his introduction)

Herman Grimm and Frank Wedekind

NOTE D: Benjamin Franklin Wedekind (1864–1918) Dramatist, essayist, short-story writer, satirist. Wedekind was a frequent
contributor to *Simplicissimus*, a popular satirical magazine, as well as
writer for and actor in *Die Elf Scharfrichter* (*The Eleven Executioners*),
a satirical cabaret at the turn of the century. Bertolt Brecht said of
Wedekind: "He was one of the great educators of the new Europe
(whose) greatest work was his personality."

An interesting corroboration of the contradictions that Steiner
observed in Wedekind's bodily expression can be found in a passage
in Wedekind's own work on humor:

The mouth would like to laugh and the eye to weep, but since each prevents the other from carrying out its intention, the lips succeed only in bringing forth a gentle smile, while the eyebrows rise almost unnoticed at both ends. The conflict so generated has a much more moving effect than either of the extremes (laughter or tears) would have; it also proves much more favorable for artistic representation. (*Gesammeltewerke*, vol. 9, p. 319, quoted by Leroy R. Shaw in *European Writers*, vol.8, Scribner, New York, 1989)

NOTE E: Christian Morgenstern (1871–1914) was a distinguished lyric poet at the turn of the century. He was also known and beloved as the creator of the *Galgenlieder* (*Songs of the Gallows*), in which one meets the charmingly ironic caricatures of intellectual officialdom in Palmström, Korff, and Palma Kunkel. Morgenstern also translated into German several dramas by Ibsen, with whom he became acquainted during visits to Norway.

It may seem strange that Morgenstern met Rudolf Steiner only in 1909. Both men lived in Berlin at the end of the nineteenth century and moved in the same literary and intellectual circles there. It seems, however, that this gifted poet had to pass through a kind of inner death in order to meet the new beginning that arose from this meeting with Steiner, in which they experienced a mutual recognition of one another.

At the New Year of 1914, just three months before his death, Morgenstern was present when, on an evening in Leipzig, Marie von Sivers recited a sequence of his poems, later published as *Wir fanden einen Pfad* (*We Found a Path*). Rudolf Steiner introduced the recitation, saying:

These poems have aura! They are permeated through and through by a spirit that penetrates and weaves in them and gives them an innermost power that can then radiate from them into our own soul.[2]

---

2. Rudolf Steiner and Marie Steiner-von Sivers, *Die Kunst der Rezitation und Deklamation*, Rudolf Steiner-Nachlaßverwaltung, Dornach, 1967, p. 209. This volume also includes two addresses by Steiner about Morgenstern.

Christian Morgenstern and Albert Steffen

NOTE F: Albert Steffen (1884–1963) was a poet, dramatist, novelist, and essayist. He was born in Murgenthal, Switzerland on December 10, the son of a country doctor and grandson of a local factory owner. Steffen was educated at the Literary Gymnasium in Bern and at universities in Lausanne, Zurich, Berlin, and Munich. In 1907 he published his first novel, *Ott, Alois und Werelsche*. Steffen met Steiner that same year in Berlin. The next year he moved to Munich, where he lived until, in 1920, he settled in Dornach.

Steiner appointed Steffen as editor of the weekly *Das Goetheanum*, the first issue of which appeared in August 1921, and he continued as its editor until his death.

When the Anthroposophical Society was reestablished at the Christmas Foundation Conference in 1923, Steiner appointed Steffen vice-president of its executive council. He also became the leader of the Section for the "*Schoene Wissenschaften*" ("sciences of the beautiful"), or Humanities. Both Steffen and Steiner assigned particular importance to understanding the proper interpenetration of art and science. Art requires spiritually grounded cognitive insight, and science needs to discover research methods and cognition grounded in living experience. Steffen published some seventy-five volumes, eighteen of which are comprised of essays that demonstrate the importance he attached to this form and to the "beautiful sciences."

NOTE G: Marie Steiner-von Sivers (1867–1948); she was the closest worker with Rudolf Steiner in the early years of the Movement and they were married in 1913. She was a member of the original *Vorstand* (Executive Council) and leader of the Section for the Arts of Speech and Music, which included speech, drama, eurythmy, and music. In 1908 she established the Philosophical-Theosophical Publishing Company (later the Philosophical-Anthroposophical Publishing Company).

Marie von Sivers met Rudolf Steiner in the winter of 1900 in Berlin. That autumn, she asked Steiner about the possibility of taking up Eastern wisdom in a way that corresponds more closely with Western spiritual life and the Christ impulse. About her inquiry, Steiner stated: "Therewith, I was given the possibility to work in the way I had always had in mind. The question had been put, and I was therefore in accordance with spiritual law and able to begin to answer the question."[3]

Marie von Sivers, who had a Baltic-German background, was born and raised in Russia. She studied recitation, declamation, and drama in Paris and St. Petersburg. While pursuing spiritual and cultural interests, she met Edouard Schuré (1841–1929) and translated his drama *Children of Lucifer* into German.[4]

In his autobiography, Rudolf Steiner says of Marie Steiner:

She was chosen by destiny at that time to take the German Section of the Theosophical Society into strong hands; the Section was founded soon after my lecturing began. Within this Section, I was now able to develop my anthroposophical activity before a continually increasing audience. (*The Course of My Life*, chap. 30)

---

3. Quoted in *From the Life of Marie Steiner-von Sivers: Biographical Contributions and a Bibliography*, H. Wiesberger, ed., Dornach, 1956.
4. Rudolf Steiner/Edouard Schuré, *The East in the Light of the West / Children of Lucifer: A Drama*, Spiritual Science Library, Blauvelt, NY, 1986.

Marie Steiner–von Sivers and Elizabeth Vreede

NOTE H: Elizabeth Vreede (1879–1943), as a member of the original Executive Council, was leader of the Section for Mathematics and Astronomy. She was born in The Hague, studied at the University of Leiden, Holland, and received a Ph.D. in mathematics. In 1900, she joined the Theosophical Society and met Steiner at the Theosophical Congress in 1902. *How to Know Higher Worlds* and Steiner's lectures on the spiritual hierarchies gave her life direction. In 1914, she moved to Dornach to work on the Goetheanum, and after 1920 she lived in Arlesheim. Vreede researched and gave lectures on mathematics and astronomy, and her work was distinguished by modesty, reticence, and exactitude. She also helped to establish the Goetheanum Archives.

NOTE I: Guenther Wachsmuth (1893–1963) was a member of the original Executive Council and Secretary-Treasurer of the General Anthroposophical Society. He was leader of the Natural Science Section of the School of Spiritual Science and author of *The Etheric Formative Forces in Cosmos, Earth, and Man* (1932) and *The Life and Work of Rudolf Steiner* (1955). He studied law and national economy at Oxford and in Germany. In 1921, he became Steiner's personal secretary and, thereafter, usually traveled with him.

Guenther Wachsmuth and Ita Wegman

NOTE J: Ita Wegman (1876–1943) was a member of the original Executive Council and leader of the Medical Section of the School of Spiritual Science. With Steiner, she co-wrote *Fundamentals of Therapy*. She founded the Klinisches-Therapeutisches Institut in Arlesheim in 1921. Born in Java of Dutch parents, Ita Wegman was introduced to Theosophy in the East Indies. She trained in gymnastics (therapeutic movement) and massage. In 1902, she opened a physical therapy center in Berlin, where she met Steiner. On his advice, she began studying medicine in Switzerland in 1905, and in 1911 received her medical degree. Wegman began a clinic and private practice in Zurich, and in 1921 moved to Basel to open a clinic in Arlesheim.

She supported and encouraged initiatives in curative education, and had a long-standing interest in the ancient mysteries. She provided Steiner with the possibility of establishing the School of Spiritual Science with a question to Steiner: Can the mysteries be renewed in our time? Together, Steiner and Wegman were responsible for the First Class of the School.

NOTE K: Rudolf Steiner as graphic artist: see Roggenkamp and Gerbert, *Bewegung und Form in der Graphik Rudolf Steiners*, Verlag Freies Geistesleben, Stuttgart, 1979 (unavailable in English). In this comprehensive introduction to Steiner's work in this field, the authors show how Steiner went farther than the search for living forms characteristic of the turn-of-the-century *Jugendstil*. He was able to unite supersensible perception of occult script with the experience of organic life in sense-perceptible form. "Steiner's achievement was to guide the striving toward the living element in graphic art (characteristic of *Jugendstil*) into the realm of soul and spirit. He was able to achieve this in such a way that the (supersensible) sources of formative power did not kill the life of the line; instead, the soul and spirit element of the graphic took on the quality (appearance) of life" (*Bewegung und Form in der Graphik Rudolf Steiners*, p. 12).

Design for The Calendar of the Soul

NOTE L: Rudolf Steiner's foreword to the second edition of *The Calendar of the Soul*:

The course of the year has its own life. The human soul can accompany this life in feeling. If what speaks so differently from week to week out of the course of the year is allowed to speak to the soul, then indeed the soul will, by accompanying the life of the year, properly find herself. She will thereby feel how forces awaken that give strength from within. The soul will notice that such forces want to awaken within through her participation in the sense and meaning of the world as it plays itself out in the course of time. The soul will, for the first time, become aware that tender but significant threads are spun between herself and the world into which she is born.

In this calendar, a verse is designed for each week so that it allows the soul to experience what occurs in a particular week as a part of the entire life of the year. What can resound in the soul when uniting with the life of the year is intended to be expressed in each verse. A healthy "finding oneself as one" with the course of nature and a strong "finding oneself" that arises from it is what one has in mind. One believes that to accompany the world's course in inner feeling, in the sense of these verses, is for every human soul something that the soul desires when she understands herself properly.[5]

Design for the weekly Das Goetheanum

---

5. *The Calendar of the Soul*, Anthroposophic Press, Hudson, NY, 1988, p. iii.

NOTE M: Structures designed by Rudolf Steiner (other than the first and second Goetheanums).[6]

The Heizhaus or Heating Plant

In a lecture given in Munich on June 14, 1908, Rudolf Steiner spoke of what it would mean for humanity if a truly contemporary artistic spirit could penetrate the architecture of practical structures. The following excerpt conveys something of what he had in mind:

The cultural means we now have at our disposal can be formed in almost limitless ways. Consequently, they could work far more educationally on human souls than they do today. We are now, for example, in the age of the railroad, but as yet have developed no architectural style for our railway stations. One has no feeling for what happens when the train arrives and

---

6. See Zimmer, *Rudolf Steiner als Architekt von Wohn- und Zweckbauten.*

departs, and has no realization that what happens through the movement of the train can be given outer expression.... One can only hope that, when human beings have mastered air travel, humanity will be so far advanced that one can connect [the plane's] departure with the place where the departure occurs, and that one will feel from its form that only an airplane can take flight from there.[7]

Duldeck House and detail; residence on Goetheanum grounds

7. From *Natur- und Geistwesen ihr Wirken in unserer sichtbaren Welt*, Rudolf Steiner Verlag, Dornach, 1983 (author trans.). See also the correspondence between the group of anthroposophical architects in Stuttgart and Eero Saarinen (1910–1961), the architect of the TWA terminal at Kennedy Airport in New York (in *Mensch und Baukunst*, 11. Jahrgang, Heft 2, 1962).

*The deJaager House; artist's studio
and residence*

NOTE N: Rudolf Steiner knew that it was essential to his life's task to bring a knowledge of reincarnation and karma to men and women in our time. He was also aware of the need for this knowledge to be presented in such a way that it could be taken up with inner freedom through individual clarity and objectivity. The Goethe work that came to him through Karl Julius Schroer during his early maturity created a detour on his life's path. Yet, as he himself realized, it led finally to an enrichment and deepening of his own spiritual-scientific work (see chap. 2).

Although Steiner, during his early anthroposophical work, laid the foundations for a modern understanding of karma and reincarnation, it was only in his final activity that he was able to develop this complex theme from many different angles. We meet this theme, for instance, in the lecture course in September, 1922, *Philosophy, Cosmology, and Religion* (Anthroposophic Press, Spring Valley, NY, 1984) and in May, 1923, *Man's Being, His Destiny and World Evolution* (Anthroposophic Press, 1984). It was only in the wake of the Christmas Foundation, however, that Steiner was free to develop this subject fully. Beginning in January, 1924, until his strength gave out at the end of September, he gave over eighty lectures on this theme. These lectures were published in eight volumes as *Karmic Relationships: Esoteric Studies* (Rudolf Steiner Press, London).

For students who wish to understand Steiner's work in this area, an especially helpful guide is Guenther Wachsmuth's *Reincarnation As a Phenomenon of Metamorphosis* (1937). Asked by Steiner to research etheric-formative forces, Wachsmuth, as a scientist, wanted especially to give an overview, from the perspective of karma, of Steiner's descriptions of the soul's passage through cosmic spheres during the life between death and rebirth. This valuable work is, unfortunately, out of print. It is therefore particularly welcome that a new introduction to Steiner's research has recently become available. *A Western Approach to Reincarnation and Karma* (Anthroposophic Press, Hudson, NY, 1997) contains an in-depth introductory essay by René Querido, a distinguished educator and lifelong student of Steiner's work. Along with his essay, he assembled eight of Steiner's lectures and writings on various aspects of reincarnation and karma.

NOTE O: Responsibility for agricultural research is incorporated within the Natural Science Section of the School of Spiritual Science, with its center at the Goetheanum in Dornach, Switzerland. The Bio-Dynamic Farming and Gardening Association, Inc., represents the agricultural work of North America. It publishes a bi-monthly magazine: *Biodynamics, Farming and Gardening in the 21st Century*. The office is located at P.O. Box550, Kimberton, PA 19442. Tel. 610-935-7797 / FAX 610-983-3196.

Annotated Bibliography

Bayes, Kenneth, *Living Architecture: Rudolf Steiner's Ideas in Practice*, Anthroposophic Press, Hudson, NY & Floris Books, Edinburgh, 1994. A small illustrated book that outlines Steiner's contributions to architecture.

Boos, Dr. Roman, ed., *Rudolf Steiner während des Weltkrieges* (Contributions of Rudolf Steiner toward mastering the tasks confronting the world as a result of the World War), Verlag der Sozialwissenschaftlichen Vereinirung am Goetheanum. (n.d.). With a foreword by A. Boos (1933), it includes two germinal essays by Steiner from 1884 and 1897, and an essay from 1915. The memoranda of June 1917 with introduction by Count Otto von Lerchenfeld are followed by a section on Helmuth von Moltke (Chief of the German General Staff in 1914) and Steiner. Also included are eight articles and essays by Steiner from the war years.

Childs, Gilbert, *Rudolf Steiner: His Life and Work: An Illustrated Biography*, Anthroposophic Press, Hudson, NY & Floris Books, Edinburgh, 1995.

Ege, Arvia MacKaye, *The Experience of the Christmas Foundation Meeting*, Adonis Press, Ghent, NY, 1981. The author was a young woman of twenty-one when she met Steiner in October 1923. She attended the Christmas Conference, which she describes very simply and beautifully. Arvia Ege (1902-1989) was an artist, sculptor, painter, and poet. Included in this slender volume is her translation of Steiner's Foundation Stone mantric verse.

Evans, Dr. Michael & Iain Roger, *Anthroposophical Medicine: Healing for Body, Soul, and Spirit*, Thorsons, London, 1992. An introduction and overview of anthroposophically-extended medicine.

Hindes, Rev. James H., *Renewing Christianity: Rudolf Steiner's Ideas in Practice*, Anthroposophic Press, Hudson, NY & Floris Books, Edinburgh,

1995. Rev. Hindes provides a concise introduction to Steiner's thought that led to the formation of The Christian Community and the "Consecration of Man," its essential sacrament.

Kühn, Hans, *Dreigliederungszeit, Rudolf Steiners Kampf für die Gesellschaftsordnung der Zukunft*, Verlag Freies Geistesleben, Stuttgart, 1978. Kühn gives the historical background of the Threefold Movement in Central Europe during the years immediately following World War One.

Luxford, Michael, *Children with Special Needs: Rudolf Steiner's Ideas in Practice*, Anthroposophic Press, Hudson, NY & Floris Books, Edinburgh, 1994. A small illustrated introduction to the practical application of Steiner's ideas for educating children with special needs.

Molt, Emil, *Emil Molt and the Beginnings of the Waldorf School Movement: Sketches from an Autobiography*, Christine Murphy, trans. & ed., Floris Books, Edinburgh, 1991. This volume gives a lively portrait of this self-made Swabian businessman and social pioneer, who is largely responsible for beginning the Waldorf school movement.

Pietzner, Cornelius, ed., *A Candle on the Hill: Images of Camphill Life*, Floris Books, Edinburgh, 1990. An illustrated, large-format book that describes the therapeutic Camphill communities, which are based on Steiner's insights on curative education and working with children with special needs.

Raab, Rex, Arne Klingborg, & Äke Fant, *Eloquent Concrete: How Rudolf Steiner Employed Reinforced Concrete*, Rudolf Steiner Press, London, 1979. Rudolf Steiner as architect and designer in concrete. Well-illustrated, it presents the history of the building project of the present Goetheanum as well as insight into the architectural and artistic intentions of Rudolf Steiner. It contains technical detail, plans, sketches, and so on, of interest to both professionals and lay-people. In addition to the Goetheanum, it includes the Heating Plant, Haus de Jaager, Haus Duldeck, Eurythmeum/Brodbeck, and the Transformer Station.

Raske, Hilde, *The Language of Color in the First Goetheanum: A Study of Rudolf Steiner's Art*, Walter Keller Verlag, Dornach, 1987. This volume, along with Carl Kemper's *Der Bau* (untranslated), constitutes the most comprehensive and meaningful introduction to the first Goetheanum through color (painting and engraved glass windows) and through structure and form. *The Language of Color* presents a wealth of color reproductions of the paintings in both the large and small cupolas, as well as black and white sketches. It offers a starting point for the serious student's understanding of Steiner's contribution to the visual arts.

Rittelmeyer, Friederich, *Rudolf Steiner Enters My Life*, Floris Books, Edinburgh, 1982. Rittelmeyer was one of the founders and the first leader of The Christian Community, founded in 1922 with Steiner's support. He was already respected and influential in the German Protestant movement and, in 1916, was called to the pastorate of the *Neue Kirche*, a leading church in Berlin. Rittelmeyer, a student of Steiner's work for a number of years, never accepted anything on faith but always tested what he encountered. This book not only gives a remarkable picture of Steiner, but expresses a truly contemporary search for a renewed religious experience.

Roggenkamp & Gerbert, *Bewegung und Form in der Graphik Rudolf Steiners*. Verlag Freies Geistesleben, Stuttgart, 1979. Contains an introductory essay by Hagen Biesantz. An artist, working together with an art historian and teachers, provides a comprehensive, many-sided introduction to this little-known side of Steiner's artistic work. Very well illustrated.

Schilthuis, Willy, *Biodynamic Agriculture: Rudolf Steiner's Ideas in Practice*, Anthroposophic Press, Hudson, NY & Floris Books, Edinburgh, 1994. Illustrated book that introduces the practical application of Steiner's ideas for agriculture.

Steffen, Albert, *On the Genesis of Rudolf Steiner's Mystery Dramas*, Verlag für Schöne Wissenschaften, Dornach, 1971. This work not only illuminates the genesis of Steiner's four mystery dramas, but also the creative process in any genuine work of art. Steffen describes the three stages during the twenty-one-year metamorphosis in Steiner's soul of Goethe's fairy tale of "The Green Snake and the Beautiful Lily." It finally emerged as his first drama, *The Portal of Initiation* (published with Goethe's fairy tale, Spiritual Science Library, Blauvelt, NY, 1981), written and performed in 1910. In all of Steffen's mature work as poet, dramatist, essayist, and novelist, he drew deeply on his experience as pupil, friend, and colleague of Steiner. This creative relationship is expressed particularly in Steffen's volume: *Meetings with Rudolf Steiner* (Verlag für Schöne Wissenschaften, 1961).

Steiner, Rudolf, *Anthroposophical Leading Thoughts: Anthroposophy as a Path of Knowledge: The Michael Mystery*, Rudolf Steiner Press, London, 1985. In the spirit of the refounding, or the renewal and transformation, of the society and anthroposophy itself, Steiner wrote a letter (a short essay) each week that went to the members of the

Society. He also crystallized what he wished to say into concentrated summaries known as "Leading Thoughts." It was Steiner's hope that they would be actively studied and thus serve to support and stimulate the renewal generated by the Christmas Conference. Beginning in August, 1924, Steiner introduced the *Michael impulse* as the theme needed to transform modern human consciousness. Week by week, always from a different point of view, Steiner wrote on the Michael theme. These essays are also published as *The Michael Mystery* (St. George Publications, Spring Valley, NY, 1984).

—— *The Anthroposophic Movement*, Rudolf Steiner Press, Bristol, 1993. These lectures provide an encompassing overview of how the Anthroposophic Movement came into existence and what it means for us today and in the future.

—— *Anthroposophy (A Fragment)*, Anthroposophic Press, Hudson, NY, 1996. Steiner's written work (never fully completed to his satisfaction), outlining a new methodology for the study of human nature. It was written in 1910, a time when Steiner was working out his ideas on psychology and physiology in relation to spirit. These ideas, though somewhat difficult, constitute the steps he took toward a truly cognitive psychology. It contains an introduction by neurologist Dr. James Dyson and a foreword by psychologist Robert Sardello.

—— *Anthroposophy and the Inner Life: An Esoteric Introduction*, Rudolf Steiner Press, Bristol, 1994 (formerly *Anthroposophy, an Introduction*). Nine lectures by Steiner to an audience largely made up of experienced students of anthroposophy and members of the Society. In this context, one can say that these lectures were not intended as an "introduction" in the usual sense, but perhaps a reintroduction, or an example how one might understand anthroposophy anew. This was the essential impulse of the refounding of the Society at the Christmas Conference, as expressed by Steiner in his "Letter to the Members" (January 20, 1924), which he concluded by asking the question: "May it not be necessary to admit that the Anthroposophical Society must work to embody *even more of anthroposophy* than hitherto? And how can this be done?"

—— *Anthroposophy in Everyday Life*, Anthroposophic Press, Hudson, NY, 1995. Contains four lectures previously available in individual pamphlets. Included are "Practical Training in Thought," "Overcoming Nervousness," "Facing Karma," and "The Four Temperaments."

—— *The Archangel Michael: His Mission and Ours*, Anthroposophic Press, Hudson, NY, 1994. This book collects much of what Steiner said concerning the Archangel Michael, from his earliest statements in 1907 until the Michael Letters.

—— *The Christmas Conference for the Foundation of the General Anthroposophical Society*, Anthroposophic Press, Hudson, NY, 1990 (foreword and conclusion by Marie Steiner). This book presents the complete proceedings of the Foundation Conference 1923-1924. It is an invaluable source for understanding Steiner's reasons for reestablishing the Society. But it may be even more important for those in search of new social forms of human community, especially spiritual communities. The ways in which Steiner characterized the intentions behind this foundation show how individual freedom may be united with a society required to deal with social, economic, and legal realities.

—— *Colour*, Rudolf Steiner Press, London, 1992. Twelve lectures on the spiritual nature of color and on Goethe's theory of color.

—— *The Course of My Life*, Anthroposophic Press, Hudson, NY, 1986; *Rudolf Steiner: An Autobiography*, Steinerbooks, Blauvelt, NY, 1977. (original title, *Mein Lebensgang*) Written and published serially in the weekly *Das Goetheanum* until his death, March 30, 1925. This autobiography records Steiner's life up to 1907. It describes his childhood and youth and his years in Vienna, Weimar, and Berlin. Written with reticence and objectivity, the reader follows the gradual unfolding of Steiner's inner life, meeting his teachers, professors, colleagues, and friends, who are often portrayed with affection, respect, and gratitude, but always with searching discernment.

—— *The Education of the Child and Early Lectures on Education*, Anthroposophic Press, Hudson, NY, 1996. First published in 1909, the essay contained in this book is based on Steiner's lectures at the time (also contained in the book) and recast by him into essay form. It can be considered the spiritual-scientific seed for what later developed as Waldorf education.

—— *The Foundations of Human Experience*, Anthroposophic Press, Hudson, NY, 1996. (originally published in English as *Study of Man*) Fourteen lectures (Aug. 21-Sept. 5, 1919, with opening address Aug. 20). Here Steiner laid the groundwork for the understanding of the human being from the aspects of soul, spirit, and body, which forms the basis of Waldorf education. This is one of three basic courses for the prospective teachers of the first Waldorf school. Included in the present edition are the two lectures that Steiner gave in Berlin, March 15 and 17, 1917, entitled "The Human Soul and the Human Body" and "Riddles of the Soul and Riddles of the Universe." These are groundbreaking lectures that for the first time describe how the human soul and spirit work directly through the organism: the brain and nervous system mirroring the thinking spirit; breathing and blood circulation serving as the instruments of the soul in feeling; and the metabolic and limb systems as instruments for the will.

—— *The Four Seasons and the Archangels: Experience of the Course of the Year in Four Cosmic Imaginations*, Rudolf Steiner Press, London, 1996. These lectures study each of the four great festivals of the year and the cosmic forces behind them. Steiner discusses alchemical processes, crystals, clouds, meteors, elemental beings in nature, and the forces of the adversaries that attempt to hinder human and cosmic evolution. He gives imaginations that help portray the activities of the archangels Michael, Gabriel, Raphael, and Uriel.

—— *Friedrich Nietzsche: Fighter for Freedom*. Spiritual Science Library, Blauvelt, NY, 1985 (first published in 1895 as *Friedrich Nietzsche, Ein Kampfer gegen seine Zeit*). Steiner characterizes Nietzsche as a profound truth seeker caught in the materialism of his time. In his autobiography, Steiner closed the chapter on his wrestling with Nietzsche's thought with the words: "Thus, in 1896, through my spiritual perception of Nietzsche's soul, I gained insight into the suffering of one who sought the spirit—suffering caused by the prevailing worldview at the end of the nineteenth century" (COML, chap. 18)

—— *Guidance in Esoteric Training: From the Esoteric School*, Rudolf Steiner Press, Bristol, 1994. Contains exercises, meditations, and practices for spiritual development as given by Steiner to his students in the Esoteric School between 1904 and 1914.

—— *How to Know Higher Worlds: A Modern Path of Initiation*, Anthroposophic Press, Hudson, NY, 1994. In this written work, Steiner sets out the conditions and methods of spiritual science, methods that, when worked with diligently, lead to a greater spiritual capacity for knowledge.

—— *An Introduction to Eurythmy*, Anthroposophic Press, Hudson, NY, 1984. Contains sixteen talks on the art of eurythmy and its place among the arts and in education.

—— *Intuitive Thinking As a Spiritual Path: A Philosophy of Freedom* (Michael Lipson, trans.), Anthroposophic Press, Hudson, NY, 1995; *The Philosophy of Spiritual Activity: A Philosophy of Freedom* (Rita Stebbing, trans.), Rudolf Steiner Press, Bristol, 1992 (original title,

Die Philosophie der Freiheit, Steiner suggested the title *Philosophy of Spiritual Activity* for the English translation). This book was published in 1894 while Steiner was editing Goethe's natural-scientific writings. The basic presentation of Steiner's philosophical and epistemological views are contained in this volume and in *The Science of Knowing: Outline of an Epistemology Implicit in the Goethean Worldview* (Mercury Press, Spring Valley, NY, 1996) and in his doctoral dissertation published as *Truth and Science* (Mercury Press, 1993). As the subtitle to his *Philosophy of Freedom* Steiner chose "Results of Soul Observation Arrived at by the Scientific Method." His basic thesis is that we need not accept the self-imposed limitation of knowledge gained through sense observation, intellectual analysis, and interpretation. Thinking, as the instrument of human cognition, can be extended through an individual's inner activity to become the primary instrument for knowledge that goes beyond the limitations of sense perception, opening the path to spiritual cognition. This capacity lies within an individual's freedom and opens the way to moral activity.

—— *Karmic Relationships: Esoteric Studies*, 8 vols., Rudolf Steiner Press, London, 1974-1997. In this series of lectures, Steiner presents the fundamental aspects of laws governing karma, as well as individual biographical insights that illustrate general karmic principles.

—— *Man and the World of Stars & The Spiritual Communion of Mankind*, Anthroposophic Press, New York, 1963. The first seven lectures in this volume deal with cosmic aspects of human existence from a variety of viewpoints. The other five lectures on the theme of spiritual communion deal with the renewal of mystery wisdom. In the final lecture, delivered on New Year's Eve, Steiner contrasts an earlier, more instinctive communion with nature with the communion possible for human beings today. He described how, through spiritual activity, contemporary human beings can create a communion for the future. This lecture closed with a verse that he introduced by saying: "Let us turn our thoughts away from the dying phenomena that confront us like old graves everywhere in modern civilization, away from New Year's Eve to New Year's Day, to the day of the Cosmic New Year. But that day will never dawn until human beings themselves decide to bring it to pass."

—— *Manifestations of Karma*, Rudolf Steiner Press, London, 1969. Eleven lectures (1910) that provide a basic introduction to Steiner's research on karma and reincarnation.

—— *An Outline of Occult Science* (H. Monges, trans.), Anthroposophic Press, Hudson, NY, 1972. This is Steiner's essential written work on cosmological and human evolution and a description of the path to higher knowledge. (*An Outline of Esoteric Science*, a new translation by Catherine Creeger, is scheduled for fall 1997.)

—— *The Origins of Natural Science*, Anthroposophic Press, Hudson, NY & Rudolf Steiner Press, London, 1965. Nine lectures given in Dornach December 24-28 and January 1-6, 1923. Owen Barfield in his introduction says that these lectures were "directed to an audience containing some professional scientists and others particularly interested in science, many of whom were members of the Anthroposophical Society.... The basic argument is that modern science, and the scientism based on it, so far from being the only possible 'reality-principle,' is merely one way of conceiving the nature of reality; a way moreover that has arisen only recently and which there is no reason to suppose will last forever." Steiner interrupted this lecture series to give three lectures on a different subject, *Man and the World of Stars & The Spiritual Communion of Mankind*. Amid these lectures, on New Year's night, the Goetheanum was destroyed by fire.

—— *Reincarnation and Karma: Two Fundamental Truths of Human Existence*, Anthroposophic Press, Hudson, NY, 1992. Five lectures in Berlin and Stuttgart (1912). In the introduction, Steiner quotes from the fifth lecture: "As human beings learning to live with the influence of ideas of reincarnation and karma, we come to realize that our life cannot be assessed based on the expression of one life between birth and death, but that a period extending over many lives must be taken into consideration."

—— *Riddles of the Soul*, Mercury Press, Spring Valley, NY, 1996. *The Case for Anthroposophy*, (Owen Barfield, trans., ed.), Rudolf Steiner Press, London, 1970. Originally published in 1917, this work (both complete and as edited by Barfield) belongs among Steiner's essential writings. It contains three essays and a series of nine notes, which Steiner described as amplifications of this work in the form of sketches. Steiner deals with the fact that contemporary humanity is at the end of a long and necessary separation of the human soul from its spiritual origins. This, however, does not necessarily mean that the soul has only a physical existence. Having gained independence, the human being can now, through its own activity, rebuild the connection that it had to lose. This was the theme of his early epistemological works in which he demonstrates how the cognitive bridge can be rebuilt. In this work Steiner extends this to the activity of feeling and of volition and shows that they are initially experienced through the body, but may be recognized as having independent life. This becomes clear when the human physical organism is viewed as three-fold in its organic and functional life and serves as the soul's instrument in the activity of thinking, feeling, and willing. For Steiner, this was the result of three decades of research, which he first presented in two lectures in Berlin in March, 1917, and condensed in the sixth note in the fourth section of *Riddles of the Soul.*

—— *A Road to Self-Knowledge and the Threshold of The Spiritual World*, Rudolf Steiner Press, London, 1975. *A Road to Self-Knowledge* (the first work in this book) is comprised of a sequence of eight meditations expressing the experience that one may gain of the fourfold body of the human being: physical, etheric, astral, and I (or thought body). It describes as well knowledge of the Guardian of the Threshold, the nature of supersensible experience, and how to experience one's repeated lives on earth. As indicated in the table of contents, each meditation in *A Road to Self-Knowledge* is "the attempt to form a true idea of" the physical body, the etheric body, repeated earthly lives, and so on. Steiner described this method as the individual's experience rather than the more general approach that characterizes his basic works, such as *How to Know Higher Worlds*, *Occult Science*, and *Theosophy.*

—— *Theosophy: An Introduction to the Spiritual Processes in Human Life and in the Cosmos*, Anthroposophic Press, Hudson, NY, 1994. Steiner describes his own supersensory experiences, which led to his understanding of the human being as a sevenfold entity of body, soul, and spirit; of the laws of reincarnation and rebirth; and of the spiritual path through which we may arrive at such understanding.

—— *Towards Social Renewal*, Rudolf Steiner Press, London, 1977. First published in the spring of 1919, this book was an essential element in the movement for social renewal that came to be known as the Three-fold Movement. A companion volume is Steiner's *The Renewal of the Social Organism* (Anthroposophic Press, Hudson, NY & Rudolf Steiner Press, London, 1985). This is a collection of articles that Steiner wrote on social issues during 1919 and 1920.

—— *Truth-Wrought-Words and Other Verses*, Arvia MacKaye Ege, trans. (with original German), Anthroposophic Press, Hudson, NY, 1979; *Verses and Meditations*, George & Mary Adams, trans. (with original German), Rudolf Steiner Press, Bristol, 1993. These two volumes comprise most of Steiner's poetic and mantric verse available in English. Steiner's *Calendar of the Soul* (available in several translations) and his *Four Mystery Dramas* (Steiner Book Centre, North Vancouver, BC, 1973) should be considered a part of his poetic work.

—— *The Spiritual Hierarchies and the Physical World: Reality and Illusion*, Anthroposophic Press, Hudson, NY, 1996. In the first ten lectures, Steiner reestablishes the human being as a participant in the evolving, dynamic universe of spiritual beings. He shows that the universe consists of consciousness—that to think of the cosmos and humanity in any terms other than consciousness is illusion. Included are five lectures on the inner aspects of evolution, or the planetary stages of cosmic development.

—— *A Western Approach to Reincarnation and Karma: Selected Lectures and Writings of Rudolf Steiner*, introduced and edited by René Querido, Anthroposophic Press, Hudson, NY, 1997. René Querido presents a historical overview of the Western perspective of karma and rebirth, which he views in relation to Steiner's spiritual-scientific research. A selection of Steiner's lectures and writings are represented, which discuss the causes and effects of karma in relation to world events, natural phenomena, illness, and so on. Steiner describes how we can come to understand our own karma in the light of past incarnations, and how we can take fuller responsibility for our own destinies.

—— *World History in the Light of Anthroposophy and as a Foundation for Knowledge of the Human Spirit*, Rudolf Steiner Press, London, 1977. Steiner gave these lectures each evening during the Christmas Conference. They present far-reaching perspectives on the evolution of human consciousness as a background to contemporary life.

Steiner, Rudolf & Ita Wegman, *Extending Practical Medicine: Fundamental Principles Based on the Science of the Spirit*, Rudolf Steiner Press, London, 1997 (previously published as *Fundamentals of Therapy*). First published in 1925, soon after Steiner's death, this volume presents from various aspects ways in which existing medical practice can be extended through insights gained by spiritual-scientific research. As such, it is an important point of reference for anthroposophically-based medical therapeutic work, which has since developed worldwide.

Unger, Carl, *The Language of the Consciousness Soul*, St. George Publications, Spring Valley, NY, 1983. This thorough and methodical book serves as an excellent study guide for the *Anthroposophical Leading Thoughts*. In short, concise chapters, Unger expands the gem-like truths contained in the aphoristic Leading Thoughts and in the Michael Letters.

Wachsmuth, Guenther, *The Life and Work of Rudolf Steiner*, Spiritual Science Library, Blauvelt, NY, 1989. This comprehensive account of Steiner's life and work spans the period from the turn of the century until his death in 1925. It builds up systematically year by year, giving a well-rounded account of Steiner's activities. Together with Steiner's autobiography, this work provides a sound biographical overview.

—— *Reincarnation as a Phenomenon of Metamorphosis*, Anthroposophic Press, New York & Rudolf Steiner Press, London, 1937. A conscientious, comprehensive survey of Steiner's research in the field of reincarnation. Wachsmuth, a scientist, researched in the field of etheric forces. He places special emphasis on the cosmological aspects that Steiner describes as the passage of the human soul and spirit through the planetary and stellar spheres during the period between death and rebirth. For the serious student of Steiner's views on reincarnation, this work is essential though, unfortunately, currently out of print.

Zimmer, Erich, *Rudolf Steiner als Architekt von Wohn- und Zweckbauten* ("Rudolf Steiner as Architect of Residential and Utility Buildings"), Verlag Freies Geistesleben, Stuttgart, 1970 (in German). A comprehensive, well-illustrated presentation of Steiner's work as designer of structures surrounding the first Goetheanum on the Dornach hill, plus the houses of Ita Wegman and Elizabeth Vreede in neighboring Arlesheim and the first Eurythmy School building in Stuttgart. The Heating Plant and the Transformer Station show Steiner's creative interest in dealing with technical structures. Photographs of models, drawings, and working plans provide insight into processes and details.

Index

· · · · · · · · · ·

For an informative catalog of the work of Rudolf Steiner
and other anthroposophical authors please contact

ANTHROPOSOPHIC PRESS
3390 Route 9, Hudson, NY 12534
TEL: 518 851 2054
FAX: 518 851 2047